£10

D1584433

THE LETTERS OF
Richard Brinsley Sheridan

Oxford University Press, Ely House, London W. 1

GLASGOW NEW YORK TORONTO MELBOURNE WELLINGTON
CAPE TOWN SALISBURY IBADAN NAIROBI LUSAKA ADDIS ABABA
BOMBAY CALCUTTA MADRAS KARACHI LAHORE DACCA
KUALA LUMPUR HONG KONG

ELIZABETH SHERIDAN
by Thomas Gainsborough
National Gallery of Art, Washington, D.C. Andrew Mellon Collection

THE LETTERS OF
Richard Brinsley Sheridan

EDITED BY

CECIL PRICE

VOLUME I

OXFORD
AT THE CLARENDON PRESS
1966

© *Oxford University Press 1966*

PRINTED IN GREAT BRITAIN

TO
JAMES MARSHALL OSBORN

ACKNOWLEDGEMENTS

I AM obliged to Her Majesty the Queen for graciously permitting me to transcribe and publish the Sheridan letters in the Royal Archives at Windsor Castle.

I wish to thank descendants of Sheridan's family for their ready help. The owner of copyright, Mary, Comtesse de Renéville, has kindly allowed me to print the letters. Mr. H. F. Brinsley Sheridan has put the material in his possession at my disposal. To the Marchioness of Dufferin and Ava and Judge John Maude I am most grateful for access to, and help in studying, the Dufferin collections. My friend W. R. LeFanu has assisted me considerably by letting me draw on his family papers and on his own extensive knowledge of their background.

A number of owners of original letters have been good enough to allow me either to publish or to check them. For these privileges I am indebted to the Duke of Norfolk, the Duke of Devonshire, Earl Spencer, the late Earl of Ilchester, Earl Grey, the Earl of Lichfield, Viscount Sidmouth, Lord Kenyon, the late Lord Bolton, Lord Cottesloe, Sir Shane Leslie, Bart., and Sir Edward Hoare. Mr. Simon Whitbread kindly allowed me to see the relevant Whitbread papers, and to print the Sheridan letters among them. Miss Margaret J. M. Grubbe generously put John Grubb's papers in my hands. To Mr. and Mrs. J. R. Blackett-Ord, Mr. Brinsley Ford, Mr. Paul M. Gilmore, Mr. Bertram Shuttleworth, Mrs. Alfred Western, and Mrs. L. A. H. Wright I am grateful for opportunities of working through much valuable background material, and for permission to print original letters. I must also thank Mr. T. S. Blakeney, Mr. Alec Clunes, Mr. George Fortescue, Mr. R. G. E. Sandbach, and the late Richard Border for similar privileges.

American scholars and collectors have been equally generous in giving me the use of their manuscripts, and I must express my sincere gratitude for this kindness to Mr. F. W. Hilles, Mr. A. A. Houghton, Jr., Mr. and Mrs. Donald Hyde, Mr. Robert E. Keighton, Mr. E. L. McAdam, Jr.,

Mr. Gordon N. Ray, Mr. Jack H. Samuels, and Mr. Robert H. Taylor. My greatest debt in this respect is inadequately acknowledged in the dedication.

Among the institutions that have granted me the privilege of working on and printing their manuscripts, I must record the names of the owners of the two largest Sheridan collections: the Harvard College Library and the British Museum. I am also grateful to the officials of the Bath Municipal Library, Bodleian Library, Brotherton Collection, Butler Library of Columbia University, Cornell University Library, Fitzwilliam Museum, the Goldsmiths' Company, Harrow School, the Historical Society of Pennsylvania, the Henry E. Huntington Library, the University of Indiana Library, the University of Kansas Library, Lehigh University Library, Maine Historical Society, the University of Michigan Library, Mitchell Library, Sydney, National Library of Ireland, National Library of Scotland, National Library of Wales, New York Public Library, Oesterreichische-Bibliotek, Pierpont Morgan Library, Princeton University Library, Public Record Office, Riksarkivet, Stockholm, the University of Rochester Library, Royal Irish Academy, Salt Library, Stafford, Saltikova-Schredin Library, Leningrad, Sheffield Public Library, Sir John Soane's Museum, the Victoria and Albert Museum, the Public Library of Victoria, Melbourne, the University of Virginia Library, and Yale University Library.

I have also received much help from the Registrar and staff of the National Register of Archives, as well as from the Archivists at the Record Offices of Bedford (Whitbread MSS.), Devon (Sidmouth MSS./D 152M), Hampshire (Tierney MSS.), Northern Ireland (Dufferin MSS.), and West Sussex (Norfolk MSS.). The staffs of the India Record Office, the Royal Academy of Arts, the Royal College of Physicians, the Prior's Kitchen, Durham University, and the City of Westminster Public Libraries have also given me much assistance. I am grateful, too, for the aid I received when working in the archives of the Duke of Devonshire at Chatsworth, and in those of the Duke of Northumberland at Alnwick.

The work of assembling the text has been greatly assisted

by the grants made to me by the Leverhulme Trust, the University College of Wales, University College, Swansea, and (from its Pilgrim Trust Fund) by the British Academy. I warmly appreciate the fellowship awarded me at the Folger Shakespeare Library, for it enabled me to find much new material, to study the account books of Drury Lane Theatre during Sheridan's management, and to enjoy the help of the Director, Dr. Louis B. Wright, and his staff.

For much personal aid and advice I must first thank Professor Gwyn Jones and Mr. D. M. Davin. For other favours I am grateful to Dr. Arthur Aspinall, Mr. F. W. Bateson, Mr. John Carter, Mr. P. J. Croft, Dr. J. L. Clifford, Dr. Giles Dawson, Mr. C. I. E. Donaldson, Miss Elizabeth C. Ford, the late Dr. E. M. Hampson, Mr. John H. Harvey, Dr. C. B. Hogan, Dr. George M. Kahrl, Miss Letitia Kennedy-Skipton, the late William Van Lennep, Dr. Wilmarth S. Lewis, Dr. J. G. McManaway, Miss Dorothy Mason, Dr. Robert F. Metzdorf, Miss Eleanor Pitcher, Mr. E. V. C. Plumtre, Miss Sybil Rosenfeld, Mr. William H. Runge, the late Michael Sadleir, Dr. Arthur Sherbo, Mr. Grzegorz Sinko, Mr. Alexander D. Wainwright, Miss Helen Willard, Mr. J. L. Williams, Miss Marjorie Wynne, and Mr. R. C. Mackworth Young.

Mr. Robert K. Black, Mr. R. J. Dobell, Miss Emily Driscoll, Messrs. F. Edwards, Messrs. Maggs Bros., Mr. Michael Papantonio, Messrs. Bernard Quaritch, Mr. Philip Robinson, and Messrs. Sotheby have kindly aided me in locating missing Sheridan letters.

For permission to publish letters that have already appeared in print, I have to thank the Controller of Her Majesty's Stationery Office, Messrs. Constable & Co., Messrs. Ernest Benn, Messrs. Maggs Bros., Sir John Murray, Miss Winifred A. Myers, Messrs. Sotheby, and The Times Publishing Company.

For material that has reached me since this book went to press, I should like to record my gratitude to the Earl of Harewood, Lord Abinger, Lady Beaverbrook and the late Lord Beaverbrook, Dr. W. H. Bond, Dr. N. E. Enkvist, Mr. P. Highfill, Jr., Dr. and Mrs. A. M. Kinloch, Dr. Eric Jacobson, Miss Patricia Sigl, the Secretary and Committee

ix

of the Garrick Club, and the Librarians of the Leeds Central Library, Liverpool City Library, and Nottingham Public Library.

Thanks are too weak to acknowledge all the assistance my wife has given me over the years, in transcription, checking readings, and preparing an index. She has pored with me over the many puzzles presented by Sheridan's handwriting, and contempt for dates. Only I know how much I owe to her accurate eye and unstinting help.

C. P.

CONTENTS

VOLUME I

VOLUME II

VOLUME III

INTRODUCTION

COLLECTIONS of letters usually attract us because they are written by great men whose lives pique our curiosity, or by lesser men who report exactly what went on in their day or express a particular outlook on life. No one will find in Sheridan's letters a satisfying philosophy, but they show gleams of his greatness as well as glimpses of the theatrical, social, and political worlds of his time.

The main interest of the letters is biographical. Sheridan's character is so full of contradictions that it is difficult to assess. His biographers have been painstaking but hardly penetrating, and it is time that readers had the opportunity of studying his correspondence so as to be able to come close to the man and make their own judgements upon him.

His first efforts of any significance belong to 1769, when he tried to imitate the letters of 'Junius' that had appeared in the *Public Advertiser* and had bitterly satirized public figures. Two of Sheridan's attempts are careless drafts; the third is reprinted for the first time from the newspaper in which it was published. Not one of them is remarkable as a literary composition, but we are bound to perceive that even at the age of eighteen, Sheridan's mind was analytical and critical, and that his chief interest in life was politics.

Another important phase in his career is seen in seven letters written between September 1770 and August 1772, when he lived with his father, brother and two sisters, at Bath. The wit in him comes out early in an amusing letter to Mrs. Angelo. The romantic gallant, who accompanied the beautiful singer, Elizabeth Linley, to France, and afterwards fought two duels with her tormentor, Thomas Mathews, is found to be irascible and legalistic, as argumentative as he was brave.

After these escapades, he was banished to Waltham Abbey to pursue his studies and forget Elizabeth Linley. It is unfortunate that his letters to her over these seven months (September 1772 to March 1773) have never come to light. Percy Fitzgerald suggested that when Sheridan came to woo his second wife, he copied from the love-letters he had written to his first, but I do not think we need take this view very seriously. Probably Sheridan learned early in his intimacy with Elizabeth a certain language of love, and used it habitually at a later date.

The correspondence of the Waltham Abbey period contains eleven letters addressed to Thomas Grenville, and they often read like essays on a set theme. Their composer (perhaps suiting himself to his correspondent) seems very earnest and even humourless in his long and didactic epistles. Yet they are revealing in the way they bring out a side of his character that is often forgotten: one that was to have its fullest expression in his play *Pizarro*.

Letters in this lofty and improving strain came to an abrupt end in April 1773, when Sheridan was married to Elizabeth Linley. In spite of his father's displeasure and his own poverty, Sheridan was a happy man at this period, and his joy is shown in the whimsical statement, 'When a man's married, it is time he should leave off speaking in metaphor'. The tone of the ten letters to his father-in-law, Thomas Linley, is as light-hearted as it is purposeful.

Some of them concern *The Duenna*. As Sheridan's chief composer of music for this ballad-opera, Linley carefully followed the hints that its author gave him, and it is interesting to see how they were conveyed. Sheridan relied considerably on his wife's musical knowledge, but he was always essentially a man of the theatre, knowing exactly what effect he wanted to achieve and where to find the necessary illustration and assistance. His ability as an organizer of other people's talents is shown at an early date.

We look in vain for anything equally important about the composition of *The Rivals*, *The School for Scandal*, or *The Critic*, and the next group of letters is largely concerned with the management of Drury Lane Theatre. Sheridan had become one of the proprietors of this playhouse because of the impression he had made on Garrick and Ford, and his connexion with Linley. He had extended his hold by buying out another of the proprietors, Willoughby Lacy. In 1778 he had also taken control (with Thomas Harris of Covent Garden Theatre) of the King's Theatre, but here he over-reached himself and the venture failed after two years. The amount of ready money Sheridan put into all three transactions was comparatively small, but he had now made such a name for himself as the author of highly profitable entertainments that it was taken for granted that he could raise ample money at any time by writing.

As the dominant partner in the proprietorship of Drury Lane Theatre, his income was soon large enough to allow him to give time to his absorbing interest, politics. After taking a leading part in the anti-Government agitations of 1778–9, he was elected member for Stafford in September 1780, and became Under-Secretary of State in the Rockingham administration of 1782, and Secretary to the Treasury in the coalition of 1783.

There are sequences of excellent letters in 1782 and 1788 that show his standing as a trusted lieutenant of Fox, and afterwards of the Prince of Wales. They disclose a delight in intrigue and in the subtle manipulation of men; they imply that Sheridan was usually wary in his political dealings. The correspondence of the last decade of the century is much less informative on these matters. There is comparatively little here concerning the French revolution, the quarrel with Burke, the split in the Whig party, the government's repressive measures, or the naval mutinies. The letters that survive deal instead with the creation of the new Drury Lane Theatre as well as with the death of his first wife and his marriage to Hester Jane Ogle.

The first marriage that had begun so romantically was marred in its closing years by Sheridan's gallantries and by Elizabeth's liaison with Lord Edward Fitzgerald. Her illness is movingly described in Sheridan's letters to the Duchess of Devonshire and Lady Duncannon, and he was completely overwhelmed by his wife's death in June 1792.

In April 1795 he was married to the nineteen-year-old daughter of the Dean of Winchester, and his early letters to her are full of affection and tender absurdity. They become more sober as time goes on, and in some of them a brooding fit of melancholy takes possession of him. 'How unceasingly', he writes, 'do I meditate on Death and how continually do I act as if the thought of it had never cross'd my mind.' These moods of self-criticism and flashes of self-knowledge give depth to offset the more superficial aspects of his character.

At these moments he deplored worldly ambitions, but the fact remains that his days were almost wholly given to them. Of these the most troublesome was the creation of the new Theatre Royal, Drury Lane. Garrick's theatre was pulled down, and after much costly delay an immense building was erected. It was designed by Henry Holland to be the finest in Europe, and to stage the most spectacular productions. All this reflected Sheridan's delight in the flamboyant. Unfortunately Holland exceeded his estimates, and Sheridan had not sufficient capital to complete the original plan. Honourably but quixotically, he took on himself all the unpaid debts of the company. Then he had to resort to all kinds of expedients to improve his finances: he borrowed from his associates, John Grubb and Thomas Shaw; raised money by the sale of boxes; neglected his backers and his creditors. His extravagant tastes and unsound management even kept him short of pocket money, and in frequent notes to the under-treasurer, Richard Peake, he pleaded in a variety of passionate cries for small advances. I have printed many of these in full because they show his characteristic energy of phrasing, and give a fair idea of the way in which Sheridan was plagued with money troubles largely because of his own heedlessness.

This state of affairs was brought to a temporary halt in 1801–2, when the future of Drury Lane Theatre was discussed in detail in the Court of Chancery. The bankers, Hammersley and Company, declared that the proprietors had misapplied the takings of the theatre; and Sheridan appeared in person to rebut the charge. By his interruptions and lengthy defence, he successfully maintained his case; but Lord Chancellor Eldon also rebuked him by applying to him Johnson's famous words about Savage: 'negligence and irregularity long continued, make knowledge useless, wit ridiculous, and genius contemptible'.

The Chancellor also made an order for the payment of the theatre's liabilities from its takings in a certain scale of priority; and he placed the concern under the control of a committee. Two of the leading figures in the new management were Sheridan's friends, Aaron Graham and Richard Wilson. More business-like methods were adopted, but control remained effectively in Sheridan's hands.

In February 1806 he found himself once again for a short time in political office, in the lucrative post of Treasurer of the Navy. The correspondence of the year is very full but chiefly concerns the Stafford election, the abortive candidature for Westminster, and the successful but very costly Westminster contest of November 1806. Sheridan went out of office with All the Talents in 1807, and his political correspondence after that date is chiefly interesting for the part he played in denying control of the government to Grey and Grenville in 1811 and 1812. As usual, he behaved with that mixture of the quixotic and the calculating that won him the confidence of nobody.

The same is true of his actions as chief proprietor of Drury Lane Theatre. His squabbles with the trustees and the bankers were patched up from time to time, and their uneasy relationship looked as if it would continue indefinitely. Then the theatre that was planned to be fireproof burned down, and a new start had to be made. Sheridan's letter to his wife about this catastrophe shows him behaving (in a slightly histrionic way) with manly philosophy. The banker, Thomas Hammersley, thought the destruction no disaster. In fact, he believed it gave Sheridan a splendid opportunity to repair his theatre and his shattered fortunes by drawing on private benefactions for rebuilding, just as J. P. Kemble had done at Covent Garden Theatre. And so it might have happened had Sheridan acted quickly, but his very proper desire for independence was only exceeded by his habitual procrastination, and nothing was done. Two years later, when an agitation for a third theatre was at its strongest, he began to act with vigour. He obtained the help of the wealthy brewer Samuel Whitbread, and persuaded him to head the Committee for rebuilding. He had a most remarkable faculty for persuading his friends to come to his rescue; but even Whitbread, with all his initial goodwill, found that potential subscribers now had to be assured, before they would consider the new propositions, that Sheridan had no concern in the management of Drury Lane Theatre. They were tired of his shifts and his dilatoriness. Sheridan was forced out of the controlling interest which he had enjoyed for thirty-five years. Still, the new proprietors had to buy this from him, and he looked forward to being paid in hard cash. Even this was denied him, and his demands were satisfied (after long discussion) in the same manner as he had fobbed off many a creditor—with shares in the theatre.

The last years (1812–16) of his life saw him out of parliament and Drury Lane. Observers cried, 'Poor Sherry!' They quoted him as a genius ruined by drink and self-indulgence. Yet it must be remembered that this was the period when he made such a striking impression on Byron. Indeed, if Sheridan was in decline the letters written in these years hardly show it, for they indicate his delight in society, his critical yet appreciative temper, his eye for the main chance, his good nature and warm heart. He occasionally grumbled at not hearing from his wife or second son, but generally his letters were cheerful and optimistic. His wife commented on this tendency 'to eat the calf in the cow's belly', and it is certain that he always hoped to realize the many schemes, extravagant or sober, that passed through his mind. Sheridan was never short of invention, even though he too seldom applied that talent to writing plays. What he lacked was the power to stop himself squandering his energies in all directions. And what was worse was that he insisted on giving to his multiplicity of activities not as much time as they required, but as much as he felt disposed to yield to them.

Towards the end of his life he read some early verses of his and remarked, 'What an ardent romantic blockhead nature made me'. Surely what he meant (and what his letters reveal) was that there was a constant conflict in him between a shrewd, practical outlook that took full advantage of every situation, and a high-minded desire to show integrity in all his dealings. He liked (though he could seldom afford it) to be completely disinterested. He has had little credit for this scrupulous side of his nature; the other side has always been obvious, and it earned him a bad name.

He sometimes excused his procrastination as a 'perverse fatality in my nature', and meant this quite seriously. The moods of melancholy, the bouts of drunkenness, the cruel tricks, shifts, and excuses, the sophistries and winning words, were beyond his control. He would have us believe (and I believe him) that he usually meant well but could seldom manage to put his meaning into action.

He tantalizes us, but there is something so human in his foibles that he remains a curiously sympathetic character. Perhaps his gift of phrase-making catches our attention; or his rueful remarks about his own shortcomings endear him to us. Yet what holds us in the end is this intimate communing with a man of genius who knows his own faults only too well but can do nothing to change his nature. In that situation lies the pathos of these letters.

They are not brilliantly written, and anyone who expects them to be worthy of the author of *The School for Scandal* will be disappointed. To achieve elegance of that kind, Sheridan had to write and rewrite. He seldom gave his letters enough attention: 'I shall confess that I write much more precipitately and triflingly often than I could wish.'

Most of them are brief. John Taylor describes an evening at the Shakespeare Tavern when Sheridan wrote 'about thirty letters, which he tied up in a handkerchief, and then resigned himself to conversation'. Edmund Kean quotes Sheridan as saying that no gentleman ever turned over the page in a letter to a friend. Charles Brinsley Sheridan looked through his father's letters and noted that 'almost all are extremely short; and he always put off writing till post'.

Sheridan knew his weakness (the product of procrastination) only too well, and made one of his most clear-sighted statements when he told Garrick 'what I write in a hurry I always feel not to be worth reading, and what I try to take pains with, I am sure never to finish'. His long letters, in later life, were usually careful attempts at special pleading.

Secrecy, too, was necessary in his world of political manœuvre, financial juggling, and fashionable intrigue. This prevented the uninhibited expression of opinion, and robbed his letters of savour. In one of them he made this clear by remarking that he preferred to reserve 'the greater part of what I meant to have written for personal communication'. Speech was less binding than writing. He knew how gifted he was in the art of oral persuasion: his genial, sympathetic manner and physical radiance all helped to convince. Sheridan was not a lazy man, but he could do so much with his tongue that his pen was always a more tedious medium. It is something of a wonder that he ever wrote any letters.

Those that remain are valuable records of the day-to-day variations of an elusive but always interesting character. They remind us sometimes of Lady Holland's comment on Sheridan, 'About him my reason and impulse are always at variance; reflection convinces me he ought to be despised for his private life and doubted for his political, but whenever I see him, if but for five minutes, a sort of cheerful frankness and pleasant wittiness puts to flight all the reasonable prejudices I entertain against him.' At other times we recall the words spoken in his own defence before the Lord Chancellor: 'I have had to struggle with the disadvantages of uncertain income. These, in all cases, are known to be great, but they are particularly formidable to a man of a sanguine temper, blessed with but a small share of resolution, who might expect much from the exertions of talent, who forms hopes which are never realised, and makes to himself promises he is unable to perform.' More rarely we recollect Byron's warm praise, '*his* very dregs are better than the first sprightly runnings of others'. Yet even if the letters too seldom show Sheridan at his best, they clearly reveal the nature of the man and are a necessary supplement to his actions, speeches, and plays.

THE TEXT

WHEN Sheridan died, his wife remarked on 'the incredible quantity of private papers' he had left behind him. Many of them were legal documents, and others were letters written to him as proprietor of Drury Lane Theatre and as a member of parliament. Some of the letters written by Sheridan himself seem to have been lent to Thomas Moore for the authorized biography, and to have been lost. Most of them were carefully preserved by Sheridan's grandson (and namesake) at Frampton Court, Dorset, and they remained in the family until they were dispersed at Sotheby's sale-rooms on 2 July 1930, 1 March 1955, and 18 February 1957. Another fine collection, gathered by Sophie, Lady Wavertree (Sheridan's great-great-granddaughter), was also sold there on 25 May 1954. These sources provide this edition with many letters. Others are drawn from the archives of the Prince Regent, C. J. Fox, Charles Grey, Samuel Whitbread, Thomas Creevey, and other public figures of the period. Sheridan's association with Drury Lane Theatre is well represented in numerous letters to his fellow manager, John Grubb, and to the Theatre's treasurer, Richard Peake. Letters to other correspondents are widely dispersed in public and private collections in this country and abroad.

I have made every effort to trace them all, but have now resigned myself to the probability that many have escaped me. It is to be hoped that when they come to light they will be found to be letters to his first wife, particularly of the Waltham Abbey period when Sheridan drafted some of the work that later made him famous.

Among the letters I have not traced are the following: eleven to Colonel Graham (sold to Spencer at Sotheby's, 1 August 1935); some in an extra-illustrated copy of Watkins's *Memoirs of . . . Sheridan* (sold by Leavitt, New York, 14 October 1878, lot 1080), and of Moore's *Memoirs of . . . Sheridan* (sold to Smythe at Sotheby's, 26 July 1923). Nor have I found the letter mentioned in Moore's memoranda (Widener MS.): 'see among Richardson's papers

Sheridan's letter to Richardson in '88 about purchasing Ford's share.'

Over the past ten years I have approached the agents of the Marchioness of Crewe on a number of occasions, about letters to Mrs. Crewe. I gather that some 'Sheridan letters' are extant, but that it is still not possible to gain access to them.

I have not included the text of two well-known letters that Sheridan signed with his friends: one was the 'Round Robin' to Johnson; the other, the address to Francis on 18 December 1787. Both are readily available in *The Correspondence of Edmund Burke*, iii (ed. G. H. Guttridge, Cambridge and Chicago, 1961), 273–4, and v (ed. H. Furber, 1965), 370–1.

While the present work has been in the press, some letters that it includes as unpublished have appeared in print. *The Correspondence of Edmund Burke*, iv (ed. J. A. Woods, 1963), 439–40, contains no. 78; volume v (ed. cit.), 121, 377–8, 457, presents nos. 89, 109, 143. Dr. N. E. Enkvist gives no. 178 in *Acta Academiae Aboensis, Humaniora*, xxvii, 3 (Åbo, 1964), 103. The first two volumes of Dr. Arthur Aspinall's edition of *The Correspondence of George, Prince of Wales, 1770–1812* (1963–4) contain sixteen letters. I list my numbers followed (in brackets) by Dr. Aspinall's: nos. 117 (290), 118 (286), 120 (346), 121 (296), 122 (334), 126 (308), 127 (309), 128 (302), 130 (311), 131 (318), 132 (292), 135 (302), 137 (369), 158 (578), 209 (844), Summary G. 3 (466).

Sotheby's sale catalogue of 21 March 1966 notes (as item 260) a letter from Sheridan to his second wife, telling her that Burdett had been 'taken by force to the Tower'. He added that he did not know what would happen but was glad she was away. His postscript noted 'much blood spilt at the Tower'.

CONVENTIONS

I HAVE printed the name of the recipient of the letter at the head of the text, and have then described the source. The names of private owners and of libraries possessing less than five Sheridan letters are quoted in full. Collections containing five or more letters are given an abbreviated title.

Unless there is an indication to the contrary, the letters are holographs. The description 'Draft' means an early version in Sheridan's hand: cancelled words have been omitted. 'Copy' refers to a Sheridan letter written in a hand not his own. Where the text is from photographic copies of original letters, that fact is indicated by the sign '[Ph.]'. Where the text is from a printed version, the earliest published form is followed.

A letter is described as published when the bulk of it has been printed elsewhere, but when brief extracts only have appeared publication is merely mentioned in footnotes. If a printed version is not named at the head of the letter or in a footnote, the letter is believed to be unpublished.

What are thought to be errors by other transcribers have usually been corrected without comment, but where the transcription remains in doubt or the alternative version has some other interest, then it is printed in a footnote.

When the date of a letter has not been placed by Sheridan at its head, the date is given in that position in italics. Dates supplied by the editor have been placed there in italics and square brackets. Abbreviated dates (e.g. 'Mond. eg.') have been expanded.

In transcribing original letters, I have tried to reproduce exactly what Sheridan wrote, but I have also compromised with this ideal by sometimes editing the text in the interests of readability. For example, all superior letters have been lowered to the line, and conventional abbreviations (including the ampersand) have been expanded. 'Mr', 'Mr', and 'Mr' are all printed as 'Mr.' I have also supplied the missing stop if followed by a capital, and the missing capital if preceded by a stop. Unclosed parentheses have been completed. Sheridan's use of 'your's' has been accepted, but 'it's' (for 'its') has been amended because of its ambiguity.

Sheridan is fond of using the dash. He also employs a very short downward stroke on the line that I have represented as a comma. His short level stroke on the line (or longer one followed by a wide space) I have shown as a point.

Of Sheridan's spelling, Moore writes: 'we find *thing* always spelt *think*—*whether*, *where* and *which* turned into *wether*, *were*, and *wich*; and double' *ms* and *s's* almost invariably reduced to "single blessedness".' The position is not quite as simple as Moore suggests, for in the very letter he alludes to, Sheridan spells 'thing' correctly and as 'think'. Sheridan is inconsistent even in his own inconsistencies, but the following generalizations have been accepted. He is confused about words containing 'ie', 'ei', and 'ai': for example, he writes 'peice', 'deceive', and 'villianous'. He sometimes metathesizes syllables, as in 'arbritation' and 'blasmephy'. 'Goverment' and 'seperate' are usual. These, and the following words, have all been normalized:

accomodation	agrieved	alltogether
allways	attonement	beautifull
benefitted	comands	compells
conexion	disapointment	disaprove
embarasment	emphaticaly	especialy
exagerated	existance	finaly
genious	infallably	inocence
inofensive	misaplied	privilige
realy	recolection	recomendation
subsistance	tranquility	tranquilize

Sometimes his spelling seems to reflect his own pronunciation: 'cridit', 'threasury', 'taching' (touching), 'deatis' (deities), 'Beiting' (biting), 'set' (said), 'begone' (begun).

Repetition of syllables (e.g. 'indepependently') and of words has been silently corrected. Nonsense words (e.g. 'insituate') have been amended, but eighteenth-century spellings (e.g. 'ideot') have been retained. Inadvertently omitted letters or words have been supplied in square brackets, and unclosed quotation marks have been silently closed. The £ sign which often appears in the manuscripts after or above the figuring has been brought to the front. Sheridan's odd spelling of some proper names has not been amended.

Where the transcription is made from copies, any eccentricities of spelling and punctuation have been normalized.

References to the dates of auction catalogues are to the first day of sale only.

Manuscripts are listed by their locations at the time when I read them. I have not attempted to record their more recent movements, though it may be worth noting that Mr. Shuttleworth's manuscripts are now in the Bodleian Library, and that the Holland House letters are in the British Museum, temporarily catalogued as Add. MS. 51641.

In the 'Summary of other Letters' (iii. 249–91), extracts from the letters themselves appear in quotation marks.

REGISTER OF LETTERS

VOLUME I

xxvii

VOLUME II

1794

1795

xlix   d

1

SUMMARY OF OTHER LETTERS

APPENDIX OF FURTHER LETTERS

ABBREVIATIONS USED IN THE NOTES

Here and throughout, place of publication is London unless
otherwise noted

Adam MS.	Manuscript owned by Captain C. K. Adam, Blair-Adam, Fifeshire.
Add. MS.	Additional MS., British Museum.
Alnwick MSS.	Manuscripts of the Duke of Northumberland, at Alnwick Castle.
Angelo	*Reminiscences of Henry Angelo* ... (1828–30, 2 vols.).
A.P.C.	*Autograph Prices Current* (ed. E. H. Courville and A. J. Herbert, 1916–22, 6 vols.).
Auckland Corr.	*The Journal and Correspondence of William Lord Auckland* (1861, 4 vols.).
Bell's W. Mess.	*Bell's Weekly Messenger*, 1796–1807.
Beresford Corr.	*The Correspondence of the Rt. Hon. John Beresford* ... (ed. W. Beresford, 1854, 2 vols.).
Black	Clementina Black, *The Linleys of Bath* (rev. ed., 1926).
Campbell	John, Lord Campbell, *The Lives of the Lord Chancellors* (1845–9, 8 vols.).
Canning MSS.	Mehitabel Canning's correspondence, owned by Mrs. Alfred Western Sadler's Butler MSS.
C.G.Th.	The Theatre Royal, Covent Garden.
Clayden	P. W. Clayden, *Rogers and His Contemporaries* (1889, 2 vols.).
Clements MS.	Manuscript in the W. L. Clements Library, University of Michigan.
Colchester Corr.	*The Diary and Correspondence of Charles Abbot, Lord Colchester* (ed. Charles Abbot, Lord Colchester, 1861, 3 vols.).
Cornwallis Corr.	*The Correspondence of Charles, first Marquis Cornwallis* (ed. C. Ross, 2nd ed., 1859, 3 vols.).
Court and Cabinets	R. P. T. N. B. C. Grenville, Duke of Buckingham and Chandos, *Memoirs of the Court and Cabinets of George the Third* (1853–5, 2 vols.).
Cradock	J. Cradock, *Literary and Miscellaneous Memoirs* (1828, 4 vols.).
Creevey Papers	*The Creevey Papers* (ed. Sir H. Maxwell, 1903, 2 vols.).
D.L.Th.	The Theatre Royal, Drury Lane.
Dock.	Docketing in a contemporary hand.

Dropmore Papers	Historical Manuscripts Commission's *Reports on the Manuscripts of J. B. Fortescue, Esq., Preserved at Dropmore* (1892–1927, 10 vols.).
Dufferin MSS.	Manuscripts of the Marchioness of Dufferin and Ava.
Egerton MS.	Egerton MS., British Museum.
Europ. Mag.	*European Magazine*, 1782–1826.
Farington	*The Farington Diary* (ed. J. Greig, 1922–8, 8 vols.).
Fitzwilliam MS.	Manuscript owned by Earl Fitzwilliam, deposited at Sheffield Public Library.
Folger MS.	Manuscript in the Folger Shakespeare Library, Washington, D.C.
Foster	J. Foster, *Alumni Oxionienses, 1751–1886* (4 vols., 1888).
Fox Corr.	*Memorials and Correspondence of Charles James Fox* (ed. Lord J. Russell, 1853–7, 4 vols.).
Fr.	Franked.
Garrick Corr.	*The Private Correspondence of David Garrick* (ed. J. Boaden, 1831–2, 2 vols.).
Georgiana	*Georgiana: Extracts from the Correspondence of Georgiana, Duchess of Devonshire* (ed. The Earl of Bessborough, 1955.)
Gent. Mag.	*Gentleman's Magazine*, 1751–1825.
Gilmore MS.	Manuscript owned by Mr. Paul M. Gilmore.
Grey MSS.	Correspondence of Charles, 2nd Earl Grey, deposited by Earl Grey at Prior's Kitchen, University of Durham, Durham.
Grubbe MS.	Manuscript owned by Miss Margaret J. M. Grubbe.
Gun	*The Harrow School Register, 1751–1800* (ed. W. J. T. Gun, 1934).
Hansard	Cobbett's (afterwards Hansard's) *Parliamentary Debates*, 1803–16.
Harrow MS.	Manuscript in the Vaughan Library, Harrow School. Where 'Rae' is also mentioned in this location, the reference is to the MS. letters there, bound in extra-illustrated volumes of Rae's *Sheridan*.
Harvard MS.	Manuscript in the Theatre Collection, Harvard College Library.
H.M.C.	Historical Manuscripts Commission.
Hist. Westm. El.	*History of the Westminster and Middlesex Elections in the Month of November, 1806* (1807).
Hodgson	Messrs. Hodgson, Chancery Lane, W.C. 2.
Holland	Henry Fox, 3rd Lord Holland, *Memoirs of the Whig Party* (1852–4, 2 vols.).

Holland House MSS.	Manuscripts of the Earl of Ilchester.
Huntington	Henry E. Huntington Library, San Marino, California.
Hyde MS.	Manuscript owned by Mr. and Mrs. Donald Hyde, Somerville, New Jersey.
Judd	Gerrit P. Judd, iv, *Members of Parliament, 1734–1832* (New Haven, 1955).
Kelly	*Reminiscences of Michael Kelly* . . . (2nd ed., 1826, 2 vols.).
Leeds' Mem.	*The Political Memoranda of the 5th Duke of Leeds* (ed. O. Browning, Camden Society, 1884).
LeFanu MS.	Manuscript owned by Mr. W. R. LeFanu.
Lefanu	Alicia Lefanu, *Memoirs of the Life and Writings of Mrs. Frances Sheridan* (1824).
Leinster Corr.	*Correspondence of Emily, Duchess of Leinster, 1731–1814* (ed. B. Fitzgerald, Irish Manuscripts Commission, Dublin, 1949–57, 3 vols.).
Letters of Geo. IV	*The Letters of King George IV, 1812–1830* (ed. A. Aspinall, 1938, 3 vols.).
Leveson Gower Corr.	*Lord Granville Leveson Gower (First Earl Granville), Private Correspondence, 1781 to 1821* (ed. Castalia, Countess Granville, 1917, 2 vols.).
Lond. Chron.	*London Chronicle*, 1769–80.
McAdam MS.	Manuscript owned by Mr. E. L. McAdam, Jr.
Maggs Catalogue	Catalogue of Messrs. Maggs Bros., London, W. 1.
Minto Corr.	*Life and Letters of Sir Gilbert Elliot, First Earl of Minto* (ed. the Countess of Minto, 1874, 3 vols.).
Moore	*Memoirs of the Life of the Right Honourable Richard Brinsley Sheridan* (2nd ed., 1825, 2 vols.).
Moore, *Journal*	*Memoirs, Journal, and Correspondence of Thomas Moore* (ed. Lord John Russell, 1853–6, 8 vols.).
Morn. Chron.	*Morning Chronicle*, 1775–1816.
Morn. Her.	*Morning Herald*, 1782–1816.
Morn. Post	*Morning Post*, 1775–1816.
Morrison Cat.	*Catalogue of the Collection of Autograph Letters and Historical Documents formed between 1865 and 1882 by Alfred Morrison* (part ed. A. Thibaudeau, 1883–92, 6 vols.).
Mrs. S.	Until 1793 this refers to Sheridan's first wife, Elizabeth Ann Sheridan (born Linley), 1754–92. After 1793 it refers to his second wife, Hester Jane Sheridan (born Ogle), *c.* 1775–1817.

Myers	Messrs. Myers, 59 High Holborn, W.C. 1; and Miss Winifred A. Myers.
New M. Mag.	*New Monthly Magazine*, 1814–71.
N.L.I. MS.	Manuscript of the National Library of Ireland, Dublin.
N.L.S. MS.	Manuscript of the National Library of Scotland, Edinburgh.
Ogle	Sir Henry A. Ogle, Bart., *Ogle and Bothal: Or, A History of the Baronies of Ogle, Bothal and Hepple . . .* (Newcastle upon Tyne, 1902).
Osborn MS.	Manuscript owned by Dr. James M. Osborn of Yale University.
Parl. Reg.	*The Parliamentary Register* (ed. J. Debrett, 1783–96, 45 vols.).
P. & S. C.	Sale catalogues of Messrs. Puttick & Simpson, London, W. 1.
Parr, *Works*	Samuel Parr, *Works* (ed. J. Johnstone, 1828, 8 vols.).
Pellew	George Pellew, *The Life and Correspondence of the Rt. Hon. Henry Addington, First Viscount Sidmouth* (1847, 3 vols.).
[Ph.]	A photographic copy of the manuscript has been the source of the text.
Pm.:	Postmark. This is printed only when it is necessary as evidence establishing the date of a letter.
Price MS.	Manuscript owned by Cecil Price.
P.R.O.	Public Record Office, London.
Pub.	Location of the first printing of the text that follows.
Pub. Adv.	*Public Advertiser*, 1769–80.
Rae	W. Fraser Rae, *Sheridan, A Biography* (1896, 2 vols.).
Rhodes	R. Crompton Rhodes, *Harlequin Sheridan* (Oxford, 1933).
Rose	George Rose, *The Diaries and Correspondence of the Rt. Hon. George Rose* (ed. L. V. Harcourt, 1860, 2 vols.).
S.	Richard Brinsley Sheridan (1751–1816).
Sadler	Michael T. H. Sadler, *The Political Career of Richard Brinsley Sheridan* (Oxford, 1912.)
Salt MS.	Manuscript of the William Salt Library, Stafford.
S.C.	Sale catalogues of Messrs. Sotheby, London, and of the varying names of the firm from 1814 to 1964.
Shuttleworth MS.	Manuscript owned by Mr. Bertram Shuttleworth.
Sichel	W. Sichel, *Sheridan* (1909, 2 vols.).

Smyth	[William Smyth], *Memoir of Mr. Sheridan* (Leeds, 1840).
Speeches	*Speeches of the late Right Honourable Richard Brinsley Sheridan* (ed. 'A Constitutional Friend' [Sir John Philippart?], 1816, 5 vols.).
Staff. Adv.	*Staffordshire Advertiser*, 1796–16.
Taylor	John Taylor, *Records of my Life* (1832, 2 vols.).
T.L.S.	*The Times Literary Supplement*, 1902–64.
Tom S.	Tom Sheridan (1775–1817).
Watkins	John Watkins, *Memoirs of the Public and Private Life of the Right Honourable R. B. Sheridan* ... (2nd ed. 1817, 2 vols.).
Whitbread MS.	Manuscript owned by Mr. Simon Whitbread.
Widener MS.	Manuscript in the Harry Elkins Widener Collection in the Harvard College Library.
Windsor MS.	Manuscript in the Royal Archives at Windsor Castle.
Winston	Manuscripts and newspaper cuttings collected by James Winston, and now in the British Museum (press-mark, C 120 h). There are fourteen boxes for the period 1776–1816, but their contents are unfoliated.
Wm.:	Dated watermark (or countermark) in the paper on which Sheridan's letter is written. This evidence is printed only when it is necessary to establish a date.
Wraxall	Sir N. W. Wraxall, *Posthumous Memoirs of His Own Times* (2nd ed. 1836, 3 vols.).
W.T.	Typescript copies of Sheridan MSS. formerly in the possession of Sophie, Lady Wavertree. These copies contain a number of obvious typing errors, and I have silently corrected them when quoting from the typescripts.
Yale MS.	Manuscript in the Yale University Library.

1. To Richard Chamberlaine[1]

Yale MS. *Pub.*: Rae, i. 72. *Address*: To Richd. Chamberlane Esqr. |
at Beauford buildings in the strand | London *Pm.*: 3 MR *Dock.*:
Answerd 8 March—1766—Saturday

March 2d: 1765 [*1766?*]

Dear Uncle

As it is not more than three weeks to the holy days, I
should be greatly obliged to you, if you could get me some
new cloaths as soon as possible, for those which I have at
present are very bad and as I have no others; I am almost
ashamed to wear them on a sunday. I fancy I shall spend my
holy days again at Harrow,[2] for I have not seen nor heard
from Mr. Akenhead[3] since August, Though I had rather
stay at Harrow than go to Richmond, Mr. Somner[4] asked
me the other day if I had heard lately from my Brother[5] and
says he has not heard from them this long time: if you have
had a letter lately I should be obliged to you would [you] let
me know how they are, and when they come to England for
I long to see them.[6]

I should be greatly obliged to you if you would let me
have some cloaths as soon as possible, for when these want
mending I have no others to wear. Mr. and Mrs. Somner[7]
are very well. I am Dear Uncle | Your affectionate Nephew |
R B Sheridan.—

---

[1] S.'s uncle, a surgeon. He frequented
the Grecian coffee-house, and was a
friend of Charles Johnstone, author of
Chrysal. He is described as a 'pleasant
little man with a good deal of anecdote' (*Gent. Mag.* xcviii (1828), pt. 2,
112).

[2] Thomas Sheridan and his family,
with the exception of S., lived in France
between Sept. 1764 and Oct. 1766. S.
had entered Harrow School in 1762 and
remained there until *c.* 1767–8. Dance's
dates (Farington, i. 133) are wrong.

[3] A friend of Thomas Sheridan. He
had a villa at Richmond and was 'well
known as an amateur of fashion in the

literature and theatrical history of the
day' (Lefanu, p. 256).

[4] Robert Carey Sumner (1729–71),
headmaster of Harrow School.

[5] Charles Francis Sheridan (1750–
1806) was at Blois with his parents and
two sisters.

[6] Forty years later, S. told Creevey
(*Creevey Papers*, i. 53) that, at Harrow,
'he was a very low-spirited boy, much
given to crying when alone, and he
attributed this . . . to his being left
without money, and often not taken
home at the regular holidays'.

[7] 'A sister of William Arden of Eton'
(*D.N.B.*).

2. To Richard Chamberlaine

Harrow MS. *Pub.*: *The Times*, 15 Feb. 1934. *Dock.*: Answered and ordered cloaths on June 24th 1766

June 1766

Dear Uncle,

I hope you will not be surprised, when I tell you that the cause of my present letter is partly my want of cloaths,[1] for my brown ones are quite gone, as I have had them almost a year, and those which I have now, being of a very light colour, and having mett with a few accidents, are not remarkably clean, though pretty decent. And as I have been some time obliged to wear them every day, I have two reasons for desiring new cloaths, first as I have lately got into the 5 form, which is the head form of the school I am under a necessity of appearing like the other 5 form boys, secondly as the sylver arrow[2] is to be shot for next thursday sevennight and most of the boys having new cloaths at that time instead of August, I should be glad, if it is convenient to you, to have them likewise, and then I should be in a condition to save them very well, by having a pretty good suit at present, which I could not do, if I were to stay u[n]till these were almost wore out. I should be also very much obliged to you, if you would lett me have a hat at the same time. If you please I will writ[e] a line to Mr. Riley how to send them to me. | Pray give my love to my Aunt.　I am | Your affectionate Nephew | R B Sheridan.

3. To Richard Chamberlaine

Yale MS. *Pub.*: Rae, i. 73.

[Oct. 1766]

Dear Uncle

It is now almost a week since Mr. Somner told me the

[1] For Thomas Sheridan's indigence at this time, see his letter in Watkins, i. 129.

[2] 'A Silver arrow value Three Pounds, to be shot [for] by twelve young gentlemen of that [school]', was the prize in the Harrow archery contest. See Gun, pp. xi–xii, and Lefanu, pp. 254–5.

melancholy news of my poor mother's death;[1] and as Mr. Somner has not heard what time my Father will be home,[2] he desires me to write to you about mourning. I have wrote To Riley, who, with your orders, will make me a suit of Black. I should be obliged to you if you would let me know what time you expect my Father.

You will excuse the shortness of my letter, as the subject is disagreeable, | from your affectionate | Nephew | R B Sheridan.

P.S. I must also have a new hat with a crape and black sto[c]kin[g]s and buckles. I should be glad of them on saturday.

4. [To the Printer of the *Public Advertiser?*][3]

Yale MS. Draft.

[*1769?*]

In submitting the following considerations to the perusal of the public I am thoroughly sensible of the difficulty of the task which I have undertaken. I am aware how much the general opinion of mankind is against me, notwithstanding which I flatter myself that I can bring such substantial argument in support of my cause as faction itself will not dare to dispute. I shall first premise that in the following essay I do not mean to appeal to your justice, but to your moderation. I shall not examine the rectitude of the action I attempt to diswade you from but its expediency and utility. 'Twould be but idle declamation to employ any time in lamenting the unfortunate situation of the noble —— my patron, sorry I

[1] Frances Sheridan (1724–66), novelist and playwright, died at Blois on 26 Sept. 1766.

[2] Writing from Paris on 13 Oct. 1766, Thomas Sheridan declared 'I set out from this in a few days for St. Quintin ... where I purpose to leave my Children in the hands of Protestants. ... As soon as I have settled them, I shall set out for London ...' (Samuel Whyte, *Poems on Various Subjects* (ed. E. A. Whyte, 3rd ed., Dublin, 1795), p. 361).

[3] Augustus Fitzroy, 3rd Duke of Grafton (1735–1811), was head of the administration from 1768 to 1770, and was strongly attacked by 'Junius' between Mar. 1769 and Nov. 1771. S.'s ironical defence of Grafton seems to belong to the earlier part of this period, and may be compared with Junius's letter of 24 Apr. 1769, as well as with the letters of 'Decius' in the *Pub. Adv.,* 18 and 23 Sept. 1769.

am that things are come to this pass, and would some abler pen had undertaken to plead his [cause] but since the lot has fallen to me my gratitude to my benefactor compels me to exert my utmost abilities in the support of it.—

I shall with utmost candour state the chief arguments me patrons adversaries bring in support of their favourite points and leave it to the judgement of the unprejudiced whether I do no[t][1] fairly refute them. The first argument is[2] found[ed] on the regard which ought to be paid to justice, and on the good effects which they affirm such an example[3] would have in suppressing the ambition of any future minister. But if I can prove that his ——— might be made a much greater example of by being suffered to live, I think I may without vanity affirm their whole argument will fall to the ground. By pursuing the methods which the[y] purpose viz. chopping off his ——— head I allow the impression would be stronger at first, but we should consider how soon that wears off; if indeed his ——— crimes were of such a nature as to entitle his head to a place on temple-Bar, I should allow some weight to their objection, but in the present case we should reflect how apt mankind are [to] relent after they have inflicted punishment so that perhaps the same men who would have detested the noble well alive and in prosperity, pointing him as a scare-crow to the children, migh[t] after being witnesses to the miserable fate that had overtaken him begin in their hearts to pity him, and from the fickleness so common to human nature, perhaps by way of compensation acquit him of part of his crimes, insinuate that he was hardly dealt with; and thus by the remembrance of their compunction on this occasion, they might be led to show more indulgence to any future offender in the same circumstances. This it is evident would be productive of the worst consequences, and the punishment so far from being a[n] example to deter others from treading his steps would become a palpable encourage-

---

1 Torn.

2 Moore prints (i. 125–7) two passages from this letter. The first begins at this point and ends with 'same circumstances'.

3 Beheading. See Junius's letter of 30 May 1769, to the Duke of Grafton:

'Sullen and severe without religion, profligate without gaiety, you live like Charles the Second, without being an amiable companion, and, for aught I know, may die as his father did, without the reputation of a martyr' (*The Letters of Junius* (ed. C. W. Everett, 1927), p. 58).

ment and for aught I know the means of establishing arbitrary power. This therefore I humbly conceive is a sufficient refutation of an argument which has or can be offered by my opponents on the above mentioned principles. But if any of the gentlemen shall think that I am biass[ed] in my judgement I beg you will do me the justice to attribute it, not to any intention of imposing on you, but to what really must be the cause, that unfeign'd regard and gratitude which I do confess I have for his Grace and which perhaps may sometimes betray into undesigned partial[ity].[1]

I shall now beg leave to touch a little on his private character, I beg his grace's friends not to be alarmed as I think I can very fairly prove that what several malicious persons have construed as crimes are in reality virtu[e]s a little misapplied. Among that number he is accused of degrading his rank by consorting with low and mean people, sur[e]ly [nothing] can be more invidious or more unchristian than such a charge, as that is evidently that christian humility only carried to a little excess. Did the saviour of mankind assort with sinners and publicans and who shall dare to blame one of his followers for following his example. I could quote various texts in scripture. I hope [I] shall be pardoned my heat on this occasion but really the malice of the world inflames. I would not dwell so much on this but in regard to the duke and in hopes that the novelty of this subject to my readers will screen me from the imputation of prolixity.

His grace has been accused of feeling . . .[1] mutability. Tho I do not positively affirm I can refute this, yet I[2] think I could bring several instances which should seem to promise the greatest steadiness and resolution. I have known him make the co[un]cil wait and the business of the whole nation Say when he has had an appointment to Newmarket. Surely this is an instance of the greatest honour and if we see him so punctual in private appointments must we not conclude that he is infinitely more so in the greater matters? Nay, when W——s[3] came over is [it] not notorious that the late Lord

---

[1] Torn.
[2] Moore's transcript begins again here, and ends with 'punctuality'.
[3] John Wilkes (1727–97) returned from his exile in France on three occasions: 11 May 1766; 28 Oct. 1766; and about 6 Feb. 1768. S. refers to the last.

Mayor[1] went to his grace on that evening, proposing a schem[e] which by securing this fire-brand might have put an end to all the troubles he has caus'd, but his Grace did not see him, no—he was a man of too much honour—he had *promised* that evening to attend Nancy Parsons[2] to renelay[3] and he would no[t] disappoint her, but made 3000 people arm in arm witnesses of punctuality. He cannot be accused of fauning on the king—he has fronted him with his whore.—Is this ambition?

5. To the Printer of the *Public Advertiser*

Yale MS. Draft. *Pub.*: *Pub. Adv.*, 16 Oct. 1769.

Oct. 1769

Sir,

Your Situation is such as must often oblige you, in order to preserve a strict Regard to Impartiality, to insert Pieces in your Paper which your free Judgment would reject: But as such fugitive Productions can neither influence the Opinions, or in the least affect the Actions of the thinking Part of Mankind, it would be madness in any one, by attempting to expose their Futility to gratify the Vanity of an Author, whose whole Object perhaps was only to indulge his own Love of Self-importance by being abused in Print.

Among that Number the tedious *Novus*[4] should have passed unnoticed, and his Essay might have remained in that impenetrable Obscurity with which he has enveloped every Sentence of it, had not the tremendous Words, *to be continued*, alarmed my Patience, and made me resolve, out of Pity to your Readers, Mr. Woodfall,[5] to persuade, if possible, the Gentleman himself to spare us the Mortification of seeing so much of your useful Paper employed in such Pro-

---

[1] Thomas Harley (1730–1804), Lord Mayor of London, 1767–8, and M.P. for Herefordshire, 1776–1802.

[2] His mistress, afterwards Lady Maynard. See 'Junius''s letters of 24 Apr., 23 June, and 22 June 1768.

[3] Ranelagh Gardens.

[4] Letters by 'Novus' appeared in the *Pub. Adv.* of 4 July, 11 Aug., 6 Oct., and 19 Oct. 1769. S. refers to that of 6 Oct.: 'On the Merits of the Present Ministry'.

[5] Henry Sampson Woodfall (1739–1805), printer of the *Public Advertiser*.

ductions as this before me. In order to do this, I am afraid it will be necessary to examine the Performance itself a little, not with an Intention to refute any Part of it, I will not pay so bad a Compliment to the Understanding of the Public, but merely to point out to the Author a few of those Absurdities which, tho' he might overlook in the Confusion of writing, he may possibly have Understanding enough to perceive, when coolly held forth to his View, stript of their pompous Epithets, specious Metaphors, and all the dazzling Decorations with which the *conceited* Writer ever gilds his Ignorance. 'Tis dirty Work, Mr. Printer, but I shall expect, as a Reward for my Letter, that our Essayist shall candidly allow he has mistaken his Talent, if I demonstrate to him that he is writing on a Subject he does not understand, that his Observations are trite to the last Degree, his Stile affected and puerile, his Meaning obscure, with not a single new Thought throughout the whole Piece, save a few which he has *made as his own*, by rendering them unintelligible.

In doing this I shall make all the Allowances which the Modesty of his Signature seems to demand, as undoubtedly an Author must be supposed to labour under some Difficulties who is giving Information to the Public on a Subject of which he is entirely ignorant. *Novus* appears to have been aware of this, and has therefore launched out into generals as much as possible; accordingly we find that the first Part of his Letter consists chiefly of undoubted sage Reflections and hackney'd Arguments, worn to the Stump by every News Paper Writer for this hundred Years past: But let us coolly examine the Fact. *Novus* is pleased facetiously to call his Letter an 'Essay on the Merits of the present Ministry', whom he scarcely ever mentions afterwards during the whole Performance. He sets out with assuring us, that political Liberty is the *Scope* of our Constitution;[1] what he means by the Scope of a Constitution, I confess I am at a Loss to conceive. The Writer must have taken some Pains here to have been unintelligible, but perhaps 'tis Policy in

---

[1] Novus begins his letter: 'In a State where political as well as civil liberty is confessedly the scope and essential Property of the Constitution, every individual naturally looks upon himself as possessed of a right to examine the conduct of the governing powers.'

him to disguise his Sentiments as much as possible, though they suffer under the Operation, on the same Principle that a poor Man who had got a laced Coat from Monmouth-street[1] would strip it of its finery that it might appear more his own. Then 'that every Individual possessed of this *Scope* of Constitution has a Right to examine the Conduct of the governing Powers;' I will leave him here to himself to make their *Right* clear, I only wish he'd throw in a Proof of their *Ability*. He then goes on for the Space of a half a Column to prove that 'he has Reason to hope he may stand excused, though a small Part of a stupendous whole, if he offers the Result of his Thoughts to the Deliberations of the Public.' The next Period consists of a Number of well-sounding Substantives, with a suitable Retinue of unmeaning Epithets: The Stile is a clumsy Imitation of Junius's[2] Manner: the pretty turn'd Period and catching Contrast. In the Space of a Dozen Lines occur the following Instances: 'The Disposition of the People capriciously passive,—Hand of Government invariably severe.—Artifice of Corruption, assisted by Threats of Violence.—Private injury subsided—Public Justice met with Disregard—Barred by the Assertion of Power,—nor deceived by the Maze of Sophistry.' This is far from being the only Place where these Prettinesses display themselves, every Sentence teems with them: But tho' I allow all possible Merit to this favourite Figure, yet I can't help thinking it a little hard that the poor remaining Part of the Sentence should, together with the trifling Circumstances of *Truth* and *Perspicuity* be generally sacrificed to the Support of it. And after all, in my Opinion, it has only this Effect, to make the Performance before us bear a strong Resemblance to an *Hasty-Pudding*[3] *stuck with Sweetmeats*.

In the many Places where *Novus* is unintelligible, I do sincerely acquit him of being intentionally so; and I will do him the Justice to believe that the Load of Epithets which burdens every Sentence, is not designed to bar all Examination into his Meaning, but that he was unhappily led into

[1] Where old clothes were sold.

[2] His trenchant criticisms of the government appeared in the *Pub. Adv.* between 21 Jan. 1769 and 21 Jan. 1772. He has not been identified with any certainty. For a summary of the cases put forward on behalf of some forty-five possible authors of his letters, see *The Letters of Junius* (ed. cit.), pp. xli-lii, 377–87. [3] A batter pudding.

this Error merely by paying too strict a Regard to an old Observation viz. *that the Difficulty of obtaining a Thing enhances its Value.* Thus it is said we esteem the Kernel of a Nut chiefly on Account of the Difficulty of obtaining it; but if after cracking, peeling, etc. our Prize should be rotten, our Expectation will certainly be succeeded by proportionable Disappointment. As this Circumstance frequently occurs in the Essay under Consideration, I am afraid, after an Attempt or two, there will be few People inclined to try the Experiment.

But let us proceed in the Examination of the Fact. After a short Dissertation on the Genius of the English Nation, and a Discovery that it will not be much to the Purpose to dwell on the Subject, *Novus* proceeds to inform us that there is one Part of it so strongly *marked*, that he can't help endeavouring to clear it[1] from the imputation of Passiveness, he says he means the *Patience of the People. The Patience* of the People is so strongly *marked*, that he can't help endeavouring to clear it from the Imputation of *Passiveness*, and a very good Reason for his Endeavours too; for certainly if the People bear *Marks* of their Patience (for in no other Sense can I understand a marked Patience) that Patience will, I am afraid, by most People be reckoned *passive*. You see I would help the Author to a little Meaning wherever I can. Well, he now proceeds to prove, that this *marked* Patience of the People was not a *passive* Patience, that is that it was an active Patience; a new kind of Patience I must confess! Which he does in the following Manner: His Words are, 'The unpopular, inexperienced Administration which guided the Counsels of our present *Sovereign* on the Demise of his *much esteemed* Grandfather.' I must just beg Leave to remark that our Essayist is here obliged to the Printer for his Wit, who is to print *present* and *much esteemed* in Italics by way of Contrast; as it is meant for a good-natured Compliment to the King, and I dare say entirely *Novus's* own, I would not have him lose the Merit of it for Want of Observation: Well, when this Ministry had 'betrayed the Deficiency of their Abilities only in inactive Absurdity at home, and manifested

---

[1] The manuscript draft at Yale begins with this word and goes on to the end of the letter. The earlier part is missing.

their Want of Integrity only in the Ruin of our Interests abroad;' a pretty modest Charge this, and very facetious: But does *Novus* know whom he attacks? He means Lord B——e,[1] etc. but unluckily forgets that Lord C——m[2] and the D—— of N——e[3] were the Ministers at the Demise of the late King. You see, Mr. Woodfall, how, Pioneer-like, I am obliged to force my way through every Sentence. When the Administration had done *only* this, 'the *patient* People *called* for a Change of Ministers.' This may be illustrated by supposing any one describing a Riot at the Theatre, and praising the Patience of the People, should say that when the first Music was playing its appointed Piece, *the patient Galleries called for Roast Beef of Old England.*[4] He then, absurdly stating a few Falsities, tells us 'the *patient* People were *roused*.' By this he does not mean that they had laid aside their Patience, for it is not till after many Pieces of Information that he assures us, that 'the *Patience* of the People is exhausted.' He surely now has gained his Point, and I hope after this no one will ever dare to accuse the good People of England of *passive Patience*. With what a masterly Hand has he wound up his Demonstration! what a beautiful Climax! what inimitable Bathos! First we see an active *Patience*, then a *calling Patience*, then a *roused Patience*, and then—no Patience at all.

In the Course of the foregoing, there is one pretty rounded Sentence, where he says, 'the *sedate Ignorance* of Lord B——e was succeeded by the turbulent Incapacity of the Duke of G——n.'[5] It *sounds* well, but I thought that Lord B——e's Enemies had always allowed him to be a Man of Knowledge,[6] and some Abilities: This is often the Case with *Novus*, which I suppose proceeds from his paying such Attention to the Structure of his Periods, that he forgets to examine on what Foundation he builds.

[1] John Stuart, 3rd Earl of Bute (1713–92), First Lord of the Treasury, 1762–3.

[2] William Pitt, 1st Earl of Chatham (1708–78).

[3] Thomas Pelham-Holles, 1st Duke of Newcastle (1693–1768).

[4] Henry Fielding's song in *The Grub Street Opera*, III. iii.

[5] Novus adds: 'and the dishonesty of the former outdone by the wickedness of the latter.'

[6] Thomas Sheridan addressed a letter to Bute on 6 Oct. 1769, asking for further support for the publication of his (Thomas Sheridan's) grammar and dictionary (Cardiff Public Library MS. 3. 615).

After a little inflammatory Declamation, *Novus* soon after concludes his Epistle without once condescending to handle the Subject on which he professes to write.

Perhaps *Novus* so far from being offended at this Attack, will be pleased to think that his future Performances may perhaps gain Consequence enough to be read by the Abuse of this: I wish so too; for it is only by their not being read that such Writers as *Novus* can scribble with any Effect; by reading I do not mean the cursory Manner in which the Eye is cast over the Generality of News paper Productions: People just see a Parcel of misleading Words, without considering their Propriety or Foundation, and they pay that Compliment to Mr. Woodfall's Taste, to suppose that there must be some Truth in whatever he admits to a Place in his Paper, without making Allowances for the Necessity he is under sometimes to oblige Blockheads, that he may seem impartial. For instance, a Man casting his Eye over the third Paragraph of *Novus's* Letter would be struck with the Sight of *Acts of Outrage—Artifice of Corruption—Threats of Violence—Violation of Rights*, etc. and then perhaps might draw a hasty Conclusion, that the Writer had some Foundation for his Assertions. But if any thing shall lead them to peruse such Performances with some Degree of Attention, their cooler Judgments will soon make them reject with Contempt whatever indigested Ideas a cursory View had left floating in their Imaginations; they will despise the Tricks of Style, nor suffer themselves to be misled by scurrilous Assertions unsupported by Facts or even Probability; on such an Examination they will find the above mentioned Paragraph to be a crude Collection of Words without Connection, and Epithets without Meaning; and the whole a confused Mass of idle Declamation and Falsity, breathed with an inflammatory Spirit, either to gratify the Blockhead's private Vanity, or promote the Interests of disappointed Faction. | Jockey

1769

6. To 'NOVUS'[1]

Yale MS.

[*After 19 Oct. 1769*]

Ecce iterum Crispinus![2]

Sir,

I would not reflect upon your understanding; but I fear you have too much spirit to suffer yourself to be influenced by conviction; Stoic-like you despise the opinion of others; and so far from profiting by the friendly admonitions conveyed to you in my last, you seem resolved to show your contempt, and disregard of them by giving me, in your second essay, a much more copious field for criticism and ridicule than even your former letter afforded. Such numerous proofs of this occur in every sentence of it, that, were not the sentiments fully suited to the language, I should suspect that you purposely neglected paying any regard to grammatical rules, or attending to the choice, or right construction of your words; in hopes by that means, to confine all criticism to your demerits as a writer, while uncontradicted[3] you might impose on the public as a politician. But[3] that gloomy seriousness in your style, that seeming consciousness of superiority, together with the consideration of the infinite pains it must have cost you to have been so elaborately wrong will not suffer me to attribute such numerous errors to anything but real ignorance, joined with most consummate vanity.

As I confined myself in my last chiefly to your pretensions as a Writer, I must now beg leave to examine your merit as an arguer and politician: tho' still I will be so far your friend, as to point out to you any other defects which shall occur to me.

---

[1] This was written in reply to Novus's letter in the *Pub. Adv.*, 19 Oct. 1769. S. took some pains over his composition, and a rough draft of it is also among the Yale MSS. I can find no evidence that any reply by 'Jockey' was printed by Woodfall, but the *Pub. Adv.*, 1 Nov. 1769, contains a note signed 'R.o.S.' [R.B.S.?], making the point that

Charles I lost his throne because of 'the spirited measures of his detested Ministers against the Laws and Constitution of their Country'.

[2] Juvenal, *Satyra*, iv, l. 1.

[3] Moore, i. 127-8, prints two brief passages from S.'s letter. The first begins after this word and runs to the end of the paragraph.

You still profess to write '*on the merits of the present ministry*'; without attempting to remove my former objection to that title, by ever once condescending to treat of what you declare is to be the subject of your essay. You persevere in the same empty, blustering style, the same dismal tautology; I should quote your first sentence as a proof of this, but that it takes up eighteen lines of Mr. Woodfall's Public Advertiser. After descanting on the opposition to '*the first Charles*' you conclude with declaring that you are '*delighted with the glorious contemplation*': your exclamation comes in here exceedingly flat; and by not being able to contain yourself within due bounds on the mere mention of Charles's name, you have so far separated the declaration of your delight from its cause, as to leave[1] it rather dubious whether you were most pleased with the glorious opposition to Charles, or the dangerous designs of that Monarch; which you emphatically call the arbitrary projects of a Stuarts nature. What do you mean by the projects of a man's *nature*? A man's natural disposition may urge him to the commission of some actions; nature may instigate and encourage, but I believe you are the first that ever made her a projector. These are trifling inac[c]uracies; I point them out merely for your own edification; and in order to perswade you to remove somewhat of that tiresome obscurity from your style; at least, 'till by these essays, like our modern Lexiphanes,[2] you have established a reputation sufficient to entitle you to wrap up your meaning in whatever cloathings you please, and like him, never to attend to perspicuity, when by the introduction of some pretty figure, or high-sounding phrase you may indulge your fancy, or display your erudition. But to proceed, how must we admire the following glorious passage!

'Let us rather contemplate that *divinity of adulation* when the contest was no longer between a powerful *monarch* on the throne and his petitioning Subjects, but when the fallen *King* was in the hands of a set of men whose souls detested him, and whose power brought him to the scaffold, etc.'

[1] Moore prints from this word to 'her a projector'.
[2] Lexiphanes was an Athenian comic poet, but S. refers to Samuel Johnson (1709–84), who as a pedant was the subject of the satire, *Lexiphanes, A Dialogue* (1767), by Archibald Campbell (1724–80).

Would common sense conceive that by *divinity of adulation* you meant nothing more than a synonymous term for Charles the 1st.—and at what time are we to view him?, when he was 'in the hands of a set of men whose souls detested him, and whose power brought him to the scaffold'? A pretty situation to contemplate a man as a divinity of adulation! So much for your meaning; but I must beg leave to hint a word or two on your mode of expression; by *divinity* of adulation you mean *Idol* of adulation; but can you really be so ignorant of the propriety of language as not to know the difference? by Idol we understand an object of worship of our own creation, and by a metaphorical allusion we apply it to men; but your *divinity* of adulation is nothing more than the deity that presides over it; as I know of no God of flattery, I have no objection to your promoting Charles to that title; but surely you might have waited 'till he had got to the skies: Inhuman Novus! to deify a King merely to furnish a subject of contemplation whilst you cut of[f] his head! You then in the most unconnected manner break out into the following modest co[n]cession: 'strongly attached as I profess myself to the cause of Liberty, the principle does not prevail so far as to make me wish for *the abolition of Law*, or desire the *extirpation of Monarchy*.' Truly a very moderate declaration! and you really, notwithstanding your love of Liberty, do not desire the abolition of law? Oh! thou hast a most glorious idea of liberty: does Liberty consist in the brutal privilege of being unconstrained in all our actions? Is to be free, to have the power of indulging every depraved inclination; to give full scope to all that's animal within us? Such I fear is Novus's opinion: had you known in what true liberty consisted, you would have seen that on law it must be founded, and by law supported: its guardian and essential: you would have been convinced that our great creator, who suffers such various passions to remain in human nature, has given us reason to establish that, which shall enable us to confine their destructive spirit, or punish the indulgence of it. So that the end of *laws* made by the general consent of a community, is the *liberty* of each individual; not the power of doing what we *will*, but what we *ought* to will; having a *right* to do whatever the laws permit. Such is Montesquieu's[1] definition of liberty; and he gives this obvious reason for it. 'If,' says he, 'a citizen could do what they forbid, he would no longer be possest of liberty, because all his fellow citizens would have the same power.'[2] But being ignorant of the principles of true liberty you form your opinion on confused notions of licentiousness, and total independence: how strange then, from such people, must all argument be on a subject, to whose very name they have annexed no precise idea!

Nor does your love of liberty carry you so far as to make you wish for the '*extirpation of monarchy*'. This is liable to the same objections as the former; and the smallest attempt to it would be absolutely subversive of our liberties. Had I any hopes of making you comprehend it, I would attempt to prove it to you.

'*The uses of this part of our mixed form*[3] *of government are evident to all lovers of their country*'—why only to lovers of their country? do you confine all common sense to patriots? —'*that we cannot but endeavour to preserve the root, tho' we lop off the injurious branches.*' By the *root* of monarchy that is to be preserved you must mean the King, the rest of the royal family are the branches; but why you'd *lop off* such harmless inoffensive twigs I cannot conceive. Really Novus If I saw a little more honesty in your writings I should suspect you to be a Turk.

'*Far be from me any attempt to justify the decollation of the condemned monarch, I rather attribute that outrage to the continuance of a popular fury, which had its rise indeed in justice, but its period in guilt, inasmuch as Charles perished not by general approbation.*'[4]

If Novus consider[s] this act by the laws of divine justice as in itself an act whether just or unjust the approbation of a part of men here can no way affect [it] if it was morally right, but as [to] the affair whether a people have a right by civil laws and institutions, to depose and put to death their monarch if it is consistent with civil justice general approba-

[1] Charles de Secondat, Baron de la Brède et de Montesquieu (1689–1755).
[2] S. quotes from the eleventh book of Thomas Nugent's translation of Montesquieu's *L'Esprit des Lois* (Geneva, 1748), which appeared as *Spirit of Laws* from 1752 onwards.
[3] 'Novus' actually writes 'forms'.
[4] The fair copy breaks off at this point. The rest of the text is from S.'s rough draft at Yale.

tion cannot alter it. If the government of bengall have a civil right to put their governor [to death] on convicting him of certain crimes, part of the . . .[1] disliking it does not alter the justice of the act, though it may the legality of the mode. But [Novus] can not be so ignorant as not to know that were the people agreeing [they] can have no civi[l] justice in killing their King. How utterly inconsistent such a proceeding is with the liberty of our constitution, which in a great measure governs civil justice, appears from Montes[qui]eu['s] opinion than whom I believe no one ever understood our constitution better as follows etc.[2] So tho the conclusion ab[out] the act was unjust the mod[e] made it doubly so. 'Quot.'[3] etc. Had you understood grammar you would have said 'effects of resentment'—(Johnson's dic.) 'Quot.'[4] 'ministerial perseverance' a new phrase. 'Quot.' but as [to] the sense what beautiful language and perspicuity suspended on ministerial dependance[5] if any gave himself the trouble of fishing for meaning[?]. Here at all [events] he would certainly conceive that their judgements were suspend[ed] on account of the dependance on the ministry 'till by the next line the[y] discover your boastful antithesis which you thought would be near it by the vulgar use of adjectives so you lugged in this figure to the support [of] your antithesis thoug[h] you forgot you became almost unintelligible. As [a] specimen of your arguing is here visible which all turns [u]pon the begin-[ning]: 'if so, why then; but if so, etc.' But had you never lugged in an 'if' any one would have been justified in supposing[6] illegalities not they who support them who accept it[7] Quot.[8] So our constitution is not establishe[d] indeed 'tis

[1] Illegible.

[2] A quotation from Montesquieu was to follow, and was marked 'ciii'.

[3] Probably Novus's statement: 'The attendant Circumstances enable me to establish my Proposition, that no Person, however exalted, is safe from the Effects of popular vengeance.'

[4] Novus writes: 'The point perhaps will not be contested even by the sincerest Advocates for ministerial Perseverance.'

[5] Novus writes: 'There are some of very moderate principles, whose judge-ments are suspended between the sophistry of ministerial dependence, and the argument of justifiable opposition.'

[6] Possibly 'opposing'.

[7] This line is almost illegible.

[8] Novus writes: 'If on the other hand it shall appear that our wrongs are not without foundation; that our interests have been given up in foreign concerns; that illegal measures have been carried into execution; that the Rights of Britons have been violated; that their Petitions have been disregarded; no Method for redressing past Grievances

time for it. Quot.[1] This to be sure is [a] very new[?] senti-ment. Ever since it was brushed up into verse in Addison['s] Cato[2] it has been crammed before our eyes in every election advertisement.

'Wrongs external and wrongs inter[nal]'[3] a villainous phrase and made rather more obscure by explanatory ——

One of the principal among the firs[t] is it seems: Quot.[4] Had you said the national honour I might in part have agreed with you, but I am afraid you'll find [it] difficult to prove that it would have been our interest to have interfere[d] in our presen[t] situation. The first origin the princi[ple] of the lat[ter][5] one the pardon [of] M'Quirk;[6] would not any imagine (I was at first in doubt) that is not meant to burlesque wrongs internal but [is] serious, the pard[on] of an . . .[7] who was convict[ed] of an electioneering riot is the princip[al] of wrong[s] internal. What a happy country is england. This is the greatest. People may judge of the res[t]. And this you mention as the greatest instance of the wickedness, and incapacity, of our ministers. Were it not for the stif[f] gloomy things which manifest you to be serious I should think you meant to burlesque the cause you have espoused—As the next sentences consist of another specimen of your Argumentation wher[e] you rais[e] up a number of spectre suppositions, from which you threat[en] to draw most blood[y] conclusions. | Jockey.

yet laid down; if this . . . shall appear every Briton will be justified not only in a determined opposition to future Ille-galities, but likewise in his resolute re-quest for the redress of former enormi-ties.'

[1] Novus writes: 'Let each man there-fore add his weight to the scale, and prosecute the establishment of our con-stitution. We received the bravely purchased blessing from our free fore-fathers, and we ought to transmit the pledge to our posterity.'

[2] *Cato*, III. i. 316–23. Addison's tragedy was first acted in Apr. 1713.

[3] Novus's 'obvious division' of the distresses caused by the ministry.

[4] Novus lists two 'wrongs external': '1. The Acts of Oppression towards our Colonies; and 2. The Sacrifice of the National Interest in the Affair of Corsica.' S. refers to the latter.

[5] S. refers to the 'wrongs internal' mentioned by 'Novus': '1. The Pardon of M'Quirk; 2. Mr. W[ilkes]'s repeated Expulsion; and 3. The Insertion of Mr. L[uttrell] in the H. of C.'

[6] Edward M'Quirk was given the royal pardon on 11 Mar. 1769. During an election riot at Brentford he had struck George Clarke who had then died. The Master and Wardens of the Surgeons' Company were asked by the Secretary of State to decide whether the blow had killed Clarke and unanimously declared that it was not the cause of death.

[7] Illegible.

P.S. you might have spare[d] yourself your N.B.s[1] with your reason for not answering my last objections. I never suspected you would. Your sarcasm of jocke[y]s wit being as character[istic] as a signature: is it absurd? What is my sig[nature] character[istic] of? Does the simple word jockey convey no intended idea?

7. To Mrs. Angelo[2]

F. W. Hilles MS. *Address*: To Mrs. Angelo | Queen-Square Court | Soho | London. *Pm.*: BATH 15 OC[3]

[*13 Oct. 1770?*]
Saturday Oct. —

May it please your Majesty

At a meeting of the Sheridanian society, in Parlour assembled, the following resolutions (amongst many others of great importance) were determined on, and I appointed to give your Majesty information of them.

Thomas Sheridan esqr. in the chair—R B S. Sec.

1. Resolved—that we are all alive. N.B. this pass'd nem. con.
2. Resolved—that her majesty be acquainted thereof.
3. Resolved—that R B S. be honoured with that commission.

Therefore I take the first opportunity of remitting to your Majesty these important, and interesting particulars, in obedience both to the resolution of the society, and, (what are still more binding) your Majesty's commands. But as it has been the fashion for Address-bearers to have a little conversation with majesty at the presentation of them; I must beg leave to take advantage of the precedent, and assume the same liberty. First then, out of zeal for your

---

[1] The postscript to the letter by 'Novus' reads: 'Your Correspondent *Jockey*'s Wit is as Characteristic as his Signature. Had he been less scurrilous, and more honest, I should not have held him altogether unworthy of an Answer.'

[2] Elizabeth Johnson was of Irish birth, and was one of the beauties of her day. She was married to Domenick Angelo (otherwise Malevolti or Tre-

manondo), the great swordsman and horseman, at St. George's, Hanover Square, on 25 Feb. 1755, and died in 1805, in her sixty-seventh year. See C. Swynnerton, 'The Angelo Family', *The Ancestor*, viii (1904), 9–16. For the friendship between the Angelos and the Sheridans, see Angelo, i. 85–90, 299–300, ii. 416–18.

[3] The Sheridans moved from London to Bath at the end of Sept. 1770.

Majesty, I cannot forbear informing you that the said Society have come to a resolution to address your Majesty to dissolve your court in Soho, and adjourn to Bath: this the[y] humbly conceive will be much to the benefit of your Majesty's health, and spirits; the latter of which they know you stand particularly in need of: to which if your Majesty does not condescend to agree, I give you warning that a motion will be made for a Thundering Remonstrance. Having given your Majesty this information, I leave you to consult your royal inclination;—provided you agree whol[l]y with this advice, not regarding your own will, but the pleasure and satisfaction of your Subjects.

But I have likewise another embassy to your Majesty; this is from King Bladud, who (as the Bath Guide inform[s] us)[1] reigned in England about 900 years before Christ, and was the first discoverer of these springs. This King keeps his state on a fine rotten post in the middle of the water, decorated with a long account of his pedigree. His Majesty whispered me the other day that having heard of your fame, he has long wished to see you; he says that, except his sister of Orange, he has not seen a royal female for a long time; and bid me at the same time assure your majesty, that tho' in his youth, about three thousand years ago, he was reckoned a man of Gallantry, yet he now never offers to take the least advantage of any lady bathing beneath his Throne, nor need the purest modesty be offended at his glances.—So says his Majesty of Bladud: and in justice I must acknowledge that he seems to be as demure, grave and inoffensive a King as ever sat upon a—post.

Having now delivered all my commissions to the Queen I must beg leave to say a little to Mrs. Angelo. First, I hope she and Mr. Angelo, with all their family[2] are in good health; if they are not, we have such plenty of it here, that 'tis only writing a line to Bath, and we'll send you enough of it; you need not fear its coming safe, for I'll fold it in a cover of Good Humour—and I am sure it will find its way to

[1] *The Bath and Bristol Guide* (4th ed., Bath [1760]), p. 1, gives Bladud as 'the first discoverer and founder of these Baths, Eight hundred and Sixty three years before Christ'. It adds that an effigy of him was set up in a niche at the King's Bath in 1699. Cf. the *New Bath Guide* (Bath [1769]), pp. 4–9, 33.

[2] At this date they had one son, Henry, and four daughters.

Mrs. Angelo. Tho' my prescription should be, to come to Bath in search of it.

We ha[v]e got a very neat house, pleasantly situated, and very cheap.¹ To describe it prettily, I should tell you that the River Avon runs not 200 yards from our door; but 'tis a female river I fancy, for it is so exceedingly shy and modest and holds its head so low, that we cant get a glimpse of it even out of our windows. But in winter we are told, when the snow has powder'd her head a little, and her beaus from the mountains (the gutters and rivulets) have come into her train, she then (as most ladies do in such circumstances) gives herself a great many airs, overflows her banks, and politely lays all our meadows under water. But to make amends for the coyness of the river, the Hills on the opposite bank seem resolved to over-look her streamship, and being prettily cultivated, form an agreeable, tho' confined prospect.

Bath is by no means full yet;² but there are however on some nights, enough to make it tolerably disagreeable; but the people are luckily all agreed in calling it pleasant, otherwise one might be apt to mistake. But the Ladies are still in great hopes of being so crowded as not to be able to walk. Tho' I must confess 'tis but policy in the present set to wish to be jumbled in a crowd, for most of those that I have seen as yet, are as ugly as Lions. But I hope, for the honour of the place, we shall soon mend, or I shall think Beauty has forsaken this spot, or that Venus is affronted at the cruel exclusion of her votaries.

This is no place for news—but there is a Mr. Linley here,³ a music master, who has a daughter that sings like an angel;⁴ perhaps you may have heard of her: the Father too sings in a particular natural stile, likewise a little daughter who has been at London.⁵ The public concerts do not begin 'till

¹ In Kingsmead Street, Bath.
² *Bath Chronicle*, Thursday, 4 Oct. 1770, reports: 'On Saturday next the Theatre Royal in this city will be opened, on Monday the Music will begin at the Pump Room, and on Tuesday will be the first Ball of the season.'
³ Thomas Linley the elder (1733–95), singing master and composer.

⁴ Elizabeth Ann Linley (1754–92), afterwards S.'s first wife. She had just returned from Salisbury, where she and Tenducci 'sang like two divine beings' (*Letters of the first Earl of Malmesbury* (1870), i. 204–5). She joined Thomas Sheridan in his 'Attic Entertainment' at Bath on 24 Nov.
⁵ Mary Linley had acted in Colman's *Man and Wife* at C.G.Th. in 1769.

after Xtmas; but we heard them at a priv[a]te[1] one in Mr. L[in]ley's hous[e.][1] As you and Mr. Angelo are so fond of music, I am sure they would give you a great deal of pleasure. The Duke of Bedford[2] is here dying, and swearing, and Lord Chesterfield[3] very little better; their ladies are here also lamenting their fates and playing Quadrille; Mr. Garrick is also here, drinking the waters, and not in very good health.

I am afraid by this time I have tired you; but I must still trouble you to tell a certain Hibernian in your house, who delights to call himself Quin,[4] that I should have writ to him, but that knowing him to be a man (or as you would say) a boy of resolution I was afraid he had set off for Ireland: but that [if] he is not too lazy, I wish, like a true Irishman he would write me word whether he is after being set out or no; for he knows if I write, and he be gone, may be he wont receive my letter in Ireland 'till after he be returned here.

I must omit all the compliments etc. from our family to you and Mr. Angelo, they are so numerous, I should scarcely have room for them; so must leave it to you to do us justice in supposing them, especially as we hope so soon to have the pleasur[e][1] of paying them to you in person, in your intended trip to Bath; which when you have fix'd we hope to be favoured with any commands you may have previous to it. If you have any reply to make to the friendly invitation of his majesty King Bladud, you must make me your ambassador, as his wooden majesty converses with no one else.

When one is engaged in an agreeable employment, 'tis difficult to break off—but I must indulge myself no farther or I shall scarcely have room to add that I am | with the greatest respect and esteem | your—(but as I am writing to a Queen, I must sa[y])[1] | Subject and Servant, R B Sheridan

[1] Manuscript torn.
[2] John, 4th Duke of Bedford (1710–71). His arrival was reported in the *Bath Chronicle*, 4 Oct. 1770. He died 15 Jan. 1771.
[3] The *Bath Journal*, 1 Oct. 1770, reports the arrival at Bath of Lord Chesterfield [P. D. Stanhope, 4th Earl (1694–1773)] and Mr. and Mrs. Garrick.

[4] Probably Thomas Quin, son of Thomas Quin of Quinsbro, Co. Kildare. He was at Harrow in 1764–5, and entered Clare College, Cambridge, 4 Feb. 1766. See Gun, p. 22. In a letter (Add. MS. 35118, f. 1) from Harrow of 18 July 1770, Mrs. Clough mentions a shirt that 'Quinn' wanted to return to S.

8. To His Father

LeFanu MS.

24 Jan. [1772?][1]

'. . . a very sincere esteem for me; and toasts at his table his *Friend in Dublin*[2] as a man for whom he has the greatest respect and esteem. Were I to say that I had now a much better opinion of this man than I had formerly I dare say you. . . .

. . . the poor little Widow *Grant.* Mrs. M'guire,[3] who was sometime ago thought to be dying, is better.

My Brother and Sisters join with me in duty and affection | Who am etc. | R B Sheridan

Friday Jan. 24.

9. To His Father

Yale MS. *Pub.*: Moore, i. 61. *Address*: To | Thomas Sheridan Esqr. | Crow-Street | Dublin *Pm.*: BATH

29 Feb. [1772]

Dear Father,

We have been for some time in hopes of receiving a letter that we might know that you had acquitted us of neglect in writing. At the same time we imagine that the time is not far when writing will be unnecessary: and we cannot help wishing to know the posture of the affairs which, as you have not talked of returning, seem probable to detain you longer than you intended. I am perpetually asked when Mr. Sheridan is to have his Patent for the Theatre, which all the Irish here take for granted,[4] and I often receive a great deal of information from them on the subject. Yet I cannot help being

---

[1] 24 Jan. was a Friday in 1772, and shortly before this date Thomas Sheridan had been acting at the Crow Street Theatre, Dublin.

[2] Thomas Sheridan.

[3] *Bath Chronicle*, 12 Dec. 1771, notes the arrival at Bath of 'Mrs. M'Guire'.

[4] Thomas Sheridan prepared a petition for an exclusive patent for the Dublin Theatre. It was described in 'a most elaborate oration, pronounced in the Musick-Hall, Feb. 22d [1772] and since published'. The petition was bitterly attacked in *An Appeal to the*

vexed when I see in the Dublin Papers such bustling accounts of the proceedings of your House of Commons, as I remember it was your argument against attempting any thing from Parliamentary authority in England. However the folks here regret you as one that is to be fixed in another Kingdom, and will scarcely believe that you will even visit Bath at all. And we are often asked if we have not received the letter which is to call us over.

I could scarsely have conceived that the Winter was so near departing, were I not now writing after Dinner by day-light. Indeed the first Winter-season is not yet over at Bath: They have Balls, Concerts, etc. at the Rooms from the old subscription still, and the Spring ones are immediately to succeed them. They are like-wise going to perform Oratorios here: Mr Linley and his whole family, down to the seven year olds are to support one set at the new Rooms,[1] and a band and Singers from London another at the old.[2]— Our weather here, or the effects of it, have been so uninviting to all kinds of Birds, that there has not been the smallest excuse to take a gun into the fields this Winter: a point more to the regret of Charles than me.[3]

We are all now in dolefuls here for the Princess Dowager: but as there was no necessity for our being dressed or weeping mourners[4] we were easily provided. Our acquaintances stand pretty much the same as when you left us: only that I think in general we are less intimate: by which I believe you will not think us great losers. Indeed, excepting Mr. Wyndham,[5] I have not met with one person with whom I would

Public, against an Intended Scheme for a Monopoly of the Stage (Dublin, 1772), obviously written to defend Barry's interest in the Crow Street Theatre. Sheridan's hopes were not fulfilled.

[1] Bath Journal, 9 Mar. 1772, contains an advertisement of performances at the New Assembly Rooms of Acis and Galatea on 3 Apr., Judas Maccabeus on 8 Apr., and Messiah on 10 Apr. The soloists were Elizabeth and Mary Linley, Thomas Linley and Thomas Linley, Jr., Corfe and Arnold.

[2] Herschel advertised a concert (Bath Journal, 19 Mar. 1772) in Gyde's Great Room on 20 Mar. The vocal part was by Signora Farinelli, 'late from the Opera at Berlin'.

[3] In later life he delighted in shooting, but, according to Uvedale Price, was a poor shot. See Clayden, i. 389.

[4] Court mourning was ordered on 8 Feb., the day of her death.

[5] Bath Journal, 13 Jan. 1772, notes: 'Arrived here . . . Mr. Wyndham.' This was probably William Windham (1750–1810), who met S. for the first time in 1771: see R. W. Ketton-Cremer, Early Life . . . of William Windham (1930), p. 183.

wish to be intimate. Tho' there was a Mr. Lutterel[1] (Brother to the Colonel[2]) who was some months ago introduced to me by an old Harrow acquaintance,[3] who made me many professions at parting, and wanted me vastly to name some way in which he could be useful to me. But the relying on *acquaintances*, or *seeking* of friendships is a fault which I think I shall always have prudence enough to avoid.

Lissy[4] begins to be tormented again with the tooth-ache. Otherwise we are all well. | I am, Sir, | Your sincerely dutiful | and affectionate Son | R B Sheridan

Friday Feb 29.

I beg you will not judge of my attention to the improvement of my handwriting by this letter as I am out of the [way] of a better pen.

10. To His Brother

Yale MS. *Pub.*: Moore, i. 68–69. *Address*: To | Charles Sheridan Esqr. | Bath | England. *Pm.*: 25 AP

April 15th[5] 1772.

Dear Brother,

Most probably you will have thought me very inexcusable for not having writ to you.[6] You will be surprised too to be told that except your letter just after we arrived we have never received one line from Bath. We suppose for certain that there are letters somewhere in which case we shall have

---

[1] James Luttrell (1751 ?–88), a captain in the Navy. M.P. from 1775.
[2] Henry Luttrell, afterwards 2nd Earl of Carhampton (1743–1821).
[3] Mrs. Clough, a woman who took a motherly interest in S. while he was at Harrow School, wrote to him on 29 July 1771 (Add. MS. 35118, f. 7) to say that a Harrovian named Watkins would call on S. on his way through Bath. The *Bath Chronicle*, 21 Nov. 1771, notes the arrival of 'Mr. and Mrs. Watkyns'.
[4] S.'s sister Alicia.

[5] Altered from 'April 16th'.
[6] Elizabeth Linley felt that her profession laid her open to unwelcome advances, and was particularly irritated by those of Thomas Mathews of Llandaff Court, a Welsh squire living at Bath. She decided to run away to France, accompanied by S. as *cavaliere servente*. They left Bath on 19 Mar. (*Lond.Chron.*, 24 Mar. 1772) on what was thought to be an elopement to Scotland. S.'s letter appears to have been written from Lille: see Rae, i. 168–9.

sent to every place almost but the right, whith[er] I hop[e]¹
I have now sent also. You will soon see me in England.
Everything on our side has at last succeeded. Miss L—— is
now fixing in a Convent² where she has been entered some
time. This has been a much more difficult point than you
could have imagined, and we have I find been extremely
fortunate. She has been ill, but is now recovered. This too
has delayed me. We would have wrote but have been kept
in the most tormenting expectation from day to day, of
receiving your letters, but as every thing is now so happily
settled here I will delay no longer giving you that information. Tho' probably I shall set out for England without
knowing a syllable of what has happened with you. All is
well I hope. And I hope too that tho' you may have been
ignorant for some time of our proceedings, *you* never could
have been uneasy that anything could³ tempt me to depart
even in a thought from the honour and consistency which
engaged me at first. I wrote to M—— above a week ago,⁴
which I think [was ne]cessary and right. I hope he has
acted the one proper Part which was left him.⁵ And to speak
from my *feelings* I cannot but say that I shall be very happy
to find to[o] no further disagreeable consequence pursuing
him. For what Brutus says of Caesar etc.⁶—if I delay one
moment longer I lose the Post.

—I have writ now too to Mr. Adams⁷ and should apologise to you for having writ to him first, and lost my time for
you. Love dear to my sisters. Miss L['s] to all | Ever,
Charles, | your affectionate Brother | R B Sheridan

I need not tell you that we altered quite our route.⁸

¹ Torn.
² Of the Ursulines? Henry Angelo's
sisters lodged in their convent at Lille,
in charge of the Prioress, 'a tall handsome English lady, Mrs. Skerrat' (H.
Angelo, *Pic-Nic* (1834), p. 84).
³ Altered by S. from 'should'.
⁴ I cannot find this letter.
⁵ Presumably, that Mathews should
have apologized for his conduct.
⁶ *Julius Caesar*, I. ii. 100–4:

'If it be aught toward the general good,
Set honour in one eye and death i' the
other,
And I will look on both indifferently.'
⁷ Lefanu, pp. 297–8, mentions an
old gentleman named Adams, who took
a fancy to S. at Bath because he was the
son of Frances Sheridan.
⁸ They appear to have travelled to
Lille via Dunkirk. See Rhodes, pp. 39,
273–4.

11. To William Wade[1]

Yale MS. *Pub.*: Moore, i. 75–76. *Address*: To | William Wade Esqr.

2 May 1772

Sir,

I ought to apologise to you for troubling you again on a subject which should concern so few.—

I find Mr. *Mathews's* behaviour to have been such that I can not be satisfied with his *concession*, as a *consequence* of an *explanation* from me. I called on Mr. *Mathews* last wednesday night at Mr. *Cachlin's* without the smallest expectation of coming to any *verbal* explanation with him.[2] A proposal of a *pacific* meeting the next day was the consequence, which ended in those advertisements, and the letter to you.[3] As for Mr. *Mathews's* honour or *Spirit* in this whole affair, I shall only add that a few hours may possibly give some proof of the latter while in my own justification I affirm that it was far from being my fault that this point now remains to be determined.

On discovering Mr. *Mathews's benevolent* interposition in my own Family I have counter-ordered the advertisements that were agreed on. As I think even an *explanation* would now misbecome me.[4] An agreement to them was the effect more of more *charity* than *judgement*. As I find it necessary to make *all* my sentiments as publick as possible, your declaring this will greatly oblige | Your very humble servant | R B Sheridan

Saturday 12 o'Clock May 2d. 1772

[1] Captain William Wade (d. 16 Mar. 1809) was the nephew of General George Wade, and became Master of the Ceremonies at Bath in 1769. There is a poem addressed to him in the *Bath Chronicle*, 28 Nov. 1771, on the theme expressed in its first line: 'You've a difficult task, my friend Wade, to perform.'

[2] The events of 29 and 30 Apr. are described by S. in full, in Letter 12.

[3] S. and Mathews seem to have agreed to send personal explanations to the Bath newspapers. Mathews's full apology was printed in the *Bath Chronicle*,

7 May 1772; but nothing by S. appeared, because in the meantime he had come to the conclusion that Mathews had deceived him.

[4] Writing to his uncle on 13 May 1772, C. F. Sheridan declared: 'Dick on coming here for the first time saw the advertisement [i.e. the 'posting'] against him, and then thought the apology then made by M——s was no concession at all for so signal an insult, this being also the opinion of everybody else, he immediately resolv'd to return to London [and] get proper satisfaction' (Yale MS.; cf. Rae, i. 183–4).

12. [To the Printer of the *Bath Chronicle*?][1]

Yale MS. *Pub.*: Moore, i. 73–75. *Dock.*: Written in the Parade coffee-house 9 o'clock Tuesday-night.

[*May–June 1772*]

It has ever been esteemed impertinent to appeal to the *publick* in concerns merely private; but there now and then occurs a *private* incident which by being explain'd, may be of *publick* advantage. This consideration, and the precedent of a *publick* appeal in this same affair, are my only apologies for the new following lines :—[2]

Mr. *T. Mathews* thought himself essentially injured by Mr. *R. Sheridan's* having co-operated in the virtuous efforts of a young Lady to escape the snares of vice and dissimulation. He wrote several most abusive threats to Mr. S. —then in France. He laboured with a cruel industry, to vilify his character in England. He publickly posted[3] him as a scoundrel and a Liar.—Mr. S. answered him from France (hurried and surprised) that he would never sleep in England 'till *he* had thank'd him as he deserved.

Mr. S. arrived at London at 9 o'clock at night.[4] At 10 he is informed by Mr. S. Ewart[5] that Mr. M. is in town. Mr. S. had sat up at Canterbury to keep his idle promise to Mr. M. He resolved to call on Mr. M. that night, as, (in case he had not found him in town he had call'd on Mr. Ewart to accompany him to *Bath*, being bound by Mr. Linley[6] not to let

[1] This is in draft form only, and a fair copy may not have been sent. I have not been able to find it in the columns of the Bath newspapers.

[2] The paragraph has been cancelled, but it is printed by Moore.

[3] Mathews advertised in the *Bath Chronicle*, 9 Apr. 1772, that because S. had run away and had made damaging insinuations against him, S. must be 'posted' a 'L[iar], and a *treacherous* S[coundrel]' (Rae, i. 173). Rhodes, p. 41, thought this instance of using the newspapers rather than the coffee-houses for posting was unique; but Sir Edward Newenham 'posted' John Beresford in the same way in Mar. 1778, and a

duel was fought. See *Beresford Corr.* i. 23.

[4] Wednesday, 29 Apr.

[5] Simon Ewart, son of John Ewart of 31 Lower Thames St., London, a brandy merchant (Rhodes, p. 36). He was an intimate friend of S. and of Charles Francis Sheridan (Lefanu, p. 343), and had helped Elizabeth Linley and S. in their flight abroad. He himself eloped to France in Mar. 1773. In 1797 a man of his name was at Calcutta (*Memoirs of W. Hickey* (ed. Spencer, 1925), iv. 155).

[6] Thomas Linley the elder persuaded his daughter to leave Lille and take up singing again.

any thing pass between him and Mr. M. 'till he had arrived thither.) Mr. S. came to Mr. Cochlins, in crutched Friars[1] (where Mr. M. was lodged,) about half after twelve.—The key of Mr. C.'s door was lost. Mr. S. was denied admittance. By 2 oclock He got in. Mr. M. had been previously down to the door and told Mr. S. he should be admitted, and had retired to bed again. He dressed—complained of the cold, endeavour'd to get heat into him, call'd Mr. S. his *dear Friend*, and *forced* him to—*sit down*.—

Mr. S. had been informed that Mr. M. had *sworn* his death, that Mr. M. had in numberless companies produced *bills* on France, whither he meant to retire on the completion of his revenge. Mr. M. had warn'd Mr. Ewart to advise his Friend not even to come in his way without a sword, as he could not answer for the consequence.

Mr. M. had left two Letters for Mr. S. in which he declares he is to be met with at *any* hour, and begs Mr. S. will not '*deprive himself of so much sleep*, or stand upon *any ceremony*.' Mr. S. called on him at the hour mentioned. Mr. S. was admitted with the *difficulty* mentioned. Mr. S. declares that on Mr. M.'s perceiving that he came with Pistols to answer *then* to his challenge he does not remember ever to have seen a *Man* behave so perfectly dastardly. Mr. M. detained Mr. S. 'till 7 o'clock the next morning. *He* (Mr. M.) said he never meant to quarrel with Mr. S. He convinced Mr. S. that his enmity ought to be directed solely against his brother, and another gentleman at Bath. Mr. S. went to Bath;[2] in an hour he found every one of Mr. M.'s assertions totally and positively disavow'd. Mr. S. staid but 3 hours in Bath. He returned to London, he sent to Mr. M. from *Hyde-parck*. He[3] came with Captain *Knight*[4] his second. He

---

[1] Close to Mark Lane. The monastery of the Friars of the Holy Cross had been situated there.

[2] Moore's transcript ends here. Rae, i. 179–82, prints the whole.

[3] Altered from 'Mr. M.'

[4] Possibly Henry Knight of Tythegston, Laleston, Glam., who appeared at the Glamorgan sessions of July 1770 for presenting a challenge to a duel. See *Cardiff Records* (ed. J. H. Matthews, Cardiff, 1911), ii. 224. Colonel Knight of Tythegston is mentioned in *The Times* of 6 Dec. 1815. The connexion between the Mathews family and the Knights is also indicated in Thomas Mathews's wife's will, where she left £200 to her god-daughter, 'the eldest daughter of my friend, James Lewis Knight, Esq.' (Glamorgan Record Office, Fonmon MSS., vi. 107).

objected *frequently* to the ground. They adjourned to the Hercules' Pillars.[1] They returned to Hyde-parck. Mr. *M. objected* to the observation of an officer. They returned to the Hercules' Pillars. They adjourned (by agreement) to the Bedford Coffee-house.[2] Mr. M. was gone to the Castel Tavern.[3] Mr. S. follow'd with Mr. E. Mr. M. made many declarations in favour of Mr. S. They engaged. Mr. M. was disarm'd. Captain K. run in, Mr. M. begg'd his life, and afterwards denied the advantage. Mr. S. was provoked by (the really well me[a]nt) interposition of Captain K. and the elusion[4] of Mr. M. He insisted since Mr. M. denied the advantage, that he should give up his sword, Mr. M. denied [again] but sooner than return to his ground he gave it up— it was broke. And Mr. M.[5] offer'd another. He was then call'd on to retract his abuse and beg Mr. S.'s pardon. With much altercation and much ill grace He complied.—The affair was settled. The sword's being broke was not to be mentioned, if Mr. M. never misrepresented the affair. Mr. S. came to Bath. He gave Mr. M. credit. Mr. *M.* came to Bath—he misrepresented the whole transaction: He wrote to all his acquaintance. He told *his own story.* Mr. S. wrote to —nobody. He contra[dic]ted whatever was told him as Mr. M.'s misrepresentation. Mr. M. found that *Truth* prevailed. He feared the aspersion of want of resolution. He grew desperate and seems resolved to *force* Mr. S. to hazard *life* (which He confesses he had once received from him) to establish his reputation. Mr. S. flatters his own charity, that he has in this representation, treated Mr. M. *most tenderly.* As to the truth of it, let their Seconds (Mr. Ewart and Captain Knight) decide | R B Sheridan.

[1] An inn at Hyde Park Corner ? One of the same name was to be found in Hercules' Pillars Alley, off Fleet Street.

[2] In the Piazza, Covent Garden.

[3] The *New M. Mag.* vi (1816), 157, ocates this tavern as on the corner of Henrietta Street and Bedford Street, and describes the duel.

[4] Manuscript 'ellusion'. Rae, i. 181, prints 'illusion'.

[5] Rae inserts 'was'.

13. To Captain Knight

Yale MS. *Pub.*: Moore, i. 78–84. *Dock.*: Copy of a Letter I sent to Captain Knight July 1772.

July 1772

Sir

On the evening preceding my last meeting with Mr. Mathews, Mr. Barnet[1] produced a paper[2] to me written by Mr. Mathews, containing an account of our former meetings in London. As I had before frequently heard of Mr. Mathews's relation of that affair, without interesting myself much in contradicting it, I should certainly have treated this in the same manner, had it not been seemingly authenticated by Mr. *Knight's* Name being subscribed to it.—My asserting that the paper contains much misrepresentation, equivocation and Falsity might make it appear strange that I should apply to you in this manner for information on the subject; but, as it likewise contradicts what I have been told were Mr. Knight's sentiments and assertions on that affair, I think I owe it to his credit, as well as my own justification first to be satisfied from himself whether he really subscribed and will support the truth of the account shewn by Mr. Mathews. Give me leave previously to relate what I have affirmed to have been a real state of our last meeting in London, and which I am now ready to support on [my ho]nor [o]r[3] my Oath; as the best account I can give [of Mr.][3] Mathews's relation, is that it is almost directly opposite to mine.

Mr. Ewart accompanied me to Hyde-Park about Six in the Evening,[4] where we met you and Mr. Mathews, and we

1 William Barnett is referred to, in the narrative of these occurrences written by S.'s sister Elizabeth, as 'Mr. Barnard'. He was 'a Gentleman lately settled in his [Mathews's] neighbourhood [i.e. Llandaff, near Cardiff]'. From the same source, we learn that he urged Mathews to fight another duel, as the only way of wiping out the shame he had incurred by his behaviour at their first encounter. Barnett accompanied Mathews to Bath and 'was the bearer of the Challenge which he had the cruelty to put into Miss [i.e. Alicia] Sheridan's hand saying it was an invitation for her Brother'. The original manuscript of this narrative has been made available to me by the Marchioness of Dufferin and Ava.   2 Cf. Sichel, i. 377.

3 Manuscript torn.

4 S. repeats his version of the occurrences described in Letter 12.

walked together to the Ring.—Mr. Mathews refusing to make any other acknowledgement than he [had] done, I observed that we were come to the Ground: Mr. Mathews objected to the Spot, and appealed to you:—we proceeded to the Back of a Building on the other side of the Ring.— The ground was there perfectly level; I called on him, and drew my sword (He having previously declined Pistols)— Mr. Ewart observed a Centinel on the other side of the Building:—We advanced to another Part of the Park; I stopped again at a seemingly convenient Place.—Mr. Mathews objected to the observation of some People at a great distance; and proposed to retire to the *Hercules'-Pillars* 'till the Park should be clear:—we did so.—In a little time we returned.—I again drew my Sword: Mr. Mathews again objected to the observation of a Person who seem'd to watch us. Mr. *Ewart* observed that the chance was equal, and engaged that no one should stop him, should [it] be necessary for him to retire to the Gate, where we had a chaise and four which was equally at his service. Mr. Mathews declared that he would not engage while any one was within sight, and proposed to defer it 'till the next morning. I turned to you and said that this was 'trifling work', that I could not admit of any delay, and engaged to remove the Gentleman (who proved to be an Officer, and who, on my going up to him, and assuring him that any interposition would be ill-timed, politely retired.) Mr. Mathews in the mean time had returned towards the Gate;—Mr. Ewart and I called to you—and follow'd. We returned to the Hercules Pillars; and went from thence by agreement to the *Bedford-Coffee-house*; where, the Master be[ing][1] alarmed, you came, and conducted us to Mr. Mathews [at][1] the *Castle Tavern*, *Henrietta-Street*. Mr. Ewart [t]ook [lights][1] up in his hand, and almost immediately on our e[nterin]g [the][1] Room we engaged. I struck Mr. Mathews's point so much out of the line that I stept up and caught hold of his wrist or the hilt of his sword, while the point of mine was at his brea[st][1]—You ran in, and caught hold of my arm, exclaiming '*do[n't][2] kill him.*'—I struggled to disengage my arm, and said his sword was in my power:—Mr. Mathews call'd out twice or thrice

---

[1] Manuscript torn.   [2] Obliterated.

—'I beg my Life'—We were parted: You immediatel[y] said—*'There He has begg'd his Life, and now there is an end of it*': and on Mr. Ewart's saying that, when his sword was in my Power, as I attempted no more, you should not have interfered, you replied *'that you were wrong*, but that you had *done it hastily, and to prevent mischief,'* or words to that effect.—Mr. Mathews then hinted that I was rather *obliged* to *your interposition* for the advantage.—You declared that *'Before you did so, both the Swords were in Mr. Sheridan's power.'* Mr. Mathews still seem'd resolv'd to give it another turn, and observed that He *had never quitted his sword.*— Provoked at this, I then swore (with too much heat perhaps) that He should either give up his sword, and I would break it, or go to his guard again. He refused. But on my persisting, either gave it into my hand, or flung it on the Table, or the ground (which I will not absolutely affirm.) I broke it, and flung the hilt to the other end of the Room.—He exclaimed at this. I took a mourning sword from Mr. Ewart, and presenting him with mine, gave me honour that what had passed should never be mentioned by me, and he might now right himself again: He replied that *'He could never draw a sword against the man who had given him his life.'* But, on his still exclaiming against the indignity of breaking his sword (which he had brought upon himself) Mr. Ewart offer'd him the Pistols; and some altercation passed between them.—Mr. Mathews said that he could never shew his Face, if it were known how his sword was broke, that such a *thing had never been* [do]ne,[1] *that* it *cancelled* all *obligation* etc. etc.—You [seemed][1] to think that it was wrong, and we both pro[posed][1] that if he never misrepresented the affair, it should not be mentioned by us.—This was settled. —I then asked Mr. Mathews, whether (as he had expressed himself sensible of, and shock'd at the injustice and indignity he had done me in his advertisement) it did not occur to him that he ow'd me another satisfaction; and that as it was now in his power to do it without discredit, I supposed He would not hesitate.—This He absolutely refused, unless conditionally I insisted on it, and said I would not leave the Room 'till it was settled.—After much

[1] Manuscript torn.

altercation, and with much ill-grace He gave the apology, which afterwards appeared.—We parted, and I returned immediately to Bath. I there to *Colonel Gould*,[1] *Captain Wade*, *Mr. Creaser*[2] and others mentioned the affair to Mr. Mathews's credit, said that Chance having given me the advantage, Mr. Mathews had consented to that apology, and mentioned nothing of the sword.—Mr. Mathews came down; and in two days I found the whole affair had been stated in a different light, and insinuations given out to the same purpose as in the Paper, which has occasioned this Trouble.—I had *undoubted authority* that these accounts proceeded from *Mr. Mathews* and likewise that Mr. *Knight* had never had any share in them I then thought I no longer owed Mr. Mathews the compliment to conceal any circumstance, and I related the affair to several Gentlemen exactly as above.—

Now, Sir, as I have put down nothing in this account but upon the most assured recollection, and, as Mr. Mathews's Paper either directly or equivocally contradicts almost every article of it, and as your Name is subscribed to that Paper, I flatter myself that I have [a] right to expect your answer to the following Questions. first

Is there any Falsity or misrepresentation in what I have advanced above?

With regard to Mr. Mathews's paper—Did I in the Park seem in the slightest article inclined to [enter] into conversation with Mr. Mathews?—He insinuates that I did.

Did Mr. Mathews *not beg* his life?—He affirms he did not.

Did I break his sword *without warning?*—He affirms I did it without warning, on his laying it on the Table.

Did I not offer him mine?—He omits it.—

Did Mr. Mathews give me the apology as a point of generosity, *on my desisting to demand it?*—He affirms he did.

I shall now give my reasons for doubting your having authenticated this Paper:—

First Because I think it full of Falsehood and misrepre-

---

[1] Nathaniel Gould (*c.* 1731–86) retired from the 3rd Foot Guards in 1765, as Lieutenant-Colonel: see *The Letters of Edward Gibbon* (ed. J. E. Norton, 1956), iii. 420.

[2] A family of this name lived at Widcombe, Bath. One Thomas Creaser, a draper of Bath, went bankrupt in 1772 (*Gent. Mag.* xlii (1772), 392).

sentation, and Mr. Knight has the character of a Man of Truth and Honour.

2d. When you were at Bath, I was informed that you had never expressed any such Sentiments.

3d. I have been told that in Wales Mr. Mathews never *told his story* in the presence of Mr. *Knight*: who had never there insinuated anything to my disadvantage.

4th. The Paper shewn me by Mr. Barnet contains (if my memory does not deceive me) three separate Sheets of writing Paper: Mr. Knight's evidence is annexed to the last, which contains chiefly a copy of our *first* proposed advertisements; which Mr. Mathews had in Mr. Knight's presence agreed should be destroy'd as totally void; and which (in a Letter to Colonel Gould by whom I had insisted on it) he declared upon his honour he knew nothing about, nor should ever make the least use of.

These, Sir, are my reasons for applying to yourself, in preference to any appeal to Mr. Ewart, my Second on that occasion, which is what I would wish to avoid.—As for Mr. Mathews's assertions, I shall never be concerned at them. I have ever avoided any verbal altercation with that Gentleman, and He has now secured himself from any other. | I am your very humble servant,[1] | R B Sheridan.

14. To His Father

LeFanu MS. *Pub.*: Rae, i. 212–14. *Address*: Thomas Sheridan Esqr. | Bath

Waltham[2] Aug 30th: 1772

Dear Father,

I arrived here on Friday evening: I am very snugly situated in the Town, tho' I should have liked it better to have been out of it.

I left you, Sir, at a time when from appearances you had reason to suppose I had not been dealing ingenuously with you. I certainly had in some degree deserved the suspicion; however some accidental occurrences served greatly to

---

[1] The subscription is not in the manuscript, but was printed by Moore.

[2] 'Farm Hill' appears to have been cancelled.

streng[t]hen it. There were circumstances attending that connexion,[1] which you so much wished me to break off, which made it almost impossible to deal with proper candour on all sides; and I can only re-assure you that what might strongly seem to be a departing from my word, and your injunctions, was sincerely, and to the best of my Judgement, enter'd on with a view to secure to myself the power of adhering effectually to both for the future. The merit or demerit of my having so involved myself, is not now a question; but I can now have no motive in solemnly declaring to you that I have extricated myself, and that on this subject you shall never again have the smallest uneasiness.

I intend to call on Mr. Adams[2] tomorrow, when I shall arrange my Studies. I believe the best specimen I can give you of a prospect of my reforming wholly in this point, is to avoid professing anything on the subject.—However my next shall furnish you with occasion to give me your sentiments on my Plan.—I have here at least one great inducement to study—Nothing else to do. And I doubt not but that a little habit founded even on that, will in no long time counteract the other habit of dissipation. And a habit I must call it, as I still affirm that I very seldom remember to have felt anything like real satisfactions in those Pleasures which constituted it.

You desired me to write to you from hence an account of what I owed. They are debts of Folly and Extravagance, some of them contracted later than they should have been, tho' to get rid of obligations of a former Date.[3] My resolutions on this head I can only date from the time I *left Bath*; as there is no inconvenience of a Debt which I have felt more than the necessity sometimes of adding to it. And had I staid there, while I ow'd a sixpence I believe I should have been incapable of fixing myself to new articles.—I expect a letter from *Bath*, when I will write you an account.

[1] With Elizabeth Linley. Thomas Linley wished to break off the relationship because he thought S. much too extravagant; Thomas Sheridan sought the same end, partly because he thought Elizabeth's name was now rather notorious, and partly because his son possessed neither fortune nor profession. S. was sent from Bath to Waltham so that he might forget Elizabeth and settle down to his studies. See Rae, i. 205–10.
[2] A tutor. See Sichel, i. 401.
[3] They are mentioned in the next letter.

I have said that where I thought myself most obliged, I have felt least capable of shewing it. I assure you, Sir, it has been so with me in regard to you. I mention this only that you may not think me insensible to what you have done, as Time, not Professions, must shew whether, by profiting by it, I am inclined to repay you.

I gave Paumier the Copy of my Letter to Captain Knight for you.[1] If no answer has arrived at Bath, He certainly intends none. In which case I should wish the fact to be mentioned and the Copy shewn. I was thinkin[g][2] of sending another Copy to M[athews in][3] Wales, lest they might have suppressed [it][2]

My Uncle and Aunt[4] are out of To[wn.][2] I packed up your Comedy by Mistake, wh[ich I will][2] send the first opportunity, with the Op[era][2] I left a Note at Mr. Horne's for.[5]

There has been a Grand Contest here between Mr. Parker, and Sir William Wake, assisted by Mr. Berrwick; in which Mr. Parker has been quite the '*Village-Hambden*':[6] and has met with all the Popular applause of a Wilkes from the Town's People, on a decision in his favour at the Sessions. He is just addressing them in a Printed Letter, to which Mrs. Parker has furnished a Latin Motto, and many severe strokes against their adversaries. I just came in time to assist at a Board of consultation over the Proof-Sheets.

They beg to be remember'd to you. Mrs. Peak and *Miss* send their Compliments to my Sisters. I shall write to them, and am | your truly affectionate and dutiful Son | R B Sheridan

---

[1] Either Letter 13 or, as seems more probable, a later note.

[2] Manuscript torn.

[3] Manuscript torn. Rae, i. 214, prints 'to Mr. Wade', which is an error.

[4] Richard Chamberlaine's wife was said by one authority (Lefanu, p. 3) to have been the daughter of Captain Pattison, commander of a man-of-war; and by another (*Gent. Mag.* xcvii (1827), pt. 2, 199–200) to be a member of a Lancashire family named North.

[5] Not identified. A letter by C. Horne to S., written from Clapham on 22 Dec. 1771 (Dufferin MS.), concerns S.'s play, *Ixion*, and the way in which Horne's brothers had enjoyed laughing at it. Sichel, i. 254, mentions that one Horne was contemporary with S. at Harrow.

[6] Edward Parker of Farm Hill, Waltham Abbey, was a friend of S.'s father. The Quarter Sessions Record Books, in the Essex Record Office, Chelmsford, reveal (Q/SB b. 270) that Parker appealed at the sessions on 14 July 1772 against part of the account presented to him by James Harden, one of the overseers of the poor in the parish of Waltham Holy Cross. Wake was a local landowner.

15. To His Sister Elizabeth

LeFanu MS. *Pub.*: Rae, i. 215–16. *Address*: Miss Elizabeth
Sheridan | Bath

30 Aug. 1772

Dear Betsy,
This Letter is wholly entre nous—and your Sister if you
will. Let me remind you, if you have not done it, to call on
Miss D'Oily for my Bill,[1] William I believe will give you
one of Mrs. Purdie's.[2] These I shall take care you shall
immediately have it in your power to pay for me, as I shall
mention it to my Father in my own Way. Will you instruct
William[3] to prevent Evil's giving his Bill[4] to my Father, as
my Note which he has is sufficient, and as my Father will
discharge that, there is no occasion for his knowing the
Particulars. Likewise let him satisfy Thwaites[5] that he shall
be paid for the Pistols, as that shall certainly be in my
account to my Father. And, considering circumstances, by
no means the most unreasonable. If anything else occurs
I must rely on you and Lissy to do the best for me and let
me know the Particulars. I left my Arts and Sciences
behind.[6] I have given them to my Friend Paumier. I wish
you could get them bound, and present them to him it
would not cost above 14 or 16 shillings.—I believe I shall
remit you some money myself: beside[s] what I mentioned
shall be given you by my Father to pay little things which he
is not to know. Out of which too Mr. Bowers[7] shall be paid.

---

[1] Miss Elsie A. Russ informs me that
Miss D'Oily had a shop adjoining the
Assembly Rooms, 1771–82.

[2] *The New Bath Guide* (new ed.,
Bath, 1787), p. 73, lists Mrs. Purdie as
a lodging-house keeper in Orange
Grove and Court. Miss Russ states that
she was the wife of William Purdie, who
ran the Spring Gardens, the fashionable
resort over the river where public break-
fasts and concerts were given.

[3] William Thompson, Thomas Sheridan's servant for many years.

[4] The original is in the Hunt collec-

tion of Bath Municipal Library, and is
printed by Rhodes, pp. 47–48.

[5] Miss Russ states that Joseph
Thwaites of Sheep Street is mentioned
in the Rate Books between 1771 and
1774.

[6] Perhaps this is E. Chambers,
*Cyclopaedia; or, An Universal Diction-
ary of Arts and Sciences* (1728, 2 vols.), or
T. H. Croker, *The Complete Dictionary
of Arts and Sciences* (1764–6, 3 vols.).
Rae, i. 215, also suggests *The History of
the Arts and Sciences* (1769).

[7] Miss Russ informs me that Thomas

By the bye I thought Mrs. Bowers seem[ed] more alarmed about the money than was necessary. 'Tis all for Flow[e]rs. And you may likewise pay her for doing ruffles what she likes. I have wrote to my Father, and shall send him the account as soon as ever I hear from Bath. He has promised me to discharge them. And I assure you I am planning Prudence and all the Cardinal Virtues. You see this is a mere letter of business for you and your Sister: never *shew* my Letters to *any* one. You may just tell me Father you have a letter from me. I shall write to Lissy next Post in a Style. Miss Peake is here.[1] Miss told Mrs. Parker she was glad to hear *I* was coming, for she'd get me to *teach her an almande*.[2] Take care of all the things I left behind me. There is an old Muff[3] which I shall seriously be obliged to you if you will put by for me. Pray write to me directly, and tell Lissy to do so too. How stands the French scheme?[4]—Remember me to Friends, acquaintances, etc., etc., etc., particularly, to the Breretonites,[5] Morganites,[6] Walshites[7] (that last word with a hyphen (-) in the middle would be a vile phrase)[8] Lynnites[9] (how like Linnets!) (whom also you must pay) and kindly to your Gentle Friend La Juliana. | Believe me your | truly affectionate Brother | R B Sheridan.

Waltham. Aug 30th. 1772

Bowers lived in Monmouth Street, Bath, 1769–75. The Bowers had a seed shop at 3 Broad Street in 1800.

[1] Sheridan appears to have intended to write 'Mrs. and Miss Peake are here'. By some confusion in his own mind, he struck out the 'Mrs. and' and penned 'is' over 'are here'. To complete the muddle, he then added 'are here'.

[2] S. enjoyed dancing. The 'allemande' was a German dance, described as 'outlandish' in *The Rivals*, III. iv. 130.

[3] Following Fielding's Tom Jones. See *Tom Jones*, bk. x, ch. v.

[4] Thomas Sheridan had intended that S. should travel to France in the autumn of 1772, in the company of his sisters.

[5] Major William Brereton was Master of Ceremonies at the Lower Rooms in later years. His son, William Brereton

(1751–87), acted at D.L.Th. from Nov. 1768. One G. Brereton is also mentioned by S.: see p. 71.

[6] Of 'Mr. Morgan's Coffee Room'? Or, possibly, the coterie of Edward Morgan, an associate of Mathews. For him, see E. Green, *Linley, Sheridan and Mathews: Their Connection with Bath* (Bath, 1903), p. 76.

[7] Mrs. Walsh seems to have kept a boarding-house. See J. Parkes and H. Merivale, *Memoirs of Sir P. Francis* (1867), i. 221, 270; and Sichel, i. 377.

[8] Omitted by Rae, i. 216.

[9] C. F. Sheridan sent a letter before 8 May 1772 to his uncle 'by Mrs. Lynn': see Rae, i. 182 (13 May), and Yale MS. The 'Linnet' reference is to the character Kitty Linnet in S. Foote's play *The Maid of Bath* (1771). It is based on Elizabeth Linley.

16. To Thomas Grenville[1]

W.T. *Pub.*: Rae, i. 217–20.

Aug. 30th. 1772—Waltham.

Dear Grenville,

That I write to you by your own desire,[2] prevents my making any observation on that kind of sudden Intimacy which excuses and demands as familiar an address. While you are no more than you are at present, I cannot be insincere in declaring how much I *feel* that I wish for your own conversation and Friendship, that it is even necessary to premise your present situation, is a strong argument in favour of what I once before observed to you, that, had it been greater, I could not have been intimate with you. A Person of an ingenuous mind, and any true spirit may have the most familiar attachment to another tho' possess'd in a superior degree of every natural endowment as well as acquired qualification, but where the accidental advantages of Rank and Fortune are added to them—I believe it to be impossible. I only mention this in order to stipulate that, as my connexion is with Mr. *Thomas Grenville*, if ever you should by any accident cease to be that Gentleman,[3] you must not be surprised if I think our correspondence dissolved. At present I have the more opinion of our acquaintance, on account of its not being founded on the common principles of Time and companionship. And tho' there was *one* incidental circumstance which served in a manner to bring forth the expression of those mutual Feelings, by which we knew one another, yet I cannot but flatter myself that some other might have answered the same purpose. As We really find in *Love* frequent proofs, of what the Novelists call a *sudden Sympathy*, I confess I have an opinion of the same in *Friendship*, and I believe the youngest Man's

[1] Thomas Grenville (1755–1846), politician and book-collector, was the third son of George Grenville. S. seems to have met him for the first time when Grenville's brother George, afterwards 1st Marquis of Buckingham (1753–1813), took lessons in elocution from Thomas Sheridan. See Rae, i. 163; Angelo, ii. 418; and *Pub. Adv.*, 5 Dec. 1787.

[2] See p. 43, 'the youngest [Grenville] desired to correspond with me'.

[3] Be ennobled. See Grenville's response, Rae, i. 221–2.

experience will furnish him with instances of his having felt a strong disposition towards a friendship with a man upon the very commencement perhaps of their acquaintance. If it so happens that they are separated soon after, most commonly the acquaintance drops, as the present mode seems to have fix'd a probation of time, exchange of services, intercourse at meals etc., as the necessary foundation of friendship and correspondence. Thus we often hear men regret that some accident should have interrupted their intercourse with Mr. Such a one, before they could grow *intimate* enough to *correspond*, tho' they'd exchanged mutual professions of regard.—For my Part I confess myself an admirer of those times when the ties of *Friendship* as well as *Love*, could with some safety be formed at the first instigation of our Hearts. It is what we call the *Civilization* of Society that has destroyed this, by making a *Fashion* of *Professions*; and still more the *Corruption* that follow'd it, which has so far blunted[1] all the nobler feelings of Man, that the test of Time and Services is become necessary to *apologise* for any mutual confidence, or *disinterested* regard.—But writing on Friendship, is not writing to my Friend: and considering that on sitting down I had apologised for not saying a word on the Subject, a double apology is due for the Trespass. But is there not a Subject nearer to you than Friendship? you say— I wish this sigh would let me deny it. I have passed two days here in excessive melancholy: and I am perfectly convinced that that unfortunate being called a Lover, if a true one, would better bear a separation from her he Loves in a Desert than a Paradise. Place me in the first and I am surrounded with one plain absolute and evident wretchedness. There is no image round me to remind me of *her*, none that I can join with her idea; nay by Heav'n I should feel myself supremely happy that *she* was not there to partake of my hardships.—But in the other, When I see a pair blest in peace and in each other Let me say, 'why am I shut out from this forever?' and 'tis torture. Let me sit in a beautiful scene, I exclaim—'what would her presence make this?' and 'tis worse than a wilderness. Let me hear musick and singing—'I cannot hear her sing and play,' and the notes become

---

[1] Rae, i. 219, also reads 'blunted'; but another Wavertree typescript reads 'blinded'.

the shrieks of the Damned. In short with my present feelings I believe I should be easy nowhere, unless I could find a Place either so perfect or so abominable, as not to admit of the idea of this torturing comparative improvement. I hope you have seen her,[1] I hope you have talk'd to her; if you *have*, and should again I am sure your own Feelings will suggest to you what I would say. Tell me she is happy; if she is otherwise, tell her to be so.—O upon my soul, it were the Part of an Angel to come down from Heaven, to watch over her, and reconcile her mind to Peace. I wish Dying could assure me of the Power to come from Heav'n to her with that Happiness, which I fear She will never know Here. It is impious to say it, but I believe I should exchange a Robe of Glory for *her* Livery. Perhaps you will think it well that I did not begin on this subject sooner. When I do I am fit for nothing Else. But the Bargain was not struck without your knowing of the Blemish. Were there any Reports about after I left Bath? I know not whether I am to charge you with compliments etc. to your Brother and Mr. Clever.[2] Adieu, Grenville, and believe me with my truest sincerity and affection | Your Friend | R. B. Sheridan.

I have promised you a certain History. And you shall have it. I will repeat the conditions.

17. To His Sister Elizabeth

N.L.I. MS. 3901, ff. 2–3. *Pub.*: W. F. Rae, 'Sheridan's Sisters', *Nineteenth Century*, cxviii (1899), 50–51. *Address*: Miss Elizabeth Sheridan | Bath

13 Sept. 1772

Dear Betsy,

Tho I have just written to your Sister,[3] I think I will take this opportunity of giving you a double reproof for not being more expeditious in your motions.—First, let me assure

---

[1] Elizabeth Linley.

[2] William Cleaver (1742–1815), afterwards Bishop of St. Asaph. He was a Fellow of Brasenose College, Oxford, at this time, and private tutor to the Grenvilles: see the *Annual Biography and Obituary* (1817), pp. 16–18, and Lefanu, p. 320.

[3] This letter has not been found.

[you], notwithstanding your boasting, that your Letter did but just come in Time, to prevent my sending you a trimming. I had received answers to all my other Letters, and I assure you I thought you a dreadful *Boar* for your Delay. The less right I have to speak on *this* Subject, you may be sure the more I should have scolded.[1] However I like your account of my commissions very well, tho' if the Phrase '*I shall*' had given into the small alteration of '*I have*' I own I should have been easier. Very *Few People* can afford to be Dilatory; and I must always *preach* at least that Delays are dangerous.—Mr. *To-Morrow* is a Gentleman liable to a variety of Accidents. He may be caught in a shower, or be invited abroad, or be kept by Visiters at home, or have the head Ache, besides he has a notorious bad Memory. In short I would never employ him in anything that can be done by honest *Jack Today*. If, tho you admit of my Doctrine, you object to the Preacher in this case, remember the Honest Clergyman's text, 'Do as I *say*, and not as I *do*.'— However excuse yourself in the true *female way*, by replying as quick as possible, and I'll pass an Amnesty.—

What you tell me of the tranquillity of Bath, astonishes me. Are you sure that all the Houses stand where they Did? Are none of the stones melted by the lamentation of the Inhabitants? Does the Silver Avon *flow on* as usual both in *mud* and *melody*? Ah! Vanité, Vanité!—

A Porpoise![2] I give you my word I never gave of either hair or Locket[3] in my Life. Did you ever know the history of those Rings?[4] If she[5] makes another mystery of this I'll inform you of a surmise that has just pop'd into my head. Indeed I wish your Friend would deal candidly with you, as I am perswaded that an habit of disingenuousness, is one of the worst weeds that can creep into a young female mind. If they go on right in life *Women never* can have occasion for address or Art.—A little trifling knack of *deceiving* in a Girl, I take to be a great advance towards being *materially deceived*.—Anything you say to her on this subject, let be only

---

[1] Betsy was fourteen.
[2] À propos? A family joke?
[3] See p. 37. Evill's bill lists, by the date 'June 10 1772', 'To 1 neat Hair

Locket—£1. 11. 6.'
[4] Rae reads 'things'.
[5] Elizabeth Linley?

from yourself. I am sorry that you are *disappointed* as to continental measures.[1] However I know you are a piece of a Philosopher, and able to recover from your vexation incontinently. Stay, tell your Sister that since you are not suffered to pursue *continentall* measures, you must agree to stay in England *incontinentaly.* Tho' by the bye No Woman *in England* can [pro]perly[2] be said to be *in Continent.*—'Why are all our Women chaste?' so you have a Conundrum.

If I write Nons[ens]ically attribute it to the Tooth-Ache—(of which, vide at large in your Sister's Letter)[3]—however the less matter there is in the place I write from to furnish a Letter, the more I shall thank you for *how*—and *abouts* in yours:—

On what grounds do you say that a Letter to Gren. senr.[4] would have been right? The youngest desired to correspond with me. His Brother told me that if any thing happened worth writing about, he would write to me. It was not my part to offer to write to him.

I assure you, Betsy, the latter Part of your letter pleased me very much! and you can not oblige me more than by informing me of any representations of my own conduct, and giving your own observations on it. And your interesting yourself in it, will always be to me more agreeable than the warmest professions, tho' I know them to be sincere; for it is a Language at least that I can never reply in Unless I sum them all up in the title of | Your ever affectionate Brother | R B Sheridan

Waltham 13 Sept. 1772.

18. To Thomas Grenville

W.T. *Pub.*: Rae, i. 224–9.

[*Late Sept. 1772*][5]

Dear Grenville,

But that it would appear too ceremonious I would begin

[1] Betsy Sheridan declares in her 'Narrative' that when Thomas Sheridan found that S. was still in touch with Elizabeth Linley, he decided that S. should stay at Waltham to prepare for the Bar, and that S.'s sisters should accompany their father to Ireland. Cf. Rae, i. 230.   [2] Manuscript torn.
[3] Not found.
[4] See p. 39, n. 1.
[5] This was S.'s reply to Grenville's letters of 21[?] Sept. (Yale MS.), and of

with apologising for not writing sooner: but wa[i]ving both
ceremony and compliment let me assure you that your's gave
me infinite Pleasure.—It gave me pleasure because it was
just such a Letter as I expected to receive from you. Every
confirmation of an agreeable Prepossession is a compliment
to one's own Penetration—but I will have done with pro-
loguesing for the future.—I thank you most sincerely for the
interest you take in my Welfare, I mean in your wishes to
recommend to me that tranquillity of Mind, which is indeed
the Health of the Soul, and which ought to be to all a consideration as superiour to bodily welfare, as the Soul is to the
Body. But I am afraid their Well-being in a most essential
degree depends equally on the original construction of the
Frames. We may diet and exercise the one to its advantage,
so may we cultivate and improve the other; We may proceed
by rule to the Body's Health, but who can 'administer to
a Mind diseas'd'?[1] For my part I take what the World calls
Philosophy to be the arrantest Quack of All. And, that 'God
never made his Work for Man to mend'[2] is an observation
I would apply not to the Body's Health but rather to the
Minds. For my own Part, unless any Soul, or Mind, or
Disposition, or Feelings, or whatever you please to call it, is
not made like other People's, I must affirm the truth of this.
For I do feel and have always felt, something within that
gives a check to my most pleasurable ideas, something that
will anticipate ovation, that contradicts my best Passions,
repines at the enjoyment of them, and cries out 'Non est
Tanti' to every Pursuit of my Life. I do not say that this
principle is always in Action, but it is sometimes so ingenious
in fixing the most foreign uneasiness on me, that I have
almost doubted, whether I am not most happy when I have
some real trouble of my own, to employ as well as distress[3]
my Mind. If a Man be unhappy, and he can tell you *what*
makes him so in my Mind he half deserves to *be* so. For if

an earlier date. Grenville did not receive
it until the first week in October, because there was a delay in forwarding it
to him in Ireland. See his letters of 4 and
10 Oct. (Osborn MSS.), addressed to S.
at 'Mr. Parker's, Farm Hill, Waltham
Abbey.'

[1] *Macbeth,* v. iii. 40: 'Canst thou not
minister to a mind diseas'd.'
[2] Dryden, 'To my Honour'd Kins-
man, John Driden . . .', l. 95.
[3] W.T. 'as will disstress'. I follow
Rae, i. 225.

his misfortune be without a remedy, let him apply to reason, and exercise his understanding: and if he has an object in view (however desperate) he may be comparatively happy in the *Pursuit*. But what is his State who is unhappy—he knows not why, who has no pursuit, and who were it possible to bid him name his wish and he should have it, would answer that he wanted nothing. This I say is Constitution; and tho' I do not say, but that it is to be counteracted, yet am I sure that it is not to be prescribed to—The Man whom the contemplation of *human Nature* itself will sometimes throw into a melancholy train of Ideas, cannot easily be put into spirits by any accidental Gifts of *Fortune*. However, these Sensations are for the most Part temporary and often go to the composition of a cheerful mind on the whole. If I have seem'd to indulge them too far, I can only say that my mind and body are in unison; tho' did I pretend to be the least of a Philosopher, it would be paying a vile compliment to the former, to suppose it liable to so irrational an influence. However the Truth is that I have been for this fortnight very much dejected by a violent cold in my head, and latterly confined and in too much pain either to employ or entertain myself. Yet let me not retract the complaints of my Despondency, as they at least show that I think an appeal to the sympathising heart of Friendship the best relief for it.

You will think perhaps that the Fire of *Love* is beneath this gloom. To convince you however that *that* is not the cause of those tormenting sensations of which I have been speaking, I will even on the mention of the subject endeavour to shake off[1] these vapours, and try to talk like a more rational being—(Without attempting a Pun—tho' probably that might be one of the best specimens I could give of my intention).

Believe me when I am most melancholy—when I am poring over Nature's large volume of affliction, I turn to the page of Love (tho' a blotted one) for consolation. I find there it is too[2] much cause for vexation, but were it a blank to *me*, I should be ten times more miserable. I am sick and without society—my love is almost the only Feeling I have alive 'Amo ergo Sum'—is the confirmation of my existence.

---

[1] W.T. 'of'.   [2] Rae prints 'true'.

However I am afraid I am giving no proof of my rationality on the subject; yet of the two it is better to tire you with Nonsense, than Complaint: at least I am sure the *former* will be no tax upon your *Sympathy*.

But what shall I say of this attachment! to hope for happiness from it, I must agree with you, *'is* and *must* be impossible'—I have received a letter from her, since I wrote to you (Counterband)[1] fill'd with the violence of Affection, and concluded with prayers, commands and entreaties that I should write to her. I did not expect such a Desire, as she had acquiesced to my determination of not corresponding. Indeed as we had always other subjects to employ us when together, she hesitated less in agreeing to a distant mortification, and I by that had less occasion to explain properly to her the Necessity of it.—I cannot now do it:—for to tell her *why* I am right is to plunge into the wrong:—to tell why I did *resolve*, is to break my resolution, yet to deny her and not excuse my denial is a hard mortification.—I am determined not to write;—not from the conviction of the necessity of such a determination, but I cannot break my solemn Promise. How strange is my situation: if I consult my Reason, or even one half of my Feelings I find conviction that I should wish to end this unfortunate connexion—what draws the knot, rejects the influence of reason, and has its full moiety of the Feelings (dearest! tenderest!) with the Passions for its hold. Perhaps then it is best that there is an artificial, but powerful bond that keeps me to the other Party.—

But, dear Grenville, what shall I say *to you* on this Subject?—could I speak on it with interest or emotion I should reap a double advantage, I should obey the dictates of my reason, and I could with *propriety*, warn *you* not to indulge a Passion which must be equally fatal to you. Yet I must say to you (while I love her) love on. Did I not, upon my soul I would turn Monitor.[2] Not that I think that at present there is any Danger, or that you can hurt yourself; nor would I deprive myself of the satisfaction I have in knowing

[1] Presumably referring to a letter written by Elizabeth Linley after she had been forbidden to correspond with S. Perhaps it is the one (now in the Widener MSS.) printed by Rae, i. 210– 12, and among those too summarily rejected by P. Fitzgerald, *Sheridan Whitewashed* (1896), pp. 17–23.

[2] This is explained on pp. 60–61.

that *She* has a Friend tho' thro' Love in the Man of my Esteem. The Feelings arising from such an attachment in a breast like yours, I am sure cannot be hurtful in their Operation: But need I say that were I free and saw you, advancing towards my present situation, I should try to hold you back, as from a Precipice. You will say perhaps, that I tho' on the Precipice have declared that I turn towards *Love* that led me there, as to a pleasant object:—'tis true, but (as I said too) 'tis only when a diseased Imagination has conjured up a more dismal Prospect on the Other Side. But I will finish the subject with requesting that if ever (and you are now treading on the heels of perilous Probabilities) you entangle yourself in a Love Net you will candidly and freely draw on me for what little experience accident or a few years may have given me in advantage over you. I would ever wish to prevent my friend from being fool'd by a Woman, but I would not give a Pin for [a] Man that was capable of being so. I will resume the subject, if it be only to show that I mean no boast by my Offer.

In regard to the memoirs[1] I must be silent at Present; but rest assur'd that I do neither retract nor *repent* of my Promise. Accuse this cold and Toothache. I have had this morning a vile tumour open'd in my upper jaw, which pained me horribly and long before I knew what it was. I am now conceivably better as you may conceive who are the first victim to my amendment.

Adieu, Grenville, but do not retort my Delay, or I shall doubly curse the cause of it. | Your's with the truest sincerity | R. B. Sheridan.

19. [To the Queen]

Yale MS. Draft.

[*1772?*]

Why should the improvement of genius and the understanding alone employ the Pens of Genius, it is better to make one Man happy than a hundred wise, and it is better to

---

[1] Presumably the 'certain History' referred to on p. 41. It may have concerned his trip abroad with Elizabeth Linley and his subsequent adventures.

make one man virtuous than a million happy. Were I ever so capable I could not employ myself in the former while I thought I could be of service in the latter, where the Heart whispers that we can be of service to promote the happiness of our fellow-Creatures, it is no Vanity to make the Attempt. Where we write in the cause of Virtue, 'tis Praise worthy even to fail.—

Giving up therefore any Pride in or attempt to the former, I hesitate not to Address the first Personage in this country as her Duty to hear me.—I do not beg your Majesty to accept my thoughts but I write to your Majesty. If I am deficient in the Form, my excuse is that my intention is to promote the welfare of your sex and children.[1]—

Before I plead the Grievances of the best, and most amiable Part of the Creation, before I shew them in the humiliating light to which our Folly and brutality have suffered Part of them to decline I may surely be excused, If I premise a Word or two on their importance

The Dispute about the Proper Sphere of Women is idle, that Man should have attempted to draw a line for them which shews that God meant them for Courts and above our jurisdiction. With them th[e] enthusiasm of Poetry, and the Idolatry of Love is the simple voice of Nature,[2] they *were* meant to polish our nature, we should be Brutes without them. They are our Angels, our Mistresses, our Souls. And He who feels not a reverence for beauty, has a vicious soul.

Philosophers are fond of recurring to a state of Nature, for foundation of their hypotheses, and those unmanly eunuchal[?] Wits, who support their titles by ridiculing Women, bring many of their examples from thence. Let us slander Nature so far as to doubt of her being our Advocate.

In a state of Nature say they Women are treated like Slaves, theirs are the employments of Labour, the Drudgery, the Care. It is true and therein let them Glory. Come let us examine these noble examples, let us draw the savage into day, or if not why then the beast he drives, perhaps will do as

---

[1] Possibly prompted by an article favouring the education of women written by S.'s relative Samuel Whyte. It appeared in *The Shamrock*, and was reprinted in the *Hibernian Magazine*, ii (1772), 267–72, 289–95.

[2] The passage, 'The Dispute . . . Nature', is quoted by Moore, i. 129–30.

well, and learn from [it] the dignity of Manhood. [To] the Eye of Reason it appears thus. When Man is scarce better than a Brute, he shews his degeneracy by his treatment of Women, but I will advance that with every ray of reason that breaks in upon his Mind, his respect for Women increases. It is a Plant that thrives in the Sun of Knowledge, and in proportion as we cheer its beams, it flourishes and repays us with its fruits. O Shame, to need the Proof. I will suppose for the reproof of these Wits, their observations were just and that they knew Geography. In Java and Japan—the Women are absolute Slaves, and as it seems a Part of our immutable Constitution, I would venture to Pronounce that their Knowledge, Virtue, and Politeness is at its Zenith. The influence that Women have over us, is as the Medium thro' [which] the finer arts act upon us, the incense of our Love and respect for them, creates the Atmosphere of our Souls, which corrects and melio[r]ates the beams of Knowledge,[1] where it is not, the Night of Ignorance shall prevail.

However in the savage countries where the Pride of Men has not fixed the first dictates of Ignorance into Law, we see the real effects of Nature, the wild Huron shall become Gentle as his weary Rein-deer to the object of Love, He shall present to her the spoil of his Bow on his knee, he shall watch the scene where she sleeps, with reward, he shall rob the Birds for feather for her hair, and dive for Pearl for her Neck, her Look shall be his Law, and her Beauties his worship.[2]—This is Nature.

Let us trace the Distinction into former times and polished Society. The two Greatest Nations in the World knew their worth. The East which has always been the seat of Tyranny to Women, has always been the seat of Barbarism and Ignorance. The honours paid to the Roman women always resembled Idolatry, and were [I] to describe the feeling of Love to [an] Anchorite, I would refer him to the rapturous humiliation of his div[in]e Transports below—and Nature appears in Milton in Nothing more than in the expression of this unaccountable influence.

---

[1] The passage, 'The influence . . . knowledge', is quoted by Moore, i. 130. [2] The passage, 'However . . . worship', is quoted by Moore, i. 130.

If we come to Modern times, we find the Effect the Same. If we ask what Nation holds the first Rank, in the opinion at least of Europe, we shall find it the Nation w[h]ere Women are most regarded. England may rank as second in both respects; Spain comes much under, and there the Women are kept like Egyptian Deities, worshipped indeed but tied to a Stake; Italy the most contemptible, to whom the epithet of *unmanly* and *effeminate* is proverbial, it is not from this falling into the methods[?] of Women, but that they have unnaturally forsook them; Holland despised for they despise women. Turkey is an Oaf among the Nations, with Eyes blinking against the beams of Learning, for their attachment is purely Animal. The Distinction between Horse Jock and Mare . . .[1] thought to be, not Man and Woman, not the Image of God and his Helpmate.—

(Love and Devotion operate in the same way the[y] both delight in Poetry and Musick etc.)

As to the Characters that have formed out this Sphere in history, I would Venture to enter the List against the Heroic, even building on the candour of History where the Men are the Painters, from Boadice[a] in our own Country to Semiramis. But we ought to blush in the contest, we shall so frequent our Heroes, and revolution[i]s[e] the effect of Female Art—Antony, Caesar, Hercules, Alexander, Ephestion, what a List. Should [we] not blush in speaking of our [heroes] to bo[a]st as their greatest excellenc[e], that they could resist the attraction of their Excellence. The Conqueror of the World meets with no greater praise than that he resisted this temptation. Scipio the good, the gallant Scipio, would thrust himself to the View, and fall and in this we Glory. Love excuses vice.

It is a coarse idea that our right over Women is found in their being of our Flesh, that God made them but *of* us. Let them take it but thus and it is true God made man of the Dust of the Earth he mould[ed] this clod into this poor devil[?] for he fashioned it thus wonderfully and fearfully, A breath of Animal Life into it, and then the divine flow[e]r of the Soul. When this was finished God saw his work imperfect, and he took from Man a Part.—He took not the original

[1] Illegible.

base Earth, but from the composition he had made and in-
spired it with [life] from his own hands. And from this part,
he moulded, and well might, a form more beautiful, more
graceful, more divine, and to this superior being did he
not breathe a Soul?—and the Soul he breathed into it, is
more beautiful, more graceful, more divine. He gave an
influence to it over the first being, and the first time he saw
it he took it for a Divinity, and would have worship[p]ed it.
And tho God himself said thou art the superior, Yet he
obey'd even to Vice the Woman, and the almight[y] found,
that he had made Man too weak, and charm'd with his own
work, to woman, he had made her too powerful. Then suffered he the first seed of Vice. Envy took root, and he let the
Man who excelled alone in brutal strength, to conceive the
genius of Woman. Yet still we find The sacred influence
prevail and in proportion as by civilities and knowledge we
polish Manners, in Proportion woman gains her Natural
ascendant. We obey tho' we know not whay, we Love even
guilt in them, and that Love almost excuse[s] guilt in us.
This was the defect of our original Creation. Since Man has
fallen it were blasphemy to suppose God had made him
Perfect.

What I have said accedes to the Subject in this Manner.
If it be granted that the Genius of Woman be thus great and
uncircumscribed; is it [to] be granted that the[y] have and
ever have had this unaccountable influence over us. It will
follow that next to the worship of our Creator, we should
turn our attention to their happiness and improvement.
Since chance and animal strength has placed the Power in
our hands how can it[1] be employ'd better than [in] perfecting
that which must govern us. The Brighter they are the more
shall we be illumined, tis reflected light that gives a double
Lustre. Were the Minds of all Women cultivated by in-
spiration, man would become wise of course, not so with
men to woman Nature will write on the Heart of man with
woman as with a Pentagraph,[2] what *she* Delineates on the
original Man will appear on the Copy,[3] and let it be their

---

[1] Moore prints 'we'.
[2] Instrument for copying a plan
mechanically (*O.E.D.*).

[3] The passage, 'How can . . . Copy',
is quoted (with some paraphrasing) by
Moore, i. 131.

essential task to perfect the lines, supply the figures, and dispose the shades. In moral Virtue it is the same, were all womanly indelic[ac]y to become Virtuous, comparatively speaking there would be no Vice in Man. Let not me be mistaken as insinuating that in Woman is the source of Vice. I would wish to advance that it is not human Nature, but in Woman is the influencing power of Virtue, if Vice be Virtue misapplied, from her too comes the influence of Vice. Adam stood not a day when Eve fell, Adam might have eat[?], and Eve not. Twas the instigations of flattery and beauty that seduced Eve, the Serpent was then an object of the completest beauty, and its voice was harmony, Yet Eve would not have listened to the same allurements from the mouth of the disgusting Toad. Hence the Devil changed his shape. This is the natural operation of Art and Beauty, these are the natural operatives of Woman, and their influence will be eternal.

The next Point then to be considered is how to prevent this influence from being perverted, and how to make it operate for the Best. In the first Place we should consider whether by the Civilization Women have suffered any unnatural inconvenience. I answer a material one. I will affirm a State of slavery, Guilt, tyranny etc. is more in Nature to Woman than a State of Poverty. (I must observe once for all that by Poverty I mean the comparative distress of any one for the convenience of Life—and by comparative I mean comparative with their make and expectations. For Instance a Young Lady bred up in elegance and . . .,[1] is in a state of Poverty and Distress should she become a Servant.—This I call unnatural) Nature points that Man was to provide for Woman as for a Limb[?][2] They are more unqualified than the female of any other Animal. And it ought to have been an Object of every society to have guarded against these emotional distresses in a Female Mind. But our Laws are most ungallant Laws. Legislators in general, have their blood too cold to make the allowances they ought. And we should blush to think how many genteel souls suffer thro the pangs of Poverty, the insult of Dependence. How many are

[1] Illegible.
[2] S. has added above the line, 'Adam was not . . . by the sweat of any lives'. The word after 'not' is illegible.

forced into the trammels of Guilt, how many droop and die in secret, who might become the ornaments of Societ[y], and the blessing of humanity.—Let me mention an Example from a Neighbouring Kingdom.

In France there is in the constitution a kind of Prevention from these Evils, Any of the Noblesse who find their fortune insufficient to Portion their Daughters, can prevent the sad perilous effects of their being left unportion'd Orphans, by shutting them in a Charity. A melancholy resource, yet I believe a fortunate one to many. Yet tho' this was the Case, There was a Woman in France,[1] who felt the sad necessity I have been complaining of. She saw how many useful members were lost to the community. She had herself felt this unnatural Process of Poverty, and her resource had been Guilt, and tho' a Crown adorn'd it, she had Virtue to wish to preserve others from the Trial. She placed herself at the head of this, she superint[end]ed their education, and made them the ornaments of Society. They were portion'd at a certain age most of them to the military, who look'd on them as their weapons[?] to fortune and Honour. This was a blessed Charity, and [though] the Foundress [had] been as sinful as the Magdalen, the grateful tears of the guarded Chorus[?] had wash'd them all away. And they did see her crown'd for it [in] Heaven if she were not so on Earth.

There is not so distressed [a] situation in the World as that of a Gentlemans Daughter in England left without Fortune. Such a Charity in France is generally speaking only snatching its object from the inactivity of [the] Cloyster, in England it would tear them from the gripe of Poverty and Vice. When I speak of Orphans, I refer only to Gentlemen's Daughters, and mostly those of Officers or Clergymen. I shall explain my reason for these.

We have no resource for them, they cannot marry. The only employment they can follow is in general branded with disgrace. They are look'd on as the lawful Prey of libertines, and the Path they tread is so thorny and so few can possibly get through with Credit, that it is regard[ed] as Presumptive

[1] Françoise d'Aubigné, Marquise de Maintenon (1635–1719), founded the Convent of St. Cyr for women of aristocratic birth who were in distressed circumstances.

Proof of Sin to be in it. The Charitable Sneers of their own Sex, when the[y] see a young Lady who has been bred to liberal expectations reduced to this situation, they kindly give her up for lost, and avoid her on the possibility. Their virtue is of that sagacious kind, tha[t] smells the storm before it appears. And feeling that their own excellence consists in no temptation thro' affluence the[y] can disjoin the ideas of Poverty and Guilt. Else every Orphan so left in a Country of Humanity will find a Parent in her wealthy Neighbour and every Woman who sees a distressed Orphan of that kind, who has it in her power to relieve, and whose heart whispers her that she ought, if she refuse let her beware that at the great Bar she may be treated as an accessory in her Guilt and misfortunes. It is Treason against the Majesty of Virtue, and not to interpose is to encourage it.

As for us we are born in a state of warfare with Poverty and Distress. The Sea of our Adversity is our Natural Element, and He that will not buffet with the Billows deserves to sink; but You, O You, by Nature form[ed] of gentler kind, can you endure the biting storm, shall ye be turn'd to the knifing[?][1] blast and not a door shall be open to give ye shelter.[2]—I will suppose a Father with his Sons who cannot provide for them when he dies, let them be of advanced age in Youth, for if the[y] are infants, as Poverty must nurse them, they will afterwards own her for their Parent. If he has educated his boys so that they have spirit to attempt to push their own way, abilities to second them, and virtue to bear the rubs they will meet with it is his own fault. But with his Daughters he cannot support them. Let Nature have deck'd them with beauty, let Education have informed them and their Danger is the Greater. They turned singl[e] on the world, all that can be done for them is like the lustre of the glow-worn, which makes [them] the more conscious prey of those that watch but to defor[m] them. This is the true style of many dear ingenious Souls who live in this kingdom. If it be the nobles[t] act of Charity to snatch[3] but one [from] such a state w[h]ere shall be the reward of her who shall avert it all.

---

[1] Moore, i. 131, prints 'nipping'.
[2] The passage, 'As for us . . . shelter',
is quoted by Moore, i. 131.
[3] Manuscript 'stretch'.

Had such a Charity as I have been speaking of existed here, the mild *Parthenia* and my poor *Laura* had [not?] fallen into untimely Grave[s].[1] But as what I have mentioned is only intended as a hint to the Genius of others, I will here[?] likewise propose a hint of a Plan for the execution of them.—I will suppose (for where Charity is the Object I shall be authorized in my supposition) that his Majesty were to grant Hampton Court, or some other Palace for this Purpose.—Let it be entitled the

Royal Sanctuary.

As it is to be immediately under your Majesty's Patronage, so should your Majesty be the first Member of it.—Let the Constitution of it be as of a University—Your Majesty Chancellor, some of the first Ladies in the Kingdom sub-Chancellors, Whose Care shall be to provide instructors of real Merit. The Classes are to be distinguished only by age —none of Degree—for as their qualification should be Gentility, they are all on a Level. The instructors should be women, excepting for the Languages. Latin and Greek should not be learned. The frown of Pedantry destroys the blush of Humility! The Practical Part of Science, as of Astronomy etc., should be [taught]. In History they would find, that there are other Passions in Man than Love. As for Novels there are some I would strongly recommend. But Romances infinitely more. The one is a representation of the Effects of the Passions as the[y] should be, tho extravagant. The other as they are. The Latter is false[ly] called Nature, it is a figure of depraved and corrupted Society. The other is the glow of Nature. Therefore I would exclude all Novels that show Human Nature depraved. However well executed the Design will disgust.[2] The next Thing to be attended to is their accomplishments. They should early be instru[ct]ed all in Dancing, and wools embroidery etc. Those whose Genius should lead to it in Musick and Poetry, and Drawing. Diversions. These are the happinesses. A well directed ima-

[1] Moore, i. 131, quotes this sentence, calling it a 'strange romantic allusion'.
[2] The passage, 'As it is . . . disgust', is quoted by Moore, i. 132–3, with the comment, 'the practical details of his plan . . . exhibit the same flightiness of language and notions'.

gination, more than an improved Understanding, or honest disposition Promotes the welfare of individuals. They should ride and walk, the younger Part be invited to exercis[e] by the little Pastimes. Dancing and Concerts, always a Spirit of Emulation kept up by Prizes. In the Winter the French petit jeus at once entertain and quicken the genius. As to the moral Duties and tone of the Heart that ever must depend on the People that conduct it. There should be a Clergyman of an uncommon Character for their Curate . . .[1] Whole Duty of Man.[2] The[y] should be taken into Life by degrees. Above all a Knowledge of Œconomy and the Management [of] a House should be inculcated as [much] as the News in France. They should in turn regard the different Officers. The want of this has hurt matrimony more than can be expressed But let them have modesty I hate [them] when Linkboy-like

Let a benevolent Mind view this Prospect and what will be his Feelings. At Present a Boarding School Education is become a term of Reproach. The Spirit of communication, indeed of the noble Uses it might be put to is contagious, and Girls are regarded, like Fruits which rot in touching. But w[h]ere would be a repository From whence The Violets[?] and the Graces would walk forth in their Own Forms and Habits and moving it thro Out see the Love, and Virtue thro' the Land.

Effects to be Expected

As one of the Effects I must previously mention why [I] have limited my Plan to the Noblesse: because the effect of the execution of it with them, would be the making it become Universal. In point of the Humanity of the thing, a Gentlemans Daughter is the Greatest Object of Compassion. There is provision for the Lowest kind, . . .[3] us if we waited 'till they should sink without the reach of Charity, tho much corrupted. Now if such a Charity were fixed for the noblesse only, something of a Similar Kind would speedily be adopted by the Trading Part of the world, tho' they in general least want it. But a Society of Merchant[s] of London would

---

[1] Three illegible words.   Cf. *The Rivals*, I. ii.
[2] By Richard Allestree (1619–81).   [3] Illegible.

quickly establish another. This example would be follow'd by the other trading Town[s], and it soon would spread. Your Majesty should be supplied from all parts of the kingdom, and the influence would be Universal.

Next let us Consider How great the Probability [is] that the Ladies thus educated would ever continue in Paths of Virtue, first they would be particularly regarded, and bound by a filia[l] respect to the Sanctuary, as well as being the adopted of your Majesty. They would come forth, with understandings to despise the Vanity of the Mode, and in the Society of Sisters whereby the Spirit of Emulation would be still Continued. They would own Every child of Distress.

The next . . .[1] would be the Powerful influence of their example, and were Your Majesty to chuse from them, the Officers of your Household this influence would be greater, and you would be . . .[1] the Queen surround[ed] by the Virtues and Graces.

But as I said that none above a certain Age, should be admitted, unless by examination—The effect of this only would be great. The Vicissitude of Life is such that none can be sure when the hand of misfortune may meet them consequent[ly] many [a] Mother would be particularly [willing] to leave her Daughter within the reach of your Majesty's Adoption. While those whose Fortunes put them above this resource, would blush to find the Children of Charity superior both in Elegance and Virtue. Thus from a Spirit of Emulation the sam[e] advantages would accrue to them.

The Effect over Men would be equal and first over their Husbands. The first Idea that would occur to me would be to endeavour to deserve the Prize. As by the Match he would be more in the way of preferment and observation He would be more careful of his Conduct. Let this at first be but the effect of Habit, and if his Wife be right it will soon be constitution. and as he will receive her from your Majesty's hands, he will take as Adam did his innocent Bride, and have a kind of religious love to her for the Majesty of the Giver.—

But beside the immediate effect on the Husband, it will operate on all the Young Men of the Age both in those who are married, and those who are introduced into Society.

[1] Illegible.

How much must each silly Macaroni blush to come into the company of Women accomplished as I have mentioned and with what contempt must they hear these Dupes of ignorance. The fine speeches that now ensnare poor Girls what paltry stuff it would appear to them! No they must indeed herd together and as the care they take of their own Persons proves that Narcissian Fondness they must admire themselves in each other being so got to one standard of Folly that each will serve as the mirror of each Other.— Upon those of genious the effect will be noble. It will be the strongest invitation to them to become worthy objects of such perfection.

Here the influencing Power of Virtue will appear in its true force. We all feel that the governing Principle in a young man of education and sensibility is a desire to be agreeable to Women. This cannot be denied 'Hoc studium'.[1] The end is the same in the Fop etc.

Then it will be a wise and virtuous incentive. The Cries[?] of Buncle[?] will be verified universally.[2] If Men now affect the character of wildness, debauching, dress and Libertinism, from a Principle of pleasing the generality of Women, it would then become a Fashion to be wise and virtuous, to be brave and honourable. Love would be their Object, their Guardian, their Instructor. Love would give them wisdom, Genius and honour. Love would bring them happiness. Love would bring them Virtue. How different is the character of Sidney[3] and Aggrippa,[4] from that of the modern man of fashion and gallantry In one there is the Soul of Honour, the true Spirit of Love, the dear delightful extravagance of Gallantry, the romance of Virtue. His Friend is as himself. His honour [is] his God. His life is the active separation of the nobler passions, and luminous feelings. But come thou contemptible wretch, on[e] worse than feminine affectation, uninstructed, a heart with[out] emotion, a countenance without expressions. Honour to a human line, politeness by chance. Philosopher in trifles. Or if they have not the greater vices neither have they the Virtues. They know not revenge

---

[1] Horace, *Epistles*, i. iii. 28: 'Hoc opus, hoc studium parvi properemus et ampli.' [2] T. Amory, *John Buncle* (1776), i. 78–80. [3] See p. 61. [4] Marcus Vipsanius Agrippa (63–12 B.C.).

nor lust, nor fury, neither know the[y] Love, nor Friendship. If these be the Polish[ed] and whouring[?] lives of Society, O give me Nature in its own rough mode and glowing in its hue. These are clip[ped] and so rubb[ed] and polish'd, that Gods image and inscription is worn from them, in this smooth world the[y] may pass comment with applause, but nail'd, to the Devils counter, the[y] shall be in a state of annihilation. Too bad for Heaven, and so far beneath the Dignity of Hell.

Let me now Address your Majesty on your known Charity. You have patronised two Charities the one for the reception of those whom Penitence or whom I fear more frequently Disease and unsuccessful Vice, fling again upon the hands of Virtue.[1] The Other for the Safeguards of those who bless the world with offspring without Gods leave.[2] Do not imagine I speak with disrespect of either. No. It is the action of a blessed hand to draw a Veil upon the blasting Cheek, altho it be the Blast of conscious Guilt, it is the action of a blessed hand to wipe the tear from Misfortunes eye, tho' it is for Vice—and blessed be the hand. Nor is it less, to serve the poor wretch At least the difficulty of the Passage through a sea of trouble, involv[ing] very existence is mark'd with Disgrace, and to cease the . . .[3] when perhaps the mind feels worse. This is the light Humanity would view it [in]—But shall that Humanity wait till Vice has made crying objects of charit[y], Shall she only[4]

20. To Thomas Grenville

Osborn MS. *Pub.*: Rae, i. 232–6. *Address*: To Thomas Grenville Esqr.

30 Oct. 1772

My dear Grenville,

I ought to be ashamed of my Tardiness in writing to you:[5] and I can no other way excuse it, than by assuring you that

---

[1] The Magdalen Hospital in Prestcot Street was established in 1758.

[2] The Foundling Hospital was built between 1742 and 1752.

[3] Illegible.

[4] The manuscript ends at this point.

[5] Replying to Grenville's letter of 10 Oct.

I deferr'd it, only to do it with the more satisfaction. I have no greater Pleasure than in hearing from, and writing to you: and therefore it is that I do not find myself inclined to the latter, when my Mind is uneasy on any account which would not be alleviated by being communicated. However I believe I may now say that in all probability, nothing of that kind will ever again cause any omission in me.

My Last was written at a time, when from bodily Indisposition, I believe I was inclined to talk too much in a desponding Strain. But the gloomy Atmosphere of a sick Room, is a vile medium to view the Prospects of Life thro'. All the Colours appear deaden'd and confused to the Eye, and every Object unsubstantial. But let the Sun of Health shine forth, and—the Patient (if he be not aware) shall talk in nonsensical Tropes and Figures for an Hour together. But I assure you I have now better Health, and mere animal Spirits, than I remember to have had. I keep regular hours, use a great deal of Exercise, and study very hard. There is a very ingenious Man here, with whom, besides, I spend two hours every Evening: In Mechanicks, Mensuration Astronomy. etc. I purpose likewise to make myself a Piece of a Sailor, which is the Conjuror's Fork: This Man has a great deal of Merit, and—a Wife and Family: is very Poor, and has taught himself everything he knows.—

There is one Point you misunderstood me in,[1] with regard to Perils and Probabilities. I did not mean anything as to Miss L., nor hint at any Peril in Particular. I meant only that a Young Man of a Warm Constitution, and of a generous Temper must in general run some risque, and probably get into some Difficulties from his intercourse with Women. I do not mean those of a low kind, For the inconveniences which mere Passion brings a Man into, are what he deserves;—I allude only to the embarrassments of the Heart. Which I believe will always be perilous where there are Passions, and at the same time too much Delicacy to relish

[1] Grenville wrote on 10 Oct.: 'I had heard the story of Miss L.'s misfortunes before I saw her. I felt for her before I saw her, and more afterwards from the reflection that so delicate a person was little calculated for such severe tryals. What I heard from you, as it increased her merit, more inclined me to lament the unhappy reward of it. But compassion with me is the strongest motive, and that compassion as I hope it is laudable wants no Monitor.'

their Gratification with Prostitutes. It was in this case that I threatned to assume the character of Monitor.—

I must repeat again, and once for all, and most sincerely that I turn to Nothing with a greater Pleasure than to our Correspondence, and the Idea I have of what our Friendship shall be. I never had met with but one Person whom I could fix in the character I had formed of Friendship. He died;—and in Proportion as I grew in acquaintance with Others, my Regret for him increased. My early acquaintance with him, gave me a delight in the Pleasures of Friendship; and when I had lost him, The recollection of that Delight made me hope that a Mind that joy'd in it, would surely find another Object for such an Intercourse. But the more (as I said) I got acquaintances, the more I found I should have *Acquaintances* only: and thus my regret for *Forbes*[1] increased; on the same Principle as a Man newly married would not so much deplore the loss of his newborn Child while he hoped that another year would Probably supply its Place. But let years roll on, and bring no appearance of a compensation, with aggravated distress, he curses the stroke that robb'd him of his First. Do not think I mean to compliment, when I say that when I was scarce acquainted with you, The Feelings of Friendship, and the Passion I had to have a Friend (which long had slumbered in me) of themselves revived. My *Heart* bid me wish to be your Friend, before my *Judgement* could inform me of your Character. And if I did not feel a Confidence that I am not mistaken, I would never trust either Heart or Judgement again.—My Speaking on this Subject in so unfashionable a Style, brings to my mind as unfashionable a Performance. I mean *Sir Philip Sidney's Arcadia.* If you have not read it (and ever read Romances) I wish you would read it. I am sure there is much of it that would charm you. For my own Part when I read for Entertainment, I had much rather view the Characters of Life as I would wish they *were* than as they *are*: therefore I hate Novels, and love Romances. The Praise of the best of the former, their being *natural*, as it is called, is to me their greatest Demerit. Thus it is with Fielding's, Smollet's etc. Why should men have a

[1] A boy named Forbes won the Silver Arrow contest at Harrow in 1769. See Gun, p. 10.

satisfaction in viewing only the mean and distorted figures of Nature? tho', truly speaking not of *Nature*, but of Vicious and corrupt Society. Whatever merit the Painter may have in his execution, an honest Mind is disgusted with the Design.—

But what made me mention this Book was, that you will there find *Friendship* as well as Love in their own noble Forms. If anyone thinks that the colouring of the Former is too high, I will deny that He can have a Soul for the Latter. He that drew them we know had for both. If you read it now, you must tell me your Opinion of some Observations I will make to you.

If I were to see you I would shew you some Idle things that I have written. However there is one of a more serious Kind, which you shall have before I do anything with it.[1]—

I fancy too I shall speedily be more seriously employ'd. But of that I will say nothing 'till I am certain.

You will observe that I have omitted saying anything de Amore, aut de Ceciliâ meâ (utinam quidem mea esset!). I have kept absolutely to my resolution. But (from a late accident) I will defer saying more 'till I see you. What you have said on the Subject has the most pleasant consolatory effect on me.

I will now continue to write to you without waiting even for answers to convince you of the truth of my former excuse. But I will not admit of excuses on your side: those who fail themselves always exact the most: so I shall notwithstanding Hope that you will retort on me with the spirit of Revenge.

I hope your Brother and Mr. Cleaver are well and that you have all brought home your Hearts and Senses from the Land of Beauties and Blunders,[2] | Believe me, dear Grenville, | ever and truly | your's | R B Sheridan.

Waltham.
    Oct 30th: 1772.

---

[1] Possibly Letter 19; but see, also, Moore, i. 103–4, and Sichel, i. 401, 412–13.

[2] In his letter of 10 Oct. Grenville stated that he would be leaving Dublin in four or five days.

21. To Thomas Grenville

Pub.: Rae, i. 236–8.

10 Nov. 1772

My dear Grenville, if anything could make me glad at not hearing from you[1] it would be the giving me an opportunity to convince you that I shall never stand upon the ceremony of waiting for an answer. I have a much higher opinion both of the utility and satisfaction of an epistolary correspondence between minds that do in some degree, from Nature or their feelings, correspond, than to confine it merely to the information of one's health, or the most trivial subjects of intelligence.

It is a common observation that the greatest excellence of familiar letter-writing consists in an easy and unpremeditated style. Hence it is not unusual for people to boast that they *write* just as in common they *speak*. Now if the correspondence be held between two ignorant and nonsensical coxcombs they will be perfectly right, as any attempt at anything of thought or observation, will in such appear an awkward and disgusting affectation. But this is also frequent with men of understanding who, to avoid the opposite extreme of a pedantic and sententious style do often labour violently to avoid the appearance of having thought in their letter, and to confine themselves to the most insignificant subjects dressed in the most familiar language.

I confess I have always regarded a correspondence of a true kind in a more serious light. I think it is a farce when it is carried on between mere acquaintances. If two men, who fancy themselves united in friendship, have so little serious understanding as never when together to discourse upon any subjects beyond the ordinary topics of chit-chat, they are certainly right at not aiming at more in their letters. But are those who delight in conversation of a more serious and improving nature to give up that satisfaction when they

---

[1] Grenville returned to Christ Church, Oxford, where he had matriculated on 9 Dec. 1771. He wrote to S. from there on 'Monday' [9 Nov.], and the postmark of the letter (Osborn MS.) is '10 NO'. S. did not receive it before writing the above.

converse in writing, that they may scribble with ease and avoid the imputation of formality? I would have every man *write* to his friend as he would *speak*. Yet not as he would speak to him at a dinner or assembly, but (if he pretends to be a man of sense) as he would speak to him in those uninterrupted, retired hours of mutual confidence and communication in which consist the spirit and enjoyment of friendship. And to such *this* will be to write with *ease*. For I do not recommend any attention in such a correspondence to language or expression. They will be right of course; it will be the language of the heart and the expression of the feelings; but I would rather court than avoid a train of serious reflection. If such do not pertinently and easily occur, it is better to lay one's head on one's hand to consider on *what* to write, than *how* to express ourselves, and the latter I believe will always be the case when we thwart the bent of our disposition in any conversation. For my own part, that [I] may not seem to discredit my own observations, I shall confess that I write much more precipitately and triflingly often than I could wish, but it is more from habit and indolence, than that I can approve of it.

I should have been running on upon this subject very impertinently, if I had not something in view to introduce by it. You must understand that I have a very high opinion of the *utility* as well as amusement of the friendly intercourse of letters. When there is a mutual confidence and esteem, I am convinced nothing could be made more highly improving. I mean more particularly among young men. Youth rejects, most universally, the experience of men of years; it is suspicious of their counsels and reserved in its communication with them. But a communication of observations and sentiments, of feeling and perceptions between young men must have a good effect. Though neither may have experience enough to be instructive, yet will the attempt throw the mind of the other into a train that, in the end, will prove so. So that all this preface tends only to this. You must not think me vain or pedantic if in future I often deliver my sentiments to you on some subjects as if I thought I could be of service to you. If you will deal the same with me, you will repay me. Friendship is the most noble of all preceptors: it courts and gives improvement. I can say no more on this subject at present, and it has for this time excluded all others.

22. To Thomas Grenville

W.T. *Pub.*: Rae, i. 238–9.

17 Nov. 1772

My dear Grenville

By the time you receive this [you will have received][1] another of mine. originally directed to Lord *Temple's*.[2] I have nothing to answer in your last, than that you may depend on it, I will see you at *Oxford* before a month is over. My last contained *nothing*, unless I were for the future to write most extremely seriously. However this shall be no Letter—it is merely a few lines, written because I feel an inclination to write to you from a Coffee-House in *London*, being just come for[3] the Play.[4]—Wherever[5] I have been at an idle and irrational amusement, whenever I have been in company with Acquaintances, and Companions (that is with fools and Coxcombs) I return with the strongest Sensations of Disgust, and I have no real Friend on whom I can turn my thoughts, I am extremely wretched. If I think that I have, I would seek a solitude to converse with him tho' but by a Letter.—Thro' this only I have taken a Pen to scribble to *you*.

The Principles of Love are the same.—A Lover (a true one) shall fly with rapture from the society of Courtezans to contemplate but the Picture of his Mistress.

I am interrupted—and can add no more than that I am | and ever will be | Your's most sincerely | R. B. Sheridan.

Bedford-Coffee-House[6]
Nov. 17th 1772

[1] Not in the W.T., but added by Rae in his transcript.

[2] In his letter of 10 Oct., Grenville had mentioned his impending return to England and had asked S. to direct his next letter to Stowe, Bucks. Presumably S. addressed Letter 21 there.

[3] Rae prints 'from'.

[4] At D.L.Th., *As You Like It* and *Harlequin's Invasion*; at C.G.Th., *The Beggar's Opera* and *The Deuce is in Him* (*General Evening Post*, 14–17 Nov. 1772). [5] Rae, 'Whenever'.

[6] A centre for literary men. See A, Ellis, *The Penny Universities* (1956), pp. 174–8.

23. To Thomas Grenville

W.T. *Pub.*: Rae, i. 239–41.

28 Nov. 1772

My Dear Grenville,

I was very lately on the Point of surprising you with a visit to Oxford; But I must now defer it for some time, tho' I believe it shall not be for long. I wrote to you a little while ago a few lines from London;[1] which I did more as an excuse to avoid joining in a company there, than that I intended to say anything. I intended to have said something on some points in your last;[2] I am writing now where I have not your letter: so of that another time.—I wish you could on any pretence come and spend a fortnight in Essex.[3] You shall hunt and Shoot and study in the prettiest rotation imaginable.—At night you shall go on stargazing Parties, and with Ladies two:[4] and conclude the Day with very good wine, and Pipes if you choose them. Then will I shew you many curious Productions,[5]—The abortions of a Fantastic or of a Melancholy Conception.—But I fear such a Plan, is scarcely among Possibilities. However I must stipulate one thing, against the time we are to meet which is, that you shall advance part of the way from Oxford, and meet me, 'thy single arm to mine', to spend one day uninterrupted before I enter the Town.

I have a great humour to talk about my own affairs. You must know that I have fixed to myself a walk in Life, for my entrance into which I shall work 'Oar and Sail'[6] as the Devil did in Milton, and when I am in, if I can't make my way on, I shall deserve to be trod on. My Plan stands thus. I am at present studying very hard, and I am determined to gain all

---

[1] Letter 22.

[2] Grenville wrote to S. from Christ Church on 17 Nov., and wanted to know when he might expect to meet S. at Oxford: see Osborn MS.

[3] At Waltham Abbey where S. remained.   [4] Rae, 'too'.

[5] See ii. 251 for S.'s recollections of writing *The Rivals* when he was 'just

past twenty-one.' R. C. Rhodes describes (in 'The Text of Sheridan', *T.L.S.*, 19 Dec. 1929, p. 1082) some notes by one of S.'s friends, to the effect that S. had written *The Rivals* at Waltham Abbey. But compare S.'s remarks on its composition on p. 85.

[6] *Paradise Lost*, II. 942.

the knowledge, that I can bring within my reach, I will make myself as much a master as I can of French and Italian; and towards Spring I would go to spend the Summer in France; and according to circumstances see as much abroad as I could.[1] Previous to this I would enter myself at the Temple (which I hope to do before a Month is over). Now I find from a third Hand that Lord Towns[h]end[2] has promised to do something handsome for me immediately. If it should be of such a Nature as would rather enable me to pursue than to impede the above Plan, I shall be extremely happy. But if I am to be sent God knows where in a prenticeship to some Minister, I shall beg to be excused. Were I once enter'd for the Bar I should not care how much I was employed; nor where, during the 5 years previous to Practice, as I should dedicate it to study, and look forward to the expiration of that term as to Independence. Any employment therefore in England, would facilitate my scheme. And I have less opinion of the other, since an Instance I have seen here. There is a Gentleman lately returned from Prussia, where he was secretary to the Envoy, (or Ambassadour I forget which) for more than *twelve* years, in which he acquitted himself so well that the Envoy who dies,[3] left him a Legacy with a particular recommendation to the Ministry. Notwithstanding which He has not the least prospect of anything, and were it not for the accidental circumstances of the Legacy, would be just where He set out. And this man had very good abilities, and is master of half hundred[4] Languages![5]

[1] As far as is known, S. never travelled abroad after this date.

[2] George, 4th Viscount, and afterwards Marquis, Townshend (1724–1807), was Lord-Lieutenant of Ireland from 1767 to Oct. 1772. He then became Master-General of the Ordnance. Lefanu, pp. 324–5, makes much of his friendly feeling towards Thomas Sheridan. Two verifiable facts are worth noting: first, that Thomas Sheridan gave instruction in elocution to Townshend's sons in 1769–70 (see his letters to Townshend of 16 Jan. 1769 and 2 Jan. 1770, owned by Mr. Brinsley Ford);

second, that Richard Chamberlaine was on friendly terms with Townshend's principal secretary, Sir George Macartney: see *Gent. Mag.* xcvii (1828), pt. 2, pp. 199–200.

[3] Rae prints 'died'. Sir Andrew Mitchell (1708–71) was Envoy Extraordinary and Plenipotentiary to Prussia, 1766–71. He died in Berlin on 28 Jan. 1771. The Secretary was Alexander Burnet. See *British Diplomatic Representatives, 1689–1789* (ed. D. B. Horn, Camden 3rd Ser., xlvi, 1932), p. 108.

[4] Rae prints 'half an hundred'.

[5] Grenville replied on 29 Nov., say-

I shall make no apology to *you* for having come to the end of my Paper with talking about my self. I hope to hear from you soon. | Your's sincerely | R. B. Sheridan.

Nov. 28th. 1772.

24. To Thomas Grenville

Jack H. Samuels MS. [Ph.] *Pub.*: Rae, i. 242–3. *Address*: Thomas Grenville Esqr. | Christ-Church | Oxford

Dec. 8th: 1772.

My Dear Grenville,

I cannot forbear writing you a line or two[1] tho' it be only to endeavour to throw off some little particle of the strongest Chagrin, distress, Astonishment, Indignation and I know not what.

I have this day had an account of the basest, meanest, and most ungrateful Piece of Treachery that ever disgraced Human Nature. *Mathews* has come to Bath and, bullying *Paumier* by attempting to call him out has made him sign some infamous Falsehoods,[2] which I am told are credited, and I am ——— such Friendship! But I hope you will Suppose that I shall not betray my self.

—I wait but for the Post from Bath, when I shall seek[3] the bottom of this Treachery[4] and If I do not revenge it, may I live to *deserve* it: by way of Consolation I find added to this Account, that *Your Friend*, Sir T. Clarges,[5] is either going to be married to or to run away with Miss L. Excuse this

ing: 'The anecdote you mention is a discouraging one; but you seem to consider such a post merely as preparatory to the embassy, it is however frequently undertaken merely with a view to engage in the constant hurry of business, and acquire that clearness and expedition which in such affairs practice only can give.' (Osborn MS.)

[1] Grenville had written to S. on 29 Nov. (Osborn MS.) and had declared he looked forward to seeing him at Oxford and reading his 'abortions': 'I do not doubt they are very pretty children.'

[2] S. had fought a second duel with Mathews at Kingsdown, near Bath, on 2 July. Paumier, who was in love with Elizabeth Linley's sister Mary, had acted as S.'s second on that occasion.

[3] Manuscript 'seek myself', but 'myself' has been cancelled. [4] See p. 74.

[5] Sir Thomas Clarges, Bart. (1751–82) corresponded with Elizabeth Linley, and when Thomas Linley wrote to S. on 15 May 1773 (Harvard MS.), he promised to take the letters out of Mrs. Linley's hands and to pass them on to S. See also Rae, i. 243, 256.

vile disjointed scrawl. I have been writing Letters these three Hours, and I am bribing the post man to wait for this. Let me have a line from you of any kind (directed to me at the *Bedford-Coffee-House*, Covent-Garden, London.) immediately on receipt of this, or I shall be in the midst of this precious Business.—

I know not what I write, for upon my soul I believe I am distracted as greatly [as] I think I am injured.—Let what will happen[1]—may all good attend you. | R B Sheridan.

25. To Thomas Grenville

Osborn MS. *Pub.*: Rae, i. 244. *Address*: Thomas Grenville Esqr. | Christ-Church | Oxford

[Mid–Dec. 1772][2]

My dear Grenville

Mr. Thornbery[3] who is to carry this is now waiting for it. So I write this only to beg a line from you immediately to know what your Stay is at Oxford; As I could now very conveniently come and spend a day with you.—

My Letters from Bath[4] tho' they do not clear up the Affair yet I believe the representation I had given me was highly exaggerated and malicious. P.[5] swears He is innocent. Your's I confess made me happy in one Point[6] but of that Hereafter.— | Your's ever | R B Sheridan

Sunday.

26. To Thomas Grenville

W.T. *Pub.*: Rae, i. 244–5.

19 Dec. 1772

Dear Grenville

I expected to receive your last[7] at the Bedford.—And I

[1] In his reply (post-marked '16 DE'), Grenville remarked, 'I am exceedingly glad to find that your immediate rage has subsided, and that a treaty of peace is on foot . . .' (Osborn MS.).

[2] See n. 1 for Grenville's reply to this letter.

[3] Possibly Nathaniel Thornbury, who matriculated at Hertford College,

Oxford, in 1766 and became a barrister-at-law in 1772 (Foster).

[4] In an undated letter of this period (now among the Widener MSS.) Elizabeth Linley praises Paumier's behaviour as 'Consistent with the strictest Friendship'.

[5] Paumier.   [6] See p. 68. n. 1.

[7] See above, n. 1

have this moment had it brought to me from Waltham. The time of my writing this, as it pleads the inexpediency of my seeing you at Oxford, prevents even my writing more at present than to inform you of my disappointment.—I must sit down and write Hymns to Patience.[1] I shall direct my next to Stowe. But if you have half an Hour before you leave Oxford, you will oblige me much by informing [me] of the circumstances which you declined to treat[2] to in your last.[3]— By that time I believe I shall be [able] to write with some degree of information on that subject—at present I am far from being satisfied or even acquainted with Particulars tho' I have had many Letters from Bath. | Your's with sincerity | and Affection | R. B. Sheridan.

London.
　Saturday Night.
　　Dec. 19th. 1772.

27. To Thomas Grenville

Jack H. Samuels MS. [Ph.] *Pub.*: Rae, i. 245–8. *Address*: Thomas Grenville Esqr.

4 Jan. 1773

Dear Grenville,

　I should have written to you before, but that I should have been glad to have had it in my power to have given you some less confused account of the late affair at Bath. But I am still very uncertain; and am really so much disgusted with the whole set of them on both sides, that I believe I shall grow very indifferent about their machinations. I expect an answer, with a copy of the Papers in his hands, every day from Wade.[4] 'Till then I shall take no further Step in the matter.—I have written for the last time to Paumier,[5] in

---

[1] Frances Sheridan's 'Ode to Patience' is printed by Watkins, i. 117–19.
[2] Rae prints 'trust'.
[3] In a letter postmarked '22 DE' (Osborn MS.), Grenville suggested that S. should take no action against

Paumier until he was sure of his facts, for Mathews would certainly have made public any corroboration by Paumier if this had been given.
[4] See p. 74.
[5] Not found.

such a manner, as, if he has the smallest pretence to Honour
or Feeling, will punish him sufficiently for his present mean
sacrifice of Both.—I shall really be ashamed to mention anything of this affair to my Father: who so often prophesied to
me that this would be my return for having so strenuously
endeavour'd to screen Paumier, and for his sake to prevent
the intended Publication of the Transaction.—I have received a Letter from this Hero, full of those equivocal
excuses, and self-sufficient assertions which always betray a
consciousness of Demerit. G. Brereton[1] I am told behaved
very well in the affair; and while He was at Bath made P. do
so to[o].—But let them go—I never now reflect on that
Place, but it puts me out of sorts for writing on other matters:
Tho' I do believe I may now say, that it can scarcely furnish
me with an agreeable subject even to think on.—However
I can find relief from most Things in study, and while the
mind is seriously employ'd we grow inattentive to the peevish
interruptions of the Feelings and the Passions. It has been
an everlasting Fashion to declaim against the Pursuits of
Ambition, and the expectation of Happiness in the scenes of
publick Life. Yet, may we not with some justice attempt to
prove, that there is to be found there a surer Foundation to
build on, than in any the most captivating roads of private,
and comparatively, solitary Enjoyments.—Envy is the
attendant on Greatness.—A Prince's Smiles are not to be
depended on—The association of Men in Power is full of
Jealousy and Distrust—The voice of the People is incon-
stant.—True—But does malice never reach a private Station? are the smiles of Friendship never deceitful? Do we
never meet with ill-will from our Companions—and does the
syren voice of Love never turn to Discord, or court other
Auditors?—Yet, let me suppose a Man possess'd of every
thing that can endear a private Station. A Woman loving
him, as much as Soul could love her; A Friend who was to
him as himself; A moderate and valuable Society; and a
Fortune to furnish the Luxuries of Study and the gratifica-

[1] G. Brereton wrote to S. from Bath
on 22 Dec. 1772 (Harvard MS.) to say
that he had returned from Ireland the
day before and had found S.'s letter
('requesting a Detail of what happened
between *Bernard, Mathews* and *Paumier*') awaiting him. He refused to give
particulars, but said that he had taken
pains to make Paumier follow his advice
'as well for your sake as his own'.

tions of Benevolence.—Yet to Minds of a certain Tone, I can conceive that there is one reflection which would embitter this Cup of Joy while at our Lips; and the completion of which in a single instance would snatch it irrecoverably from our Hands. A man in such a retirement rests his happiness on Persons, not Things. Of all others, He is least happy on Principle, or from within himself.—Let his Mistress, or his Friend die, or let him but fear they will, or that they may change, and He is at on[c]e completely miserable. The Calm and secluded mode of his Living, which formed one of its chief comforts, must in that case be one of the chief causes of his extreme disquiet. His Feelings unex[er]cised by sorrow, or even by the contemplation of it, will be torn to pieces by the first Attack. While the Strings that sounded to the Harmony of his soul, being known to the touch of so few hands, will never more make but Discord, when they are cold.—

> —Ask the Fond Youth
> Why the cold Urn of Her whom long he lov'd,
> So often fills his arms!

Could our natural Stock of Benevolence be intended to be thus circumscribed? Was it meant that we should shrink from the active Principles of Virtue, and consequent[ly] of true Happiness and indolently insure them both on others' Lives? Nor can such a Life be the Sphere of true Benevolence. He who returns to Solitude (unless convinc'd that He is fit for no other station) and thinks that He does much in relieving the few objects of distress that groan within his hearing, does really but gratify himself in removing what must annoy him, on the same principle as He does Dunghills and Ruins.—True Ambition can never be disappointed—it hopes most when most oppressed and the very scene which presents it with its misfortunes, denies it time to feel, or opportunity to indulge them. Then its object is as immortal as the source of it. Our Enjoyments here will never depend upon our selves, and our own abilities, in the other They can exist but on the verge of accident, and others' Caprice. Death can not touch the object of the one, The other must live a Slave to the dread of his Dart. In short—I am to be enter'd next week in the Temple[1] (which I take to be the great Gate of Power) and I am at Present much disposed to say 'Hence! idle Joys!'[2] to every thing but Study and the pursuits of Business.—I find what led me into these Pages, was an intention to apologize to you for breaking off at the second.—However as you are to enter the same Gate,[3] I hope you will not insist on my retracting what I have said, as be[ing] ever so inconclusive, and perhaps unintelligible.— I must observe to you tho' here, that were I as you are I should endeavour to enter at on[e] of the Inns as soon as possible—as there are 5 years allow'd to keep the Terms in it can be of no disadvantage; and may save time hereafter, without preventing your pursuing anything else for the Present.

Adieu, dear Grenville, I shall expect to hear soon from you, and much too and when you return to Oxford I will fix a time for seeing you—sans fail. | your's sincerely | and with true affection | R B Sheridan

Waltham-Abbey
Jan. 4th. 1773.

28. To William Barnett[4]

Yale MS. *Pub.*: Moore, i. 93–97. *Address*: To William Barnett, Esqr.

[*1773?*]

Sir,

It has always appear'd to me so impertinent for Individuals

---

[1] He was not entered in the Record of Admissions to the Middle Temple until 6 Apr. 1773. See Rae, i. 261.

[2] Cf. Milton's line, 'Hence, vain deluding Joys' ('Il Penseroso', l. 1).

[3] Grenville was admitted to Lincoln's Inn on 19 Jan. 1774. See *The Records . . . of Lincoln's Inn, Admissions* (1896), i. 474.

[4] At Mathews's request, Barnett had drawn up an 'Exact Narrative' of what had occurred during the second duel. It is printed by Moore, i. 88–92.

Mathews asked William Brereton (the elder ?) to inquire if Paumier agreed with it. In a letter of 24 Oct. (probably to Wade), Brereton reported that Paumier thought it 'true and impartial', except in a 'few immaterial circumstances'. Both these documents are Yale MSS., and the Brereton letter is certified by Wade as 'A True Copy. Bath Jany. 6th. 1773'. This makes me suppose that the copies were obtained for S. so that he could make the above representations.

to appeal to the Public on Transactions merely private,[1] that
I own the most apparent necessity does not prevent my
entering, into such a Dispute with[out] an auk[w]ard consciousness of its Impropriety. Indeed I am not without some
apprehension that I may have no right to plead your having
led the way in my excuse; as it appears not improbable that
some Ill-wisher to you Sir, and the c[ause you][2] have been
engaged in, betray'd you first [into this][2] *exact Narrative* and
then exposed it to the public eye, under the pretence of
vindicating your Friend. However as it is the opinion of some
of my Friends, that I ought not to suffer these Papers to pass
wholly unnoticed, I shall make a few observations on them
with that moderation which becomes one who is highly conscious of the impropriety of staking his single assertion
against the apparent testimony of three. This I say would be
an impropriety, as I am supposed to write to those who are
not acquainted with the Parties. I had some time ago a copy
of these Papers from Captain Wade, who informed me that
they were lodged in his hands to be made public only if called
for by judicial Authority.[3] I wrote to you Sir, on the subject,
to have from yourself an avowal that the Account was yours;
but as I received no Answer I have reason to compliment
you with the supposition that you are not the Author of it.
[How][2]ever as the name *William Barnett* is subscribed to it,
you must accept of my apologies for making use of that as
the ostensible signature of the Writer: as Mr. Paumier likewise (The Gentleman who went out with me on that occasion
in the character of a Second) has assented to every thing
material in it, I shall suppose the whole Account likewise to
be his. And as there are some circumstances which could
come from no one but Mr. Mathews, I shall (without meaning to take from its authority) suppose it to be Mr. Mathews's
also. As it is highly indifferent to me whether the account I
am to observe on, be consider[ed] as accurately true or not,

[1] A draft with the heading, 'Being told this Paper had great weight', is also among the Yale MSS. It uses some of the phrases of the above letter, but also contains other material. For instance, S. asserts that 'Mr. M. has thrice appear'd in print'. See Moore, i. 97–98.

[2] Manuscript torn.

[3] Barnett's narrative is dated 'October, 1772'. The reference to 'judicial Authority' gives support to the statement that Thomas Sheridan wanted to institute proceedings against Mathews. See Rae, i. 206.

and as I believe it is of very little consequence to any one else, I shall make those observations just in the same manner as I conceive any indifferent Person of common sense, who should think it worth his while to peruse the matter with any degree of attention. In this light the *Truth* of the Articles which are asserted under Mr. Barnett's name is what I have no business to meddle with; but if it should appear that this *accura[te]*[1] *narrative* frequently contradicts itself [as well][1] as all probability, and that there are some [posi]tive[1] Facts against it, which do not depend upon any one's assertion, I must repeat that I shall either compliment Mr. Barnett['s][1] judgement in supposing it not his, or his *humanity* in proving the *Narrative* to partake of that confusion and uncertainty, which his well-wishers will plead to have possessed him in the *transaction*.—On this account what I shall say on the subject need be no further addressed [to] you: and indeed it is idle in my opinion to address even the Publisher of a newspaper on a Point that can concern so few and ought to have been forgotten even by Them.—This you must take as my excuse for having neglected the *Matter* so long.

The first Point in Mr. Barnett's Narrative that is of the least consequence to take notice of, is where Mr. M. is represented as having repeatedly signified his Desire to use Pistols prior to swords from a conviction that Mr. Sheridan would run in upon him and an ungentlemanlike scuffle probably be the con[sequ]¹ence. This is one of those articles which [eviden]¹tly must be given to Mr. Mathews. For [as] Mr. B.'s part is simply to relate a matter of Fact of which he was an eye witness, He is by no means to answer for Mr. Mathews's *private convictions*. As this insinuation bears an obscure allusion to a past transaction of Mr. M.'s[2] I doubt not but He will be surprised at my indifference in not taking the trouble even to explain it. However I cannot forbear to observe here, that had I, at the period which this Passage alludes to, known what was the Theory which Mr. M. held of *gentlemanly scuffle*, I might possibly have been so unhappy as [to] have put it out of his Power ever to have brought it into practice.

Mr. B. now charges me with having cut short a number

---

[1] Manuscript torn. [2] See p. 32.

of pretty preliminaries concerning which He was treating with Captain Paumier, by drawing my Sword and in a vaunting manner desiring Mr. M. to draw: Tho I acknowledge (with deference to these Gentlemen) the full right of interference which Seconds have on such occasion, yet I may remind Mr. B. that He was acquainted with my determination with regard to Pistols, before we went on the Down,[1] nor could I have expected it to have been proposed.—'Mr. M. drew; Mr. S. advanced etc.'—Here let me remind Mr. B. of a circumstance which I am convinced his Memory will at once acknowledge.[2]

29. To Thomas Grenville

Jack H. Samuels MS. [Ph.] *Pub.*: Rae, i. 249–51. *Address*: Thomas Grenville Esqr. | Christ-Church | Oxford.

24 February 1773

Dear Grenville,

I am very much ashamed of the Neglect with which the Post between Waltham and Oxford is conducted.[3] But I must confess that I was not sorry to find that you had observed it so much as to inform me of it. The Purpose of my delay was at first only to ensure my Letter's finding you at Oxford: and I really did not think so much time had elapsed: but as I had said in my last that I thought in a week to have been enter'd at the Temple,—the Point which delay'd that, likewise made me defer writing to you 'till it should be accomplished. However as I am afraid you will not admit of this as an excuse, I will procrastinate no longer though I am not certain but that my Plea still continues. My Father had at one time, I believe, absolutely changed his intentions with regard to my following the Law and my not hearing from him on the subject occasioned me the highest chagrin: however it is now once more fixed: and I hope this week to put my Name in the Books. He has likewise changed his idea of my passing the Summer in France, yet at the same time pro-

---

[1] Kingsdown, near Bath.
[2] The letter breaks off at this point.
[3] Grenville wrote to S. on 14 Feb.

(Osborn MS.) apologizing for the fact that he had not written to him since 'Decbr. or beginning of January'.

poses to me that I should retire a few hundred miles North-ward on a party with Messrs. Coke, Blackstone and Co.[1] Had He pursued this notion as expeditiously as I expected, I should not have been altogether at a loss to account for it: as I conceived that it might have originated from his Apprehension that all the Counties in the Neighbourhood of London were within the magic Circle of a certain formidable Enchantress, who was to keep her Lent there:[2] or else that He feared some revival of my Dispute with M.[3] or his party. But as he is convinced of my peaceable disposition with regard to the latter Point, and has not been alert enough to prevent the effects which might have followed the near Approach of this Charmer, I have some reason to suppose He has re-altered his mind. But it is a matter of little moment to me, as I can sincerely say that it is very indifferent to me what the Latitude of the Spot of ground is where I am to eat drink and Sleep. My sole Idea is to qualify myself so that it shall not be indifferent to the place where I hope to do something more and apropos to this, I intended to have made a violent reply to some passages in your last wherein you talk most profanely of certain *Spheres in which God has placed us*.[4] I shall one of these days learnedly confute the idea that God could ever have intended individuals to fill up any particular Stations in which the accidents of Birth or Fortune may have flung them. The Track of a Comet is as regular to the eye of God as the orbit of a Planet. *The Station* in which it has pleas'd God to place us, (or whatever the words are) is not properly interpreted. And as God very often pleases to let down great Folks from the elevated Stations which they might claim as their Birth-right, there can be no reason for us to suppose that He does not mean that others should ascend etc. etc.

[1] Writing from Dublin on 15 Mar. 1773 to C. F. Sheridan, Thomas Sheridan stated: 'Your brother is . . . preparing to set out for Yorkshire, upon a proposal of his own. He has pressed so earnestly to have his name entered in the Temple, and has given such solemn assurances of his determined application to the study of the law, that I have at last consented to it. . . .' (W.T.; Rae, i. 258.)

[2] Elizabeth Linley sang in *Judas Maccabeus* on 3 Mar. 1773, at D.L.Th. She completed her performances by singing at the Foundling Hospital on 6 Apr., and at the Lock Hospital on 7 Apr. (*The Gazetteer*, 3 Mar. and 9 Apr. 1773).   [3] Mathews.

[4] In a letter post-marked '8 MR' (Osborn MS.) Grenville said that S. had misunderstood him on this point.

My Father informs me that all Lord Townshend's fine Promises are come to nothing.—I have placed him down in one of my very dark-brown books, for there was something very cruel in the manner in which He has (unsolicited) raised my Father's expectations, and employed his Time and attention, as if he sought a pleasure in wantonly disappointing one whom He had made his sanguine applauder.

—Eliza is within an hour's ride of me,[1] and must have been for some time. Yet upon my honour, I have and do industriously avoid even knowing the particular Place that is blest with her inhabiting.—I was obliged to go to London the other day—and I protest to you, no country Girl passing alone through a church-yard at midnight, ever dreaded more the appearance of a Ghost than I did to encounter this (for once I'll say) *terrest*[r]*ial* being.—But—I can't not say anything on this subject on paper.

As I am daily in expectation of a commission to sally forth in quest of Adventures, I must again observe that it would give me the highest satisfaction to spend—if it were only a few hours with you.—If I am bound northward I shall appoint a place within some 12 or 20 miles of Oxford for a *congress*—on which I beg your sentiments. It will vex me highly to go far off for any length of time without holding a *Talk* with you, and tho' I flatter myself you will continue to correspond with me, yet have we conversed so little vivâ voce, that I shall fancy I am hearing from a friend in the shades, and think ours like *The Letters from the Dead to the Living*.[2] But at all events, never let any seeming omission of mine prevent your continuing to hold me as one who is and I hope ever will be your true and sincere friend. | Richard Brinsley Sheridan

Waltham-Abbey
   Feb. 24th: 1773.

[1] S. lived for some time at Waltham Cross, and 'was in bad health, but used to steal up to town to see and hear Miss Lindley in publick, though he was under an engagement with her family not to pursue her any more in private' (*Creevey Papers*, i. 55).

[2] Either *Letters from the Dead to the Living by Mr. Thos. Brown, Capt. Ayloff* . . . (1702), or *Friendship in Death, in twenty Letters from the Dead to the Living* (1728) by Elizabeth Rowe (1674–1737).

30. To Thomas Linley the Elder

N.L.S. MS. 582, f. 130, contains the last four lines of the text. *Pub.*: Moore, i. 115–19.

East Burnham, May 12. 1773.

Dear Sir,

I purposely deferred writing to you till I should have settled *all* matters in London, and in some degree settled ourselves at our little home.[1] Some unforeseen delays prevented my finishing with Swale[2] till Thursday last, when every thing was concluded. I likewise settled with him for his own account, as he brought it to me, and, for a *friendly* bill, it is pretty decent.—Yours of the 3d instant did not reach me till yesterday, by reason of its missing us at Morden.[3] As to the principal point it treats of, I had given my answer some days ago to Mr. Isaac[4] of Worcester. He had inclosed a letter to Storace[5] for my wife, in which he dwells much on the nature of the agreement you had made for her eight months ago, and adds, that 'as this is no new application, but a request that you (Mrs. S.) will fulfil a positive engagement, the breach of which would prove of fatal consequence to our Meeting, I hope Mr. Sheridan will think his honour in some degree concerned in fulfilling it.'—Mr. Storace, in order to enforce Mr. Isaac's argument, showed me his letter on the same subject to him, which begins with saying, 'We must

---

[1] S. and Elizabeth Linley were married at Marylebone Church on 13 Apr. 1773. For a full description of their first home, see Letter 31.

[2] John Swale was the solicitor who had 'many consultations with Mr. Linley and Mr. Sheridan on the treaty of marriage' between S. and Elizabeth Linley. His bill for arranging the settlement came to £25. 11. 6; and to it was added a further £50 lent to S. The receipted bill (dated 6 May 1773) is among the Harvard MSS. Swale was a witness at the marriage ceremony, and a trustee for the settlement: see Sichel, i. 424, 426.

[3] After their marriage, S. and his wife were left 'at a gentleman's house in Mitcham, to consummate their nuptials' (*Bath Journal*, 19 Apr. 1773).

[4] Conductor of the Three Choirs' Festival at Worcester in Sept. 1773: see the *Worcester Journal*, 19 Aug. 1773.

[5] Storace (or Sorace), the bass-player, who at one time kept the Marylebone Gardens. He was father of the composer, Stephen Storace, and the singer, Anna Storace. He was on friendly terms with Linley, and tickets for the Linley concerts could be obtained 'from Mr. Linley at Mr. Storace's, in High Street, Marylebone' (*Pub. Adv.*, 12 Apr. 1773). Perhaps the Linleys boarded with him. Cf. Kelly, i. 95; Moore, i. 121.

have Mrs. Sheridan, somehow or other, if possible!'—the plain English of which is that, if her husband is not willing to let her perform, we will persuade him that he acts *dishonourably* in preventing her from fulfilling a *positive engagement*. This I conceive to be the very worst mode of application that could have been taken; as there really is not common sense in the idea that my *honour* can be concerned in my wife's fulfilling an engagement, which it is impossible she should ever have made.—Nor (as I wrote to Mr. Isaac) can you, who gave the promise, whatever it was, be in the least charged with the breach of it, as your daughter's marriage was an event which must always have been looked to by them as quite as natural a period to your right over her as her death. And, in my opinion, it would have been just as reasonable to have applied to you to fulfil your engagement in the latter case as in the former. As to the *imprudence* of declining this engagement, I do not think, even were we to suppose that my wife should ever on any occasion appear again in public,[1] there would be the least at present. For instance, I have had a gentleman with me from Oxford (where they do not claim the least *right* as from an engagement), who has endeavoured to place the idea of my complimenting the University with Betsey's performance in the strongest light of advantage to me. This he said, on my declining to let her perform on any agreement. He likewise informed me, that he had just left Lord North (the Chancellor),[2] who, he assured me, would look upon it as the highest compliment, and had expressed himself so to him. Now, should it be a point of inclination or convenience to me to break my resolution with regard to Betsey's performing, there surely would be more sense in obliging Lord North (and probably from *his own* application) and the University, than Lord Coventry[3]

[1] Her performances at Worcester, 8–10 Sept. 1773, were her last in public: see *Worcester Journal*, 9 Sept. 1773, S. refused the offer of £2,000 a year for seven years for her services, and even refused to allow her to sing at a royal concert: see *New M. Mag.* vi. 245.

[2] In the event, she sang at the concert after the Convocation. The effect of her performance then (9 July 1773) is well described by James Beattie in his *London Diary, 1773* (ed. R. S. Walker, Aberdeen, 1946), p. 69.

[3] George, 6th Earl of Coventry (1722–1809). His letter inviting the Sheridans to stay with him at Croome, whilst at the Three Choirs meeting, is Add. MS. 35118, f. 13. He was one of the Stewards of the festival: see *Worcester Journal*, 19 Aug. 1773.

and Mr. Isaac. For, were she to sing at Worcester, there would not be the least compliment in her performing at Oxford. Indeed, they would have a right to *claim it*—particularly, as that is the mode of application they have chosen from Worcester. I have mentioned the Oxford matter merely as an argument, that I can have no kind of inducement to accept of the proposal from Worcester. And, as I have written fully on the subject to Mr. Isaac, I think there will be no occasion for you[1] to give any further reasons to Lord Coventry—only that I am sorry I cannot accept of his proposal, civilities, etc. etc., and refer him for my motives to Mr. Isaac, as what I have said to you on the subject I mean for you only, and, if more remains to be argued on the subject in general, we must defer it till we meet, which you have given us reason to hope will not be long first.

As this is a letter of business chiefly, I shall say little of our situation and arrangement of affairs, but that I think we are as happy as those who wish us best could desire. There is but one thing that has the least weight upon me, though it is one I was prepared for. But time, while it strengthens the other blessings we possess, will, I hope, add that to the number. You will know that I speak with regard to my father.[2] Betsey informs me you have written to him again—have you heard from him?[3] * * *[4]

I should hope to hear from you very soon, and I assure you, you shall now find me a very exact correspondent; though I hope you will not give me leave to confirm my character in that respect before we meet.

As there is with this a Letter for Polly[5] and you, I shall

[1] Linley replied on 15 May 1773 (Harvard MS.) saying that if Mrs. S. sang at Oxford she must also sing at Worcester. He urged S. to think carefully about the problem, because it would be unwise to make enemies by refusing these two requests; and added that S. might think it prudent to wait on Lord Coventry and Lord North.

[2] Thomas Sheridan was so irritated by S.'s marriage to Elizabeth Linley that he declined to meet him, and wrote to Charles Francis Sheridan on 20 Apr.

1773: '. . . I consider myself now as having no Son but *you*, and therefore my anxiety about you is the greater' (W.T.).

[3] Linley reported in his letter of 15 May that he had written to Thomas Sheridan in the way S. had suggested, but that there was 'small Prospect of a Reconciliation'. Linley added that Thomas Sheridan could not 'be easily induced to forgive . . . her [Mrs. S.]'.

[4] Passage omitted by Moore.

[5] Mary Linley, Mrs. S.'s favourite sister.

only charge you with mine and Betsy's best love to her Mother, and Tom, etc. etc. and believe me | your sincere Friend, and affectionate Son | R B Sheridan

31. To Thomas Grenville

W.T. *Pub.*: Rae, i. 266–8.

East Burnham, Bucks.
May 14th.
—73

My dear Tom,

I know not whether you will reckon me tardy in writing to you, or accuse yourself of some little Delay in not having written before this to me.[1] Were I to plead the seducing Avocations of what Folks call The Honey-Moon, perhaps you would seize the same Plea, and say that you imagined that even the Voice of Friendship would sound ungrateful were it to intrude upon that ambrosial Month of Love. But as I am now four Days gone in a simple twel[f]th part of a Year, I give up all excuse myself, and demand the same of you. You must not conclude from this that this Moon sheds less Honey on me, than the last; yet I would never wish my Love to have his Wings so clogg'd with Sweets that[2] I could borrow one quill from them for the service of Friendship.— Were I to continue this Style much longer I am afraid you would think that the Moon had another more serious effect upon Married Men.—To write then like a Married Man, I should inform you first that I have for some time been fixed in a grand little Mansion situate at a Place called *East-Burnham*, about 2 mile and ½ from Salt-Hill; which as an Etonian you must be acquainted with. Had I hunted five years I don't believe I could have hit in a Place more to my mind, or more adapted to my present situation: were I in a descriptive vein, I would draw you some of the prettiest Scenes imaginable. I likewise waive the opportunity of displaying the rational and delightful scheme on which our

---

[1] Grenville's letter of congratulation (Osborn MS.) mentions that he does not know where to find S. but desires to see him in Bolton Street. 'Joy Joy to you.' It is not dated.

[2] Rae prints 'but that'.

Hours proceed.—On the whole I will assure you, as I believe
it will give you more pleasure, that I feel myself absolutely
and perfectly happy.—As for the little Clouds which the
peering eye of Prudence would descry to be gathering against
the Progress of the Lune, I have a consoling Cherub that
whispers me, that before They threaten an adverse Shower,
a slight gale or two of Fortune will disperse them.—But
when a Man's married 'tis time he should leave of[f] speaking in Metaphor. If I thought it would be entertaining to
you I would send you an account of the arrangement of my
Household which I assure [you] is conducted quite in the
manner of plain Mortals, with all due attention to the Bread-
and-Cheese—Feelings—I have laid aside my Design of
turning Cupid into a Turnspit's Wheel, and my Meat
undergoes the indignity of a Cook's handling. I have even
been so far Diffident of my Wife's musical Abilities as to
have Carrots and Cab[b]ages put into the Garden-Ground;
and finding that whatever effect her Voice might have upon
the Sheep on the Common, The Mutton still obstinately
continued stationary at the Butchers, I have design'd to
become indebted to the Brute's Abilities.[1]

My Paper puts me in mind to conclude for the present.—
I must mind[2] tho' that I[3] considerably advanced on the road
to Oxford, and If we don't meet soon I shall say with
Falstaf[f] 'you're not the Man I took thee for.'—[4]

P.S. I beg a letter sans delay

[1] The Sheridans began married life
on money given Mrs. S. by Walter Long,
to whom she had been engaged. For the
circumstances and discussion of them,
see C. Price, 'Hymen and Hirco: A
Vision', *T.L.S.*, 11 July 1958, p. 396.
By the terms of the marriage settlement
(dated 10 Apr. 1773), £1,050 3 per cent.
Consols 'was transferred to Swale and
Linley In Trust, to pay the Dividends
to Mrs. Sheridan for her Life'. For this,
and alternative provisions, see Add.
MS. 44919, ff. 44–45. They lived, S.
told Creevey, 'most happily, a gig and
horse being their principal luxury, with
a man to look after both the master and
his horse' (*Creevey Papers*, i. 55). On
3 Dec. 1773 S. signed an agreement for
the sale and repurchase for £150 of a
pair of diamond ear-rings and a neck-
lace: see S. C., 27 Feb. 1882, lot 76.
[2] Rae reads 'hint'.
[3] Rae reads 'I am now considerably'.
[4] The sense is to be found in Falstaff's
'There's neither honesty, manhood, nor
good fellowship in thee . . . if thou
dar'st not stand for ten shillings' (*1
Henry IV*, i. ii. 132–6), but the nearest
wording is 'They are not the men you
took them for' (*Much Ado About Nothing*, iii. iii. 44). See *Complete Works
of Shakespeare* (ed. P. Alexander, 1951),
pp. 151, 483.

32. To Mr. Dinwoody

Widener MS. *Address*: – Dinwoody, Esqr. | at Mr. Pigot's | No. 23 | Holborn.

24 Feb. 1774

Mr. Sheridan presents his Compliments to Mr. Dinwoody[1]—begs leave to trouble him for the character of George *Renauld*, lately in his Service—

Febry. 24 —74
Orchard-Street—No. 28[2]
Portman-Square.—

33. To Thomas Linley the Elder

Pub.: Moore, i. 121–4.

Nov. 17th, 1774.

Dear Sir,

If I were to attempt to make as many apologies as my long omission in writing to you requires, I should have no room for any other subject. One excuse only I shall bring forward, which is, that I have been exceedingly employed, and I believe *very profitably*. However, before I explain how, I must ease my mind on a subject, that much more nearly concerns me than any point of business or profit. I must premise to you that Betsey is now very well, before I tell you abruptly that she has encountered another disappointment and consequent indisposition.[3]* * *[4] However she is not getting entirely over it, and she shall never take any journey of the kind again. I inform you of this now, that you may not be alarmed by any accounts from some other quarter, which

---

[1] Possibly William Dinwoody who held an appointment in the Excise Office until 1783. See *Gent. Mag.* lxxv (1805), 491, 872.

[2] The *Morn. Post*, 4 Feb. 1774, mentioned that S. had 'taken a house in Orchard Street, where he purposes, if his wife recovers, to give concerts twice a week to the nobility'.

[3] Mrs. S. had several miscarriages. In a letter of 26 June 1774 (Widener MS.), Linley warned S. about her 'seminal weakness' and wrote 'you must absolutely keep from her, for every time you touch her, you drive a Nail in her Coffin'.

[4] Passage omitted by Moore.

might lead you to fear she was going to have such an illness as last year,[1] of which I assure you, upon my honour, there is not the least apprehension. If I did not write now, Betsey would write herself, and in a day she will make you quite easy on this head.

I have been very seriously at work on a book,[2] which I am just now sending to the press, and which I think will do me some credit, if it leads to nothing else. However, the profitable affair is of another nature. There will be a *Comedy*[3] of mine in rehearsal at Covent-Garden within a few days. I did not set to work on it till within a few days of my setting out for *Crome*,[4] so you may think I have not, for these last six weeks, been very idle. I have done it at Mr. Harris's (the manager's)[5] own request; it is now complete in his hands, and preparing for the stage. He, and some of his friends also who have heard it, assure me in the most flattering terms that there is not a doubt of its success. It will be very well played, and Harris tells me that the least shilling I shall get (if it succeeds) will be six hundred pounds.[6] I shall make no secret of it towards the time of representation, that it may not lose any support my friends can give it. I had not written a line of it two months ago, except a scene or two, which I believe you have seen in an odd act of a little farce.[7]

Mr. Stanley[8] was with me a day or two ago on the subject of the oratorios. I find Mr. Smith[9] has declined, and is re-tiring to Bath. Mr. Stanley informed me that on his applying to the King for the continuance of his favour, he was de-

[1] In a letter of 15 Nov. 1773 (Bath Municipal Library MS.), Linley wrote, 'We are all in great anxiety to hear from you in regard to Betsy's health.'

[2] Not identified with any certainty. Rhodes (in *Plays and Poems of . . . S.* (Oxford, 1928), iii. 170) suggests that it is *A Familiar Epistle*, but this was reviewed in the April issue of the *Critical Review*, xxxvii (1774), 314.

[3] *The Rivals*.

[4] Croome, Worcestershire: the seat of the Earl of Coventry.

[5] Thomas Harris, a proprietor of C.G.Th. from 1767.

[6] See R. C. Rhodes, 'Some Aspects of Sheridan Bibliography,' *The Library*, 4th Ser., ix (1929), 244–5.

[7] Possibly S.'s revision of Frances Sheridan's *A Trip to Bath*, in *A Journey to Bath*. See Rhodes, pp. 55–57.

[8] John Stanley (1713–86), musician, managed the Lent oratorios at Covent Garden, with Smith, from 1760. See *Europ. Mag.* x (1786), 80.

[9] John Christopher Smith (1712–95), musician. In an unpublished letter (Bath Municipal Library MS.) Linley wrote to S. on 15 Nov. 1773, to say, 'I am not satisfied with Smith, who appears to me to be a cunning man.'

sired by His Majesty to make me an offer of Mr. Smith's situation and partnership in them, and that he should continue his protection, etc.—I declined the matter very civilly and very peremptorily. I should imagine that Mr. Stanley would apply to you;—I started the subject to him, and said you had twenty Mrs. Sheridans more. However, he said very little:—if he does, and you wish to make an alteration in your system at once, I should think you may stand in Smith's place. I would not listen to him on any other terms, and I should think the King might be made to signify his pleasure for such an arrangement. On this you will reflect, and if any way strikes you that I can move in it, I need not add how happy I shall be in its success.
* * *[1]

I hope you will let me have the pleasure to hear from you soon, as I shall think any delay unfair,—unless you can plead[2] that you are writing an opera, and a folio on music[2] beside. Accept Betsey's love and duty. | Your sincere and affectionate | R. B. Sheridan.

34. To Thomas Linley the Elder

Pub.: Moore, i. 157–9.

Oct. 1775[3]

Dear Sir,
    We received your songs to-day, with which we are exceedingly pleased. I shall profit by your proposed alterations;[4] but I'd have you to know that we are much too chaste in London to admit such strains as your Bath spring inspires. We dare not propose a peep beyond the ancle on any account; for the critics in the pit at a new play are much greater prudes[5] than the ladies in the boxes. Betsey intended to have troubled you with some music for correction and I with some

---

[1] Passage omitted by Moore.
[2] His 'Letters upon Music' appeared in a morning paper and were afterwards reprinted in the *Europ. Mag.* xxiii (1793), 262–4, 332–4, 409–12.
[3] Moore's date from the manuscript.
[4] On 22 Sept. 1775, Linley wrote from Bath: '. . . I have engaged to assist my son-in-law Sheridan in composing an opera [*The Duenna*], which he is to bring out at Covent-Garden this winter' (*Garrick Corr.* ii. 100).
[5] A lesson S. had learnt at the first performance of *The Rivals*. See *The Rivals* (ed. R. L. Purdy, Oxford, 1935), pp. xxviii–xxxi.

stanzas,[1] but an interview with Harris to-day has put me from the thoughts of it, and bent me upon a much more important petition. You may easily suppose it is nothing else than what I said I would not ask in my last. But, in short, unless you can give us three days in town, I fear our opera will stand a chance to be ruined. Harris is extravagantly sanguine of its success as to plot and dialogue, which is to be rehearsed next Wednesday at the theatre. They will exert themselves to the utmost in the scenery, etc., but I never saw any one so disconcerted as he was at the idea of there being no one to put them in the right way as to music. They have no one there whom he has any opinion of—as to Fisher[2] (one of the managers) he don't choose he should meddle with it. He entreated me in the most pressing terms to write instantly to you, and wanted, if he thought it could be any weight, to write himself. Is it impossible to contrive this? couldn't you leave Tom[3] to superintend the concert[4] for a few days? If you can manage it, you will really do me the greatest service in the world. As to the state of the music, I want but three more airs, but there are some glees and quintets in the last act, that will be inevitably ruined, if we have no one to set the performers at least in the right way. Harris has set his heart so much on my succeeding in this application, that he still flatters himself we may have a rehearsal of the music in Orchard Street[5] to-morrow se'n-night. Every hour's delay is a material injury both to the opera and the theatre, so that if you can come and relieve us from this perplexity, the return of the post must only forerun your arrival; or (what will make us much happier) might it not bring *you*? I shall say nothing at present about the lady 'with the soft look and manner,'[6] because I am full of more than hopes of seeing you. For the same reason I shall delay to speak about G———;[7] only this much I will say, that I am

[1] Not necessarily for *The Duenna*. William Linley said that S. wrote twelve 'beautiful ballads' for Linley at this time (*Notes and Queries*, 11th Ser., x (1914), 62).

[2] John Abraham Fisher (1744–1806), violinist and leader of C.G.Th. band.

[3] Thomas Linley the younger (1756–78), violinist and composer, was Lin-

ley's second son, a gifted musician, and a friend of Mozart.

[4] At Bath New Assembly Rooms.

[5] S.'s home.   [6] S.'s wife?

[7] David Garrick. He had frequently talked of retiring and selling his interest in D.L.Th. This is S.'s first reference to the idea of buying a share in the management.

more than ever positive I could make good my part of the matter; but that I still remain an infidel as to G.'s retiring, or parting with his share, though I confess he *seems* to come closer to the point in naming his price. | Your ever sincere and affectionate | R. B. Sheridan.[1]

35. To Thomas Linley the Elder

Pub.: Moore, i. 160–2.

[*Oct. ?1775*]

Dear Sir,

Mr. Harris wishes so much for us to get you to town, that I could not at first convince him that your proposal of not coming till the music was in rehearsal, was certainly the best, as you could stay but so short a time. The truth is, that what you mention of my getting a *master* to teach the performers is the very point where the matter sticks, there being no such person as a master among them. Harris is sensible there ought to be such a person; however, at present, every body sings there according to their own ideas, or what chance instruction they can come at. We are, however, to follow your plan in the matter; but can at no rate relinquish the hopes of seeing you in eight or ten days from the date of this; when the music (by the specimen of expedition you have given me) will be advanced as far as you mention. The parts are all writ out and doubled, etc. as we go on, as I have assistance from the theatre with me.

My intention was to have closed the first act with a song, but I find it is not thought so well. Hence I trust you with one of the inclosed papers; and, at the same time, you must excuse my impertinence in adding an idea of the cast I would wish the music to have; as I think I have heard you say you never heard Leoni,[2] and I cannot briefly explain to you the character and situation of the persons on the stage with him.[3]

[1] Mrs. S. added the note: 'Dearest father, I shall have no spirits or hopes of the opera, unless we see you. Eliza Ann Sheridan.'

[2] Michael Leoni, or Myer Lyon (d. 1797), tenor singer, had made his first appearance at C.G.Th. in 1775 as Arbaces in *Artaxerxes*. He was Don Carlos in *The Duenna*.

[3] On 28 Sept. Linley had written to Garrick, '... No musician can set a song properly unless he understands the cha-

The first (a dialogue between Quick and Mrs. Mattocks),[1] I would wish to be a pert, sprightly air; for, though some of the words mayn't seem suited to it, I should mention that they are neither of them in earnest in what they say. Leoni takes it up seriously, and I want him to show himself advantageously in the six lines, beginning 'Gentle maid.'[2] I should tell you, that he sings nothing well but in a plaintive or pastoral style; and his voice is such as appears to me always to be hurt by much accompaniment. I have observed, too, that he never gets so much applause as when he makes a cadence.[3] Therefore my idea is, that he should make a flourish at 'Shall I grieve thee?' and return to 'Gentle maid,' and so sing that part of the tune again. After that, the two last lines,[4] sung by the three, with the persons only varied, may get them off with as much spirit as possible. The second act ends with a *slow* glee,[5] therefore I should think the two last lines in question had better be brisk, especially as Quick and Mrs. Mattocks are concerned in it.

The other is a song of Wilson's in the third act.[6] I have written it to your tune, which you put some words to, beginning, 'Prithee, prithee pretty man!' I think it will do vastly well for the words: Don Jerome sings them when he is in particular spirits; therefore the tune is not too light, though it might seem so by the last stanza—but he does not mean to be grave there, and I like particularly the returning to 'O the days when I was young!' We have mislaid the notes, but Tom remembers it. If you don't like it for words, will you give us one? but it must go back to 'O the days,' and

racter and knows the performer who is to exhibit it' (*Garrick Corr.* ii. 101). See also Rhodes, pp. 58–59.

[1] Isaac Mendoza and Donna Louisa. This is the duet for baritone and soprano at the end of Act I. Quick usually played 'testy old gullible' men, and Mrs. Mattocks, 'widows of distinction': see Boaden, *Memoirs of . . . John Philip Kemble* (1825), i. 73, 84.

[2] 'Gentle maid, ah! why suspect me?' Don Carlos's air at the end of Act I.

[3] Cadenza.

[4] The trio at the end of Act I, on the two lines:

Never mayst thou happy be,
If in aught thou'rt false to me.

[5] 'Soft pity never leaves the gentle breast', sung by Don Carlos, Antonio, and Louisa.

[6] Wilson 'was respectable in the characters of old men; but his continual embarrassments prevented him from ever retaining a situation' (*Thespian Dictionary*, 1805). He played Don Jerome. The song alluded to is his only solo in Act III: 'Oh, the days when I was young' (Sc. 1).

be *funny*. I have not done troubling you yet, but must wait till Monday.

36. To Thomas Linley the Elder

Pub.: Moore, i. 162–6.

[*23–27 Oct. ?1775*]

Dear Sir,

Sunday evening next[1] is fixed for our first musical rehearsal, and I was in great hopes we might have completed the score. The songs you have sent up of 'Banna's Banks', and 'Deil take the Wars',[2] I had made words for before they arrived, which answer excessively well; and this was my reason for wishing for the next in the same manner, as it saves so much time. They are to sing 'Wind, gentle evergreen' just as you sing it (only with other words), and I wanted only such support from the instruments, or such joining in, as you should think would help to set off and assist the effort. I inclose the words I had made for 'Wind, gentle evergreen,' which will be sung, as a catch,[3] by Mrs. Mattocks, Dubellamy,[4] and Leoni. I don't mind the words not fitting the notes so well as the original ones. 'How merrily we live,' and 'Let's drink and let's sing,'[5] are to be sung by a company of *friars* over their wine. The words will be parodied, and the chief effect I expect from them must arise from their being *known*; for the joke will be much less for these jolly fathers to sing anything new, than to give what the audience are used to annex the idea of jollity to. For the other things Betsy mentioned, I only wish to have them with such accompaniment as you would put to their *present* words, and I shall have got words to my liking for them by the time they reach me.

My immediate wish at present is to give the performers their parts in the music (which they expect on Sunday night),

[1] 29 Oct. ?

[2] See Rhodes, pp. 61–62, for S.'s use of these well-known airs.

[3] The trio ('Soft pity . . .') at the conclusion of Act II.

[4] 'A favourite performer in the vocal line' (*Thespian Dictionary*, 1805). He

was a tenor and played Antonio in *The Duenna*.

[5] Presumably for *The Duenna*, III. v. Moore, i. 163, notes: 'For these was afterwards substituted Mr. Linley's lively glee, "This bottle's the sun of our table".'

and for any assistance the orchestra can give to help the effect of the glees, etc., that may be judged of and added at a rehearsal, or, as you say, on enquiring how they have been done; though I don't think it follows that what Dr. Arne's[1] method is must be the best. If it were possible for Saturday and Sunday's post to bring us what we asked for in our last letters, and what I now enclose, we should still go through it on Sunday, and the performers should have their parts complete by Monday night. We have had our rehearsal of the speaking part, and are to have another on Saturday. I want Dr. Harrington's[2] catch, but, as the sense must be the same, I am at a loss how to put other words. Can't the under part ('A smoky house,' etc.) be sung by one person and the other two change? The situation is—Quick and Dubellamy, two lovers, carrying away Father Paul (Reinold) in great raptures, to marry them:—the Friar has before warned them of the ills of a married life, and they break out into this.[3] The catch is particularly calculated for a stage effect; but I don't like to take another person's words, and I don't see how I can put others, keeping the same idea ('of seven squalling brats,' etc.) in which the whole affair lies. However, I shall be glad of the notes, with Reinold's[4] part, if it is possible, as I mentioned.

I have literally and really not had time to write the words of any thing more first[5] and then send them to you, and this obliges me to use this apparently awkward way. * * *[6]

My father was astonishingly well received on Saturday night in Cato:[7] I think it will not be many days before we are reconciled.

The inclosed are the words for 'Wind, gentle evergreen;' a passionate song for Mattocks,[8] and another for Miss

---

[1] Thomas Arne (1710–78) was appointed composer to D.L.Th. in 1744, and went to C.G.Th. in 1760.

[2] Henry Harington (1727–1816), physician and composer. He lived at 4 Northumberland Buildings, Bath.

[3] Moore, i. 164, notes that this idea was relinquished.

[4] Frederich Reinhold, on the musical staff of C.G.Th., 'was a respectable performer in the vocal line' (*Thespian*

Dictionary, 1805). The part of Father Paul seems to have been played not by him, but by Robert Mahon.

[5] A slip either by S. or by Moore?

[6] Passage omitted by Moore.

[7] Thomas Sheridan made his first appearance for sixteen years at C.G.Th. on 21 Oct.: see J. Genest, *Some Account of the English Stage* (Bath, 1832), v. 513.

[8] Moore, i. 165, says this song ('Sharp is the woe') is seldom found in

Brown,[1] which solicit to be clothed with melody by you, and are all I want. Mattocks's I could wish to be a broken, passionate affair, and the first two lines may be recitative, or what you please, uncommon. Miss Brown sings hers in a joyful mood: we want her to show in it as much execution as she is capable of, which is pretty well; and, for variety, we want Mr. Simpson's hautboy to cut a figure, with replying passages, etc., in the way of Fisher's '*M'ami, il bel idol mio*,'[2] to abet which I have lugged in 'Echo', who is always allowed to play her part. I have not a moment more. Yours ever sincerely.

37. To Thomas Linley the Elder

Pub.: Moore, i. 166.

Nov 2. 1775

Our music is now all finished and rehearsing, but we are greatly impatient to see *you*. We hold your coming to be *necessary* beyond conception. You say you are at our service after Tuesday next; then 'I conjure you by that you do possess,'[3] in which I include all the powers that preside over harmony, to come next Thursday night (this day se'nnight) and we will fix a rehearsal for Friday morning. From what I see of their rehearsing at present, I am become still more anxious to see you.

We have received all your songs, and are vastly pleased with them. You misunderstood me as to the hautboy song;

editions of *The Duenna*, and quotes its four lines. Mattocks, a tenor, played Don Ferdinand.

[1] Soprano. She played Donna Clara, and was later well known under her married name—Mrs. Cargill. Moore suggests that the song is 'Adieu, thou dreary pile' (*The Duenna*, III. iv).

[2] Used for Donna Clara's farewell to the convent (III. iv):

Adieu, thou dreary pile, where never dies
The sullen echo of repentant sighs!

'Fisher' is probably John Christian Fischer, oboeist, who married Thomas Gainsborough's daughter, Mary. Dr. Roger Fiske informs me that Fischer wrote no operas and that S. means that Fischer played the very difficult oboe obbligato in this song. See, on this point and for the detailed sources of the musical score, R. Fiske, 'A Score for *The Duenna*', *Music and Letters*, xlii (1961), 132–41.

[3] *Macbeth*, IV. i. 50: 'I conjure you, by what you do profess.'

I had not the least intention to fix on 'Bel idol mio.' However, I think it is particularly well adapted, and, I doubt not, will have a great effect. * * *[1]

38. To Thomas Linley the Elder

Pub.: Moore, i. 181–4.

Sunday, Dec. 31. 1775

Dear Sir,

I was always one of the slowest letter-writers in the world, though I have had more excuses than usual for my delay in this instance. The principal matter of business, on which I was to have written to you, related to our embryo negotiation with Garrick, of which I will now give you an account.

Since you left town, Mrs. Ewart has been so ill, as to continue near three weeks at the point of death. This, of course, has prevented Mr. E.[2] from seeing any body on business, or from accompanying me to Garrick's. However, about ten days ago, I talked the matter over with him by myself, and the result was, appointing Thursday evening last to meet him, and to bring Ewart, which I did accordingly. On the whole of our conversation that evening, I began (for the first time) to think him *really serious* in the business. He still, however, kept the reserve of giving the refusal to Colman,[3] though at the same time he did not hesitate to assert his confidence that Colman would decline it. I was determined to push him on this point, (as it was really farcical for us to treat with him under such an evasion,) and

---

[1] The rest of the letter is omitted by Moore, and has not been found.

[2] Either Simon Ewart or his father, John Ewart, brandy merchant. 'S. G. Ewart' is catalogued as one of the signatories of the agreement (dated 17 Jan. 1776) for the purchase of Garrick's share in D.L.Th.: see P. and S.C., 16 Mar. 1852, lot 801; and is the author of an undated note (Harvard MS.), promising to call on S. at East Burnham in the next week. See also Moore, i. 101.

[3] On 29 Dec. Garrick wrote to George Colman the elder (1732–94) offering him his share in D.L.Th.: '. . . I saw a gentleman yesterday of great property, and who has no objection to the price, viz.: £35,000 for my part. I must desire you to speak out.' Colman replied next day, saying that he was only interested in the whole, and not merely in Garrick's share: see *Garrick Corr.* ii. 118, and E. R. Page, *George Colman the Elder* (New York, 1935), p. 235.

at last he promised to put the question to Colman, and to give me a decisive answer by the ensuing Sunday (to-day).— Accordingly, within this hour, I have received a note from him, which (as I meant to show it my father) I here transcribe for you.

'*Mr. Garrick presents his compliments to Mr. Sheridan, and as he is obliged to go into the country for three days, he should be glad to see him upon his return to town, either on Wednesday about 6 or 7 o'clock, or whenever he pleases. The party has no objection to the whole, but chooses no partner but Mr. G.—Not a word of this yet. Mr. G. sent a messenger on purpose.*[1] *He would call upon Mr. S. but he is confined at home. Your name is upon our list.*'

This *decisive answer* may be taken two ways. However, as Mr. G. informed Mr. Ewart and me, that he had no authority or pretensions to treat for *the whole*,[2] it appears to me that Mr. Garrick's meaning in this note is, that Mr. Colman *declines* the purchase of *Mr. Garrick's share*,[3] which is the point in debate, and the only part at present to be sold. I shall, therefore, wait on G. at the time mentioned, and if I understand him right, we shall certainly without delay appoint two men of business and the law to meet on the matter, and come to a conclusion without further delay.

According to his demand, the whole is valued at £70,000. He appears very shy of letting his books be looked into, as the test of the profits on this sum, but says it must be, in its nature, a purchase on speculation. However, he has promised me a rough estimate, of *his own*, of the entire receipts for the last seven years. But, after all, it must certainly be *a purchase on speculation*, without *money's worth* being *made out*. One point he solemnly avers, which is, that he will never part with it under the price above-mentioned.

This is all I can say on the subject till Wednesday, though I can't help adding, that I think we might *safely* give five thousand pounds more on this purchase than richer people. The whole valued at £70,000, the annual interest is £3,500;

---

[1] Moore adds 'i.e. to Colman'.
[2] Garrick owned one moiety, Willoughby Lacy the other. According to *The Gazetteer*, 14 Oct. 1776, Garrick gave Lacy first option in buying his share, but Lacy declined it and refused to sell his own. Cf. p. 96.
[3] A correct deduction by S.

while this is *cleared*, the proprietors are *safe*,—but I think it must be *infernal* management indeed that does not double it.

I suppose Mr. Stanley has written to you relative to your oratorio orchestra.[1] The demand, I reckon, will be diminished one third, and the appearance remain very handsome, which, if the other affair takes place, you will find your account in; and, if you discontinue your partnership with Stanley at Drury Lane, the orchestra may revert to whichever wants it, on the other's paying his proportion for the use of it this year. This is Mr. Garrick's idea, and, as he says, might in that case be settled by arbitration.

You have heard of our losing Miss Brown;[2] however, we have missed her so little in The Duenna, that the managers have not tried to regain her, which I believe they might have done. I have had some books of the music these many days to send you down. I wanted to put Tom's name in the new music, and begged Mrs. L. to ask you, and let me have a line on her arrival, for which purpose I kept back the index of the songs. If you or he have no objection, pray, let me know.—I'll send the music to-morrow.

I am finishing a two act comedy for Covent-Garden, which will be in rehearsal in a week.[3] We have given The Duenna a respite this Christmas,[4] but nothing else at present brings money. We have every place in the house taken for the three next nights, and shall, at least, play it fifty nights, with only the Friday's intermission.[5]

My best love and the compliments of the season to all your fire-side.

Your grandson is a very magnificent fellow.[6] | Yours ever sincerely, | R. B. Sheridan.

[1] The Lent oratorios at D.L.Th.

[2] Her attempted elopement on 5 Dec. failed, but she succeeded in getting away with her lover on 14 Dec. Her part, Donna Clara, was taken by her understudy, Miss Dayes (*Morn. Post*, 6 and 15 Dec.; *Morn. Chron.*, 15 Dec. 1775; *Gazetteer*, 16 Dec. 1775).

[3] Not identified.

[4] Its twenty-third performance was given on 23 Dec., but for the week after Christmas the theatre reverted to stock tragedies and comedies.

[5] *Morn. Chron.*, 25 Nov. 1775: 'It can never be performed on a Friday, on account of Leoni's engagement with the Synagogue.'

[6] Tom S. was born on 17 Nov. 1775. See Sichel, i. 504.

39. To Thomas Linley the Elder

Pub.: Moore, i. 185–8.

January 4. 1776.

Dear Sir,

I left Garrick last night too late to write to you. He has offered Colman the refusal, and showed me his answer; which was (as in the note) that he was willing to purchase the whole, but would have no partner but Garrick. On this, Mr. Garrick appointed a meeting with his partner, young Leasy,[1] and, in presence of their solicitor,[2] treasurer,[3] etc., declared to him that he was absolutely on the point of settling, and, if *he* was willing, he might have the same price for his share; but that if he (Leasy) would not sell, Mr. Garrick would, instantly, to another party. The result was, Leasy's declaring his intention of not parting with his share. Of this Garrick again informed Colman, who immediately gave up the whole matter.

Garrick was extremely explicit, and, in short, we came to a final resolution. So that, if the necessary matters are made out to all our satisfactions, we may sign and seal a previous agreement within a fortnight.

I meet him again to-morrow evening, when we are to name a day for a conveyancer on our side, to meet his solicitor, Wallace. I have pitched on a Mr. Phips,[4] at the recommendation and by the advice of Dr. Ford.[5] The three first steps to be taken are these,—our lawyer is to look into the titles, tenures, etc. of the house and adjoining estate, the extent and limitations of the patent, etc. We should then employ a builder (I think, Mr. Collins,)[6] to survey the state

[1] Willoughby Lacy appears in an indenture of 1780 (Add. MS. 38607, f. 134) under that name and as Willoughby Lacy Morris. His father, James Lacy, had been Garrick's partner, and, dying in 1774, left his moiety to his son, a wildly extravagant but pleasant person.

[2] Albany Wallis (1713?–1800), of the firm of Wallis & Troward.

[3] Benjamin Victor is mentioned as Treasurer of D.L.Th. until his death in 1778, but the work seems to have been carried out by Thomas Westley.

[4] Probably Samuel Phipps of Lincoln's Inn New Square.

[5] James Ford (1717–95), physician and 'man-midwife'.

[6] When S. sought a house in London in Dec. 1773, 'Mr. Collins, Bernard Street' acted as intermediary (Add. MS. 35118, ff. 15–19).

and repair in which the whole premises are, to which G. entirely assents. Mr. G. will then give us a fair and attested estimate from his books of what the profits have been, at an average, for these last seven years. This he has shown me in rough, and valuing the property at £70,000, the interest has exceeded ten per cent.

We should, after this, certainly, make an interest to get the King's promise, that, while the theatre is well conducted, etc. he will grant no patent for a third,—though G. seems confident that he never will. If there is any truth in professions and appearances, G. seems likely always to continue our friend, and to give every assistance in his power.

The method of our sharing the purchase, I should think, may be thus,—Ewart to take £10,000, you £10,000, and I, £10,000—Dr. Ford agrees, with the greatest pleasure, to embark the other five; and, if you do not choose to venture so much, will, I dare say, share it with you. Ewart is preparing his money, and I have a certainty of my part.[1] We shall have a very useful ally in Doctor Ford; and my father offers his services on our own terms.[2] We cannot unite Garrick[3] to our interests too firmly; and I am convinced his influence will bring Leasy to our terms, if he should be ill-advised enough to desire to interfere in what he is totally unqualified for.

I'll write to you to-morrow, relative to Leasy's mortgage (which Garrick has, and advises us to take,) and many other particulars. When matters are in a certain train (which I hope will be in a week), I suppose you will not hesitate to come to town for a day or two. Garrick proposes, when we are satisfied with the bargain, to sign a previous article, with a penalty of ten thousand pounds on the parties who break from fulfilling the purchase. When we are once satisfied and determined in the business (which, I own, is my case) the sooner that is done the better. I must urge it particularly, as

---

[1] From Dr. Ford.

[2] In 1783 Thomas Sheridan gave his point of view on the matter: 'Garrick's retiring, whose jealousy had long shut the London theatres against me, such an open[ing] was made for me both as manager and actor as might soon have retrieved my affairs, and in no long space of time have placed me in easy circumstances' (Rae, ii. 4).

[3] Garrick's income from the theatre in 1775–6 had been: as author, £400; as actor, £800; as manager, £500 (Moore, i. 186).

my confidential connection with the other house is peculiarly distressing, till I can with prudence reveal my situation, and such a treaty (however prudently managed) cannot long be kept secret, especially as Leasy is now convinced of Garrick's resolution.

I am exceedingly hurried at present, so excuse omissions, and do not flag, when we come to the point. I'll answer for it, we shall see many golden campaigns. | Yours ever, | R. B. Sheridan.

You have heard, I suppose, that Foote[1] is likely never to show his face again.

40. To Robert Crispin[2]

Pierpont Morgan Library MS. *Pub.*: *The Autographic Mirror* (1865), p. 194. *Address*: Mr. Crispin *Dock.*: 12. Jany. 1776 | Mr. Sheridan's Letter

12 Jan. 1776

Dear Sir,

I have gone over the Draught with Dr. Ford, which appears extremely well calculated for the Purpose. I think relative to the moiety of the Debts due from the Performers—which we are to take—it should not be as they shall stand on *the 24th: June*, but at their *present* amount—on our signing this Agreement. We think likewise that the Term allow'd for us to take the Mortgage from Mr. Garrick, need only be *three months* (instead of a year) from the time of Lacy's giving notice that He does not mean to pay it off—(should that be the case)—as we wish to have it in our Power as soon as possible—and should certainly take it from G. directly.— We think it will not be worth while to stipulate anything

---

[1] Samuel Foote (1720–77), actor and wit. A scurrilous newspaper had accused him of sexual perversion. On 9 Dec. 1776 Foote was acquitted at Westminster Hall of having made an unnatural attack on his footman. 'Obscure hints and innuendos' had appeared earlier: see W. Cooke, *Memoirs of Samuel Foote* (1805), i. 218–20.

[2] Of the firm of Crispin & Exley, attorneys, 3 New Square. See Add. MS. 44919, ff. 39–43, for his legal charges to the new proprietors in the sale of the D.L.Th. moiety.

relative to the Box given up to G.[1]—I understand there is another mortgage on Lacy's share—I suppose the Register will inform us whether Garrick's is not the first.—[2]

I have added our Names etc.—and wish much Mr. Wallis may have it as soon as possible—as G. goes from Town Sunday—and we hope to have matters finally adjusted on Tuesday Evening.

I'll appoint a Time for our meeting with Mr. Ewart—on the Article which we are [to] sign with each other—which you'll be so good to have a Draught of.

I Hope you are recover'd from your [in]Disposition—tho' the Weather is so much against going abroad, and there is no alteration in the Articles material enough to require our meeting. | I am, Sir, | Your very | obedient | R B Sheridan

Orchard Street
Jan. 12th: 76.

41. To ——

Pub.: American Art Association—Anderson Galleries Sale Catalogue, 18 March 1936, lot 485. Cf. S.C., 11 May 1905, lot 128.

January 16, 1776

[Containing a promise to write a prologue, which, according to the note on the verso, was never done.]

42. To Thomas Linley the Elder

Robert H. Taylor MS. *Pub.*: Moore, i. 188–90.

Jan. 31st. 76

Dear Sir,

I am glad you have found a Person who will let you have

---

[1] 'The new proprietors, as an act of their own, have stipulated, that Mr. Garrick shall continue to keep that box which has of late years been set apart for the accommodation of his family' (*Lady's Magazine* (1776), p. 54).

[2] In an indenture of 1780 (Add. MS. 38607, f. 150) Lacy's moiety is said to be subject to a mortgage of £22,000 to Garrick, and of £5,000 to Raphael Franco.

the money at 4 per Cent.[1] The Security will be very clear, but as there is some degree of Risk, as in case of Fire, I think 4 per Cent uncommonly reasonable, as it will scarcely be any advantage to pay it off—for your Houses and Chapel I suppose bring in much more.[2] Therefore while you can raise money at 4 per Cent on the security of your theatrical share *only*, you will be right to alter as little as you can the present Disposition of your Property. As to your quitting Bath I cannot see why you should doubt a moment about it. Surely the undertaking in which you embark such a sum as £10,000 ought to be the chief object of your Attention: and supposing you did *not chuse* to give up all your Time to the Theatre you may certainly employ yourself more profitably in London than in Bath. But if you are willing (as I suppose you will be) to make the Theatre the great object of your Attention, rely on it you may lay aside every Doubt of not finding your account in it.[3] For the Fact is we shall have nothing but our own Equity to consult in making and obtaining any Demand for exclusive Trouble.—Leasy is utterly unequal to any Department in the Theatre. He has an opinion of me, and is very willing to let the whole Burthen and ostensibility be taken off his Shoulders—but I certainly should not give up my Time and Labour (for his superior advantage having so much greater a share) without some

[1] The *Morn. Chron.*, 18 Jan. 1776, stated: 'It is currently reported that David Garrick, Esq; has sold his share of the Patent and Property of Drury Lane Theatre for £36,000 to four gentlemen, one of whom is said to be Mr. Richard Sheridan, the successful author of The Duenna. Report adds, that the writings were signed Tuesday evening [i.e. 16th].' As late as 24 Jan. it was said that Ewart was one of the patentees (*Lady's Magazine* (1776), p. 54). By the time the contract with Garrick was completed (in June), he had assigned his share to Ford.

[2] Linley's share cost him £10,000, which he raised by granting Garrick a mortgage on property he owned at Bath (detailed in Egerton MS. 1975, f. 22) and on his share in the theatre (Add. MS. 42720, f. 132).

[3] The way in which S. raised the money for his share has been the subject of much discussion, but Add. MS. 42720, ff. 132–5, makes his position clear. His share cost him £10,000, of which James Ford advanced him £7,700 on a mortgage on S.'s share of D.L.Th. S. found £2,300 himself and so became controller of the theatre. Sichel, i. 524–5, states that £1,000 of this amount was obtained by a mortgage of two annuities to Garrick's solicitors. It is little wonder that Bagehot spoke of S.'s 'managing shrewdness', for S. had no financial resources and in this same year had to borrow £100 from Garrick: see the promissory note listed in S.C., 5 Aug. 1851, lot 31. This was probably for an advance to Crispin, whose bill for £238 7s. 2d. was not settled until 15 Feb. 1793: see Add. MS. 44919, f. 43.

exclusive advantage. Yet I should by no means make the Demand 'till I had shewn myself equal to the Task. My Father purposes to be with us but one year—and that only to give me what advantage He can from his experience.[1] He certainly must be paid for his trouble: and so certainly must you. You have experience and character equal to the line you would undertake, and it never can enter into anybody's Head that you were to give your time or any Part of your Attention gratis because you had a share in the Theatre.[2] I have spoke on this subject both to Garrick and Leasy, and you will find no demurr on any side to your gaining a *certain* Income from the Theatre, greater I think than you could make out of it—and in this the Theatre I am sure will be acting only for its own advantage. At the same time you may always make Leisure for a few select Scholars—whose interest may also serve the greater cause of your Patentee-ship.

I have had a young man with me who wants to appear as a Singer in Plays or Oratorios—.I think you'll find him likely to be serviceable in either. He is not one and twenty, and has no conceit. He has a good Tenor Voice—very good ear and a great deal of execution, and of the right kind. He reads Notes very quick, and can accompany himself.—This is Betsey's Verdict, who sat in Judgement on him on sunday last.—I have given him no answer—but engaged him to wait 'till you come to Town.—You mustn't regard the Reports in the Paper about a third Theatre[3]—that's all Nonsense.

Mr. Collins has been disappointed in two Houses which he expected would have been Empty by this time—but they will not be so this month. He will look out, as I will— and you need not doubt being suited for the time and at the Price you want. There is a small House in a malbro'-Street that we are to see tomorrow.[4]—

Betsey's and my Love to all. Your Grandson astonishes everybody by his vivacity his talents for musick and Poetry and the most perfect integrity of mind.[5] | Yours most sincerely | R B Sheridan

[1] They quarrelled again before the season began, and Thomas Sheridan withdrew from all participation. See *Morn. Post*, 24 Aug. 1776; Rae, ii. 4.
[2] Nominally, Linley had £10,000, Ford had £15,000, and S. had £10,000.
[3] A constant menace to the proprietors of the two patent theatres. See p. 117.
[4] Moore omits this paragraph.
[5] Tom S., aged two months.

1776

43. To Thomas Linley the Elder

Pub.: Moore, i. 195–8.

[*1776*]¹

Dear Sir,

You write to me, though you tell me you have nothing to say—now, I have reversed the case, and have not wrote to you, because I have had so much to say. However, I find I have delayed too long to attempt now to transmit you a long detail of our theatrical manœuvres; but you must not attribute my not writing to idleness, but on the contrary to my *not* having been idle.

You represent your situation of mind between *hopes* and *fears*. I am afraid I should argue in vain (as I have often on this point before) were I to tell you, that it is always better to encourage the former than the latter. It may be very prudent to mix a little *fear* by way of alloy with a good solid mass of *hope*; but you, on the contrary, always deal in *apprehension* by the pound, and take *confidence* by the grain, and spread as thin as leaf gold. In fact, though a metaphor mayn't explain it, the truth is, that, in all undertakings which depend principally on ourselves, the surest way not to fail is to *determine to succeed*.

It would be endless to say more at present about theatrical matters, only, that every thing is going on very well. Lacy promised me to write to you, which I suppose, however, he has not done. At our first meeting after you left town, he cleared away all my doubts about his sincerity; and I dare swear we shall never have the least misunderstanding again, nor do I believe he will ever take any distinct council in future. Relative to your affair he has not the shade of an objection remaining, and is only anxious that you may not take amiss his boggling at first. We have, by and with the advice of the privy council,² concluded to have Noverre³

¹ Moore dates the letter '1776' but confuses the reader by stating that it was written in the spring of the year after the squabble (Oct. 1776) between Lacy and S. I accept '1776' from the allusions to Noverre and to the weaning of S.'s son.

² The new proprietors, and Garrick.
³ Jean-Georges Noverre (1727–1810), the great ballet-master. He had promised Garrick that he would perform at D.L.Th. in the coming season (D. Lynham, *The Chevalier Noverre* (1950),

over, and there is a species of pantomime to be shortly put on foot, which is to draw all the human kind to Drury. This is become absolutely necessary on account of a marvellous preparation of the kind which is making at Covent-Garden.[1]

Touching the tragedies you mention, if you speak of them merely as certain tragedies that may be had, I should think it impossible we could find the least room, as you know Garrick saddles us with one which we *must* bring out.[2] But, if you have any particular desire that one of them should be done, it is another affair, and I should be glad to see them. Otherwise, I would much rather you would save me the disagreeableness of giving my opinion to a fresh tragic bard, being already in disgrace with about nine of that irascible fraternity.

Betsey has been alarmed about Tom,[3] but without reason. He is in my opinion better than when you left him, at least to appearance, and the cold he caught is gone. We sent to see him at Battersea, and would have persuaded him to remove to Orchard Street; but he thinks the air does him good, and he seems with people where he is at home, and may divert himself, which, perhaps, will do him more good than the air,—but he is to be with us soon.

Ormsby[4] has sent me a silver branch on the score of The Duenna. This will cost me, what of all things I am least free of, a letter; and it should have been a poetical one, too, if the present had been any piece of plate, but a candlestick!—

pp. 78–79). S. then conducted the negotiations through C. Greville, who wrote in an undated letter: 'I called on you that I might give you the earliest intelligence about Noverre. It happens that he will come for one Year Certain, and according to the demand he makes the establishment will amount to full £3000' (Salt MS.). The *London Packet*, 17–19 July 1776, commented on the engagement: 'Musick and dancing are the plans of the new managers; for which purpose a chevalier dancer is procured, at an enormous salary . . . the very identical Knight of the Toe that made Mr. Garrick's Chinese festival so agreeable . . . he hath already ruined three princes.' But Noverre took up the post of ballet-master to the Paris Opéra and did not come to London.

[1] *Harlequin's Frolics*.

[2] On 18 Dec. 1777, Shirley's *The Roman Sacrifice* was performed: 'this Tragedy had been accepted by Mr. Garrick before his retirement from the theatre, and left, by engagement, to be brought out by the present managers' ([W. C. Oulton], *The History of the Theatres of London . . . 1771 to 1795* (1796), i. 67).

[3] Her brother.

[4] ? Captain Ormsby of the 45th Regiment, son of Charles Ormsby of Cloghans, Co. Mayo: see J. and J. B. Burke, *Extinct and Dormant Baronetcies* (1838), p. 393.

I believe I must melt it into a bowl to make verses on it, for there is no possibility of bringing candle, candlestick, or snuffers, into metre. However, as the gift was owing to the muse, and the manner of it very friendly, I believe I shall try to jingle a little on the occasion; at least, a few such stanzas as might gain a cup of tea from the urn at Bath-Easton.[1]

Betsey is very well, and on the point of giving Tom up to feed like a Christian and a gentleman, or, in other words, of weaning, waining, or weening him. As for the young gentleman himself, his progress is so rapid, that one may plainly see the astonishment the sun is in of a morning, at the improvement of the night. Our loves to all. | Yours ever, and truly, | R. B. Sheridan.

44. To David Garrick

Victoria and Albert Museum MS., Garrick Correspondence, 22, ff. 5–8. *Pub.: Garrick Corr.* ii. 180–2.

15–16 Oct. 1776

My dear Sir,

I should have written to you yesterday but as I found Mr. Wallis had sent you an account of our situation I thought I might as well defer it 'till I could give you some more decisive Intelligence.[2]—I have never been to the Theatre nor interfer'd with the Business of it since I saw you.—A Resolution which at first appear'd precipitate even to our own Party and particularly to our Friend Wallis. However They are now convinced that it was positively the only step which could have prevented Lacey's signing with the Parties,[3] or have put us on the footing which I hope We shall be on after a meeting we are to have tomorrow.

[1] Anna Miller's literary coterie met at her home at Batheaston and placed poems in an antique Roman urn. After a public breakfast, she presented a myrtle wreath to the writer of the best lines.

[2] When Garrick retired in June, S. became manager of D.L.Th. The winter season had only been running for three weeks when performances ceased because of a disagreement among the proprietors.

[3] Garrick had sent Lacy a notice to discharge his mortgage; and on 27 Sept. 1776, Lacy wrote him a letter (Folger MS. CS 907, f. 95) asking for time. Lacy then determined to sell his share to Langford and Thompson, but Albany Wallis declared he ought to give first refusal to his partners. For other reasons brought forward, see [W. C. Oulton], op. cit. ii. 188–9.

I was convinced that everything had passed between
Lacey, Thompson,[1] and Langford[2] on Friday except the
actually having executed the Deeds, and I had reason to
think that the next Day was appointed for this to be done.—
It was not to be supposed that argument or indeed any consideration whatever would prevail with Captain T. to quit
his Hold, (when He had so much at stake) if he could by
any means maintain it—the only method therefore which
the exigence admitted of, was to convince those who were
to find the money that they were going to embark their
Property on a vessel that was on Flames: and at the same
time to let Lacey see that by thus dividing his share He
would ruin the whole of it.—Accordingly after I left you
I wrote a long letter[3] to Langford and Thompson stating
the injustice and illegality of the Business and informing
them of my Determination if they persisted in it. This Mr.
W.[4] delivered to Langford before five o'clock. At eight I
sent Hopkins[5] to Lacey with a more formal and written
Notice to provide for the Business and management by
himself. He scarcely believed 'till then that I would actually
do this—and sent Hopkins back to me etc., but as I would
not talk [?] even relative to the Theatre—He return'd to L.
who was in great confusion—Mrs A.[6] having refused to
play, and the Xmas Tale[7] not being ready from the evening
Rehearsal which had waited for my coming being stop't.—
At 12 Richard and the Pantomime were fix'd—the Performers not having heard anything of our Change[8]—the next
day[9] (which I am convinced was the Day they would other-

[1] Edward Thompson (1738 ?–86)
was a naval man and author of occa-
sional verse. He earned Garrick's ani-
mosity by spreading a rumour that he
had tried to damn Thompson's masque,
The Syrens, produced at C.G.Th. on
26 Feb. 1776.

[2] Robert Langford, auctioneer. Add.
MS. 38607, f. 150, reveals that by 1778
Lacy was so much in debt to Langford
as to have to secure him an annuity of
£500. He also made over to him Eynsham Hall before 1785: see *The Tor-
rington Diaries* (ed. Andrews, 1934), i.
215.   [3] Not found.

[4] Albany Wallis.
[5] The prompter. He has a line in *The
Critic*, ii. ii.
[6] Frances Abington (1737–1815), the
original performer—six months after
the above occurrences—of Lady Teazle.
[7] By Garrick. It was first performed
at D.L.Th. on 27 Dec. 1773.
[8] They heard of it next morning:
'nothing could exceed the confusion
which ensued at Drury-Lane theatre on
Saturday morning, on its being known
that Mr. S. had given up his share in
the management' (*Morn. Chron.*, 14 Oct.
1776).   [9] Saturday, 12 Oct.

wise have sign'd and seal'd on) Hopkins found them all three in great confusion and Perturbation—Mr: *Langford particularly* on hearing from H. that he did not think He could keep the House open a week. However T. spirited hem as much as possible to stand to the Business, but (as I suppose Langford began to have Qualms about advancing the money) it was determined to try what a civil Letter[1] to me would do—which they sent hoping to be friendly, with a compliment to my Abilities and so forth. And at Night and again on sunday morning Lacey sent by Hopkins to entreat I would return to the management and that He would do everything in his Power to procure matters to be settled to my satisfaction, and would give up the Point if He could prevail on them. As I was aware of this—and felt on what secure ground I stood I still declined hearing anything on the Subject—so that they soon found that the whole of their stock, after changing their Play several Times, was reduced to the *Committee*[2] and that after Tuesday they had not one Play which they could perform. This appear'd to have a great effect in settling the matter—and in consequence (tho' our meeting yesterday ended in nothing) we were to Day very friendly together[3]—and received a positive promise that the Point should be given up—and Mr. Lacey's word that He would never Part with his share or any Part of it but to us. We are to meet at Night at Mr. Wallis—where we are to receive a Letter from Captain T. and Mr. L. renouncing the Business—tho I do not expect we shall come to the Point 'till tomorrow.—I have seen none of the Performers (purposely) except Mr. Smith[4] and Mr. King[5] who call'd on me in Orchard-Street since the Affair

[1] Not found.

[2] On Tuesday, 15 Oct. Fawcett and Mrs. Bradshaw played in *The Committee* at D.L.Th., and Bannister and Mrs. Wrighten took part in *The Waterman*; but King, Smith, and Dodd, as well as Mrs. Abington, Mrs. Yates, and Mrs. Baddeley, were absent from the theatre.

[3] 'Mr. Lacey also declared that he was not in the least influenced ... by ... any difference with Mr. Sheridan, for whom he has the greatest esteem, and whose conduct towards him had ever been polite, honourable and disinterested' (*Universal Magazine*, lix (1776), 209).

[4] William Smith (1730?–1819), 'Gentleman' Smith, the great performer of Charles Surface.

[5] Thomas King (1730–1805), the original Sir Peter Teazle, was acting manager of D.L.Th. He appears to have led the actors' rebellion against Lacy's proposals: 'the *acting-manager* has fled the stage—with the Muses in his train, and the performers seem inclined soon to follow' (*Morn. Post*, 14 Oct. 1776).

happen'd. King has acted particularly well. However, from one motive or other almost all the Principal Performers declined playing on various Pretences[1]—even one or two who I believe L. thought would stand forward have been taken ill—. Indeed there never was known such an uncommonly epidemick Disorder as has raged among our unfortunate Company—it differs from the Plague by attacking the better sort first—the manner too in which they are seiz'd I am told is very extraordinary—many who were in perfect Health at one moment, on receiving a Billet from the Prompter to summon them to their Business are seiz'd with sudden Qualms—and before they can get thro' the contents are absolutely unfit to leave their Rooms. So that Hopkins's Notes seem to operate like what we hear of Italian-poison'd Letters which strike with sickness those to whom they are address'd. In short if a successful Author had given the Company a Dinner at Salt-Hill[2]—the effects could not be more injurious to our Dramatic Repre[se]ntations.—And what has been still more alarming is that those who being indisposed sent for our Doctor, found themselves on the first visit (an effect which Doctors often produce) worse than they were before—with this difference only in the Process that instead of hearing his Patient's Case, He related his own. However I hope we shall be able to procure a *Bill of Health* very soon: and as their confinement stands entirely on the Ground of their Dislike of playing under they knew not whose management, I shall be particularly cautious that there shall be no precedent for sickness, as I have been from giving any Authority for it and indeed I believe they were most of them actuated by the same considerations and obvious foresight of the event which had influenced me to desist from my Part in the Direction.—

I shall not seal this Letter 'till we have met to Night—

---

[1] The *Morn. Chron.*, 14 Oct. 1776, reported that by the evening of 12 Oct. ten actors were hoarse, four seized with sudden fevers; six of the actresses had hysterics, and three suffered from the falling sickness.

[2] Mrs. Thrale noted in 1777: '*We* were at Salthill on our way to Bath and dined at Middlecott's; the other house having a strange Accident happen to it some time ago, when a large Company of Gentlemen were poysoned in an unaccountable manner' (*Thraliana* (ed. K. C. Balderston, Oxford, 1942), i. 125).

when it is possible I may have the Pleasure to tell you that matters are firmly accommodated.—

Oct 15th: 76.—

Oct 16th. Wednesday morning

I had not an opportunity last Night to get at my Letter— and indeed what I could have said was not decisive enough to have made me anxious for it.—The Business of the House is all stopt, by Lacey's Desire sooner than let it be known to his proposed Partners (which another Play the effect of my interfering must have informed them of) that we were already agreed on our old Terms. We dine together to Day at Wallis—when the Affair must be decided—but I will not keep this—as Mr. Wallis will have time more fully to inform you of the event.[1]—As I speculate on Rehearsing the Xmas Tale at 10 o'clock for Friday. I have run this vile scrawl (which I beg you will excuse being written in Haste) to such a Length I have scarcely Room to say how much we feel your Friendship in this Business, and how sincerely | I am your obliged Friend | and humble Servant | R B Sheridan.

I beg mine and Mrs. S.'s Compliments to Mrs. Garrick.

45. To Carr[2]

Salt MS.

[*1776?*]
Thursday Night

Mr. Sheridan presents his Compliments to Mr. Carr. He has read the Tragedy He did him the Favor to leave at his House and thinks the Fable and management of the

---

[1] The *Morn. Post*, 18 Oct. 1776, reported: 'We are assured the late disputes between the managers of Drury-lane were on Wednesday accommodated, to the satisfaction of all parties; Mr. Lacey being convinced of the impropriety of disposing of any part of his theatrical property, without offering Mr. Sheridan, Mr. Linley, and Dr. Ford, the refusal of it.' He sold out to them in 1778.

[2] See T. Gilliland, *The Dramatic Mirror* (1808), i. 283, for Robert Carr who may possibly be the person to whom the letter was written. In 1766 he had joined with Samuel Hayes in writing a tragedy called *Eugenia*.

Plot extremely judicious—but as far as He can pretend to judge, the Language and versification appear to require a good deal of revisal.—

As to the *receiving* any Piece for Drury-Lane-Theatre Mr. Sheridan thinks it proper in the first instance to inform Mr. Carr that the Proprietors have come to a Resolution to have all Pieces which Authors may Favor them with the offer of, sent anonymously to the Theatre, and an answer will be given to the Direction left, as speedily as possible, a method which Mr. S. recommends to Mr. Carr, tho' as He told Mr. Carr the circumstances of the company have made two tragedies stand over already to the next season.

46. To ——

Folger MS.

19 Jan[?] [*1777*][1]

Sir,

The Note you received yesterday from me was given by the Servant in a mistake, and indeed I have been in an error relative to the little Piece you did me the favor to leave at my House from the first—owing to its having been mislaid by a very stupid Servant, and to my having since received a Letter with a signature nearly similar to your's accompanied by a Comedy: of which I conceived myself to be speaking when I had the Pleasure of seeing you at the Theatre.— The Fact is that I did not get your Packet 'till after repeated Enquiries on Receipt of your Letter yesterday. I have since read the Piece and beg leave to assure you, without a compliment, that as far as my judgement extends, it has particular merit—and if I am writing (as I presume from your Letter and appearance is the case) to an author whose first dramatic Attempt is this *New Year's Trifle*[2]— I will venture to assert that you cannot fail of success.—The real embarrassments our Theatre is under at present from promises to different Authors will I am afraid make it impossible for

---

[1] If we accept the date as Sunday, 19 Jan., then the year must be 1777 or 1783. S. lived in Great Queen Street in Nov. 1776 (Widener MS.) and for some years afterwards, but had left the street by July 1782.   [2] Unidentified.

me to speak on the subject of having your Piece Performed this Season—but if you will name any time when you will do me the Favor to call in Great-Queen-Street—I shall be happy to be acquainted with its Author—who I am afraid must have thought me either very inattentive or impolite, not to have perused so short a manuscript, introduced by a Letter which He must have supposed me to have read, and which I should have been unpardonable to have neglected. | I am, Sir, | Your very Humble | and obedient Servant | R B Sheridan.

G—Queen-Street
    Sunday-Night,
        Jan[?] 19th:

47. [To the Licencer of Plays]

Huntington MS. LA 426. [Ph.] Subscription only in S.'s hand.

17 Feb. 1777

Sir

If the following Comedy call'd *A Trip to Scarborough* (alter'd from Sir John Vanbrugh) meets the Approbation of the Lord Chamberlain we shall have it perform'd at the Theatre Royal in Drury Lane.[1] | R B Sheridan | For self and Partners.

17 February 1777

48. [To the Licencer of Plays]

Yale MS. Subscription only in S.'s hand. *Pub.*: W. Van Lennep, 'The Chetwynd Manuscript of *The School for Scandal*', *Theatre Notebook*, vi (1951), 10–11.

7 May 1777

Sir

If the following Comedy calld *The School for Scandal*[2]

[1] It was given its first performance at D.L.Th. on 24 Feb. 1777. According to D. E. Baker, *Biographia Dramatica* (new ed., 1782), ii. 379, S. owned that he had spoiled Vanbrugh's play in his adaptation.

[2] First performed on 8 May 1777 at D.L.Th.

meets the Approbation of The Lord Chamberlain we shall have it perform'd at The Theatre Royal in Drury Lan[e.] | R B Sheridan | For self and Partners

May 7th 1777

49. [To the Proprietors of Drury Lane Theatre]

Folger MS.

[*Sept. 1777?*]

Remarks etc.[1]

Dressers and Dressing Rooms

The Number of Performers being reduced—the Number of Rooms and Dressers ought to be reduced also. On representing this to *Kirk*[2] (whose province it is) he said they had been exceedingly distressed last Year, by our taking away the two Rooms for Mr. Giles and that he had been oblidged to let People dress in his own Room:—I have this Year taken away another Room adjoining to the property Room, which it is hoped has made that department convenient.

There are 20 Dressing Rooms (besides the shifting Room) a Dresser is allotted to each—these are to attend every night and to assist in other Rooms if not wanted in their own (they might be useful on the Stage on such Nights in Processions etc.)

The Dressers have had a Perquisite of the Candles left in their Rooms (this custom ought to be abolished as many bad consequences may arise from it)

Supernumeraries were risen in 1775 from 1s. to 1s. 6d. per Night (viz. those who go on as Gents). These should be brought back to their old Price. No Dresser to be allowed a Share in a Benefit in future.

Waiting Women—more than Six are never wanting at a Time.

---

[1] They appear on ff. 49–53 of a notebook lettered by S. 'Memorandum Book'. This reveals that D.L.Th. employed 48 actors on salary, 37 actresses, 18 adult and two child dancers, 30 dressers, 14 door-keepers, 7 box-keepers, 4 lobby-keepers and messengers, 2 numberers, 1 candle woman, 3 box inspectors, 7 office-keepers, and two pensioners.

[2] Housekeeper at D.L.Th.

1777

Porters—One only was found sufficient and did the business before last Year (1776–7).[1] (Why not at present?) Performers who live at a certain distance from the House to pay a Porter for themselves—or to appoint a Place of Call within the Limits assigned—remote distances very inconvenient to the general Business—and ought to be discouraged

The Business of the Bills etc. to be considered

There are about 30 Days in the Season when the House is not opened—the printing hand Bills on those Days etc. unnecessary. And how do the Fruit women and Shops get their Bills?

Several Encroachments have been made on us such as

    Stockings for Dancers
    Gloves (Moody)[2]
    Supernumeraries
    Lobby Sweepers
    Barge[3]
    Goodwine[4]
    Cartage for Oil
    Sanderson[5]
    Perquisites of Candles
    3 Treasurers[6]—two sufficient—

The Plot of every Play should be transcribed in a Book to be kept by the Proprietors.

The Property plot-Book should be copied for them.

Fosbrook[7]—to give in the Names of such men who are employed to keep Places—any Person appointed to go on the Stage being absent to keep places at such time to be severely forfeited.[8]

New Performers—and old ones on new Salaries to provide their own *white*-silk stockings (and Gloves?) as at Covent Garden.

[1] The porter or call-man visited actors' lodgings every morning to tell them when they would be needed for rehearsals. See E. C. Everard, *Memoirs of an Unfortunate Son of Thespis* (Edinburgh, 1818), p. 40. One Hughes was employed by D.L.Th. for 'extra-calling.'

[2] John Moody (1727?–1812), Irish comic actor.

[3] A Sweeper.
[4] Lampman.
[5] Carpenter.
[6] Victor, Westley, Thomas Evans.
[7] Numberer at D.L.Th.
[8] The 'Memorandum Book' contains a list (in S.'s hand) of forfeits for absence from the chorus and orchestra.

Buff Gloves and Hats should be returned to the Wardrobe.

Stockings should be stamped with the Actors Name

Office and Doorkeepers not to quit their Stations till the Performances are quite ended.

1777

Certain great Expences which are to be provided for
in the first 132 Nights or 22 full Weeks—

	£
Proprietors—	2200
House rent and taxes—	900
Oil Coals and Candles—	1500
Lord W[alpole]—[1]	315
Abington ⎫	
Yates and ⎬ Benefits—	600[2]
King ⎭	
For the Summer—1778—	1000
	£6515

£50 per Night 22 W[eeks]			6600
25	.	. 30 W	4500
28	.	. 30 W	5056

which is nearly our Debt

£103
————
  8 per Night Renters
————
111

Some Provision should also be made for losses on Benefit but not so much as last year, as many Benefits will be raised to £105—the Pay List includes all other *certain* Expences and *contingencies* make up the rest of the Account.

[1] D.L.Th. paid 'a clear yearly sum of £315 unto the Hon. Robert Walpole for 21 years to be computed from the second day of Sept. 1774' (Add. MS. 38607, f. 153). Walpole (1736–1810) was the son of Horatio, 1st Lord Walpole of Wolterton, and was at one time Clerk of the Privy Council.

[2] In the previous season they had received £200 each in lieu of benefits: see D.L.Th. 'Receipts and Payments, 1776–7' (Folger MS.) under 29 Mar., 14 Apr., and 26 May. Mrs. Mary Ann Yates (1728–87) played leading tragic roles.

Stated Salaries

to be provided for in 180 Nights, or 30 full Weeks; and should be put in the pay List.

	£.	s.	d
The Manager—			
Mrs. Linley—	500.	0.	0
Loutherbourg[1]—	500.	0.	0
Yates[2]—*	800.	0.	0
King—*	500.	0.	0
M. Gallet[3]—*	500.	0.	0
M. Dupres—*	400.	0.	0
Sigr. Tenducci[4]	500.	0.	0
M. Roye[5]	150.	0.	0
S. French	120.	0.	0
T. French	70.	0.	0
Miss Armstrong	50.	0.	0
Mr. Giles	50.	0.	0
Mr. Kirk &[c.]	40.	0.	0
	£4180.	0.	0

Yates, King, Gallet, Dupres were in the pay List of last year—but Gallets salary is increased £100 as Ballet Master, Tenducci was also paid, but not in the pay List.

N.B. there is above £300 added to the Debt which Dr. Ford has advanced for the Summer Payments.

N.B. Not one Tradesmans Bill (excepting for Oil) provided for the current year in the Enormous Expence—
   In Jan. 1777 The Pay List was £100.6.3 per Diem or £601.17.6 per Week—
   In *that* List was included—£28 per Week for the Pro-

---

[1] Philippe Jacques de Loutherbourg (1740–1812), painter. He was scene designer at D.L.Th., 1773–81.
[2] Richard Yates (1706 ?–96), comedian and the original Sir Oliver Surface. The *Pub. Adv.*, 13 Nov. 1776, stated that 'Mr. and Mrs. Yates's income from the stage does not fall short of the sum of £1600'.

[3] The *Morn. Post*, 24 Sept. 1776, reported that the dancing at D.L.Th. was under the direction of Gallet and Slingsby. The Duprés were dancers.
[4] Giusto Tenducci (1736–?), Italian composer and male soprano.
[5] Pierre Royer (or Royé), Samuel French, and Thomas French were all painters at D.L.Th.

prietors and £31.10.0 per Week to the Sinking Fund, or nearly £10.0.0 per Day.

This year's Pay List not being complete (to a certainty) no *exact* calculation can be made—there have been great strikings off—and some new ones added—

From the present Mode of carrying the Sums on the other side to Account, there will be a considerable change on the first Appearance of the Accounts—for instance Rent and Taxes—Oil and Coal Bills etc. and most of the stated Salaries, were brought under the article of *contingencies*; and the *Proprietors Subsistance* and *sinking Fund* were included in the pay List.

There are several *certain* and not *inconsiderable constant* Expences to be provided for and paid *Weekly*, which being variable cannot be brought under any *certain* Head such as the Carpenter's, House-keepers, Printers, Lamplighters, and Bill Sticker's, Taylor's and Mantua-Makers Bills.

If with this plain Account before us we are inattentive or extravagant—shall we not deserve the Ruin which MUST *follow?*

The Property Man (viz. he who makes the Property) Not to make any Thing new but what is ordered by the Board.—No Power to be delegated —

The Under Offices of the House are much more lucrative than they at first appear to be. No Person whatever to be employed in the House without the knowledge and Examination of the Board.

Those whose Business is confined to the Morning only may have an Evening Employment—for the fewer Servants the better and their Places will be more valuable.—No Person should hold two Places the Business of which can possibly interfere in respect to Time.

Every Person should be discharged as soon as discovered to be drunken or disorderly—

Workmen should be kept out as much as possible for little single Jobs as it has been found productive of great Impositions.

One Old House cost a great deal in Repairs and one [was] underlet. All Salaries to be fixed at the commencement of the Season.

Costly After Pieces should not be made common as the Extra Expences are great.[1]

The Captain of the Supernumeraries should send in every Morning a copy of the Prompters List.—

A List of the Properties should be delivered and often overlooked, as neglect and Embezzlement are liable to creep on this Department.

50. [To the Proprietors of the Drury Lane and Covent Garden Theatres]

Harvard MS. Copy. A draft is in W.T. *Pub.*: Moore, ii. 373–7.[2] *Dock.*: Proposed Plan of 3d. Theatre

1777

Gentlemen

According to your desire the Plan of the proposed *Assistant Theatre*[3] is here explained in Writing for your further consideration.

From our situations in the Theatres Royal of Drury Lane and Covent Garden, we have had opportunities of observing many circumstances relative to our general Property which must have escaped those who do not materially interfere in the management of that Property—One point in particular has lately weigh'd extremely in our Opinions which is an Apprehension of a new Theatre being erected for some species or other of Dramatic Entertainment. Were this

[1] An example may be found in D.L.Th. 'Receipts and Payments, 1778–9' (Folger MS.) in connexion with *The Camp*: 'Oct. 31: Children for Practices of Camp £6.10.0; Oct. 16: Super[numeraries] and Sol[diers] for Camp £35.5.6; Oct. 28: Mr. Burnett for Extra Music in Camp in 23d inclusive £18.7.6.'

[2] Moore prints a completed version tallying with the draft in W.T.; and both differ from the text in the Harvard MS.

[3] On 29 Nov. 1777, George Colman the elder wrote, 'A third Winter Theatre is in agitation, to be opened and established by the other two. Harris and

Sheridan are the projectors . . .' (LeFanu MS.). On 6 Jan. 1778, Tom King stated that S. had 'devoted himself much of late to his darling scheme of a third theatre' (Folger MS. D. a. 82, f. 6). But no new building was erected, and the scheme as outlined above was somewhat modified. On 4 Feb. 1778, Harris and S. purchased the King's Theatre, and opened it with opera in the autumn. The venture did not pay, and at the end of the first season, Harris withdrew from the management. S. himself sold out to William Taylor on 7 Nov. 1781. See Harris's memorial to the Earl of Salisbury in P.R.O., L.C.7/3.

Event to take place on an opposing Interest[1] in all probability the contest that would ensue would speedily end in the absolute ruin of one of the present Established Theatres,—We have reason it is true from His Majesty's gracious Patronage to the Present Houses to hope that another Patent for an opposing[2] Theatre is not likely[3] to be obtained[4]—but the motives which appear to call for one, are so many and those of such nature as to encrease every Day—that we cannot on the maturest consideration of the subject divest ourselves of the dread of such an event.[5] With this Apprehension before us—We have naturally fallen into a joint consideration of the means either of preventing so fatal a Blow to the present Theatres or of deriving a general advantage from a Circumstance which might otherwise be their ruin[6]—

Some of the leading motives for the establishment of a third Theatre are as follows—

1st: The great extent of the Town and encreased Residence of a higher class of People who on account of many inconveniences seldom frequent the Theatres—

2d: The distant situation of the Theatres from the Politer Streets[7]— and the difficulty with which Ladies reach their Carriages or Chairs.

3d: The small number of side Boxes, where only by the uncontroulable influence of Fashion Ladies of any Rank can be induced to sit.

4th: The earliness of the hour, which renders it absolutely impossible for those who attend Parliament, live at any distance, or indeed for any Person who dines at the prevailing hour to reach the Theatre before the Performance is half over.—

These considerations have lately been strongly urged to

[1] W.T. adds 'our Property would sink in value one half and'.

[2] W.T. prints 'a winter Theatre'.

[3] W.T. 'easily'.

[4] For the way in which the managers of the patent theatres clung to their privileges, see W. Nicholson, *The Struggle for a Free Stage in London* (1906), pp. 85–97, 103–10, 142–8.

[5] W.T. 'that such an event may not be very remote'.

[6] In a letter to Garrick of *c.* Mar. 1778, Lacy wrote, 'If any fears for the safety of your money had arose on the idea of *a third theatre* . . .' (*Garrick Corr.* ii. 292).

[7] The King's Theatre was not open to this objection, because it was in the Haymarket.

me by many leading Persons of Rank—There has also prevailed, as appears by the number of private Plays at Gentlemen's seats an unusual Fashion for Theatrical entertainment among the politer Class of People—and it it not to be
wondered at that they finding themselves, (from the causes
before enumerated) in a manner excluded from our Theatres,
shou'd persevere in an endeavour to establish some Plan of
similar entertainment on Principles of superior elegance
and accommodation—

In proof of this disposition and the effects to be apprehended from it we need but instance one fact, among many
which might be produced, and that is the well known
circumstance of a subscription having actually been begun
last Winter, with a very powerfull Patronage for the im-
portation of a French Company of Comedians[1]—a scheme
which tho' it might not have answered to the undertakers
would certainly have been the Foundation of other Entertainments whose opposition we shou'd speedily have experienced—

The Question then upon a full view of our situation
appears to be whether The Proprietors of the present
Theatres will contentedly wait till some other Person takes
advantage of the prevailing wish for a third Theatre or
having the remedy in their power profit by a turn of fashion
which they cannot controul—

A full conviction that the latter is the only line of conduct
which can give security to the Patents of Drury Lane and
Covent Garden Theatres and yield a probability of future
advantage in the exercise of them, has prompted us to endeavour at modelling this Plan which we conceive the
Theatres may unite in the support of a third to the general
and mutual advantage of all the Proprietors.

Proposals—

The Proprietors of the Theatre Royal in Covent Garden
appear to be[2] possessed of two Patents[3] for the Privilege of

[1] See the two satirical stanzas entitled 'To the Encouragers of the
Troop of Comedians expected soon to
arrive from France' in the *Lond. Chron.*,
28–30 Jan. 1777.

[2] In the margin another hand suggests altering this to 'are'.

[3] Charles II granted letters patent, in
1660 (and separately in 1662), to
Thomas Killigrew and Sir William

acting Plays etc.—under one of which the above mention'd Theatre is open'd—the other lying Dormant and useless. It is proposed that this dormant patent shall be exercised (with his Majesty's approbation) in order to licence the Dramatic Performances of the New Theatre to be erected—

It is proposed That the Performances at this New Theatre shall be supported from the united establishments of the two present Theatres—so that the unemploy'd part of each company may exert themselves for the advantage of the whole.

As the object of this assistant Theatre will be to reimburse the proprietors of the other two at the full season for the expensive establishment they are obliged to maintain when the Town is almost empty, it is supposed that the scheme of Business to be adopted in the New Theatre shall differ as much as possible from that of the other two and that the Performances at the New House shall be exhibited at a superior price and shall commence at a later hour—

If a Theatre for these purposes is hired or to be built (being the Property of the Builder or Builders) it must be for an agreed on Rent with security for a Term of Years, in this case the Proprietors of the two present Theatres shall jointly and severally engage in the whole of the risk and the Proposers are ready on equitable Terms to undertake the Management of it—But if the proposers find themselves enabled either on their own credit or by the Assistance of their Friends on a plan of subscription, the mode being devised and the security given by themselves to become the Builders of the Theatre,[1] The Proposers will in that case undertake that no Rent shall be demanded for the Performances therein to be exhibited for the mutual advantage of the two present Theatres[2]—Reserving to themselves

Davenant, for theatrical performances in London. William III issued a further patent to Betterton in 1695. In later years Killigrew's licence became known as 'the dormant patent', attached to but not used by C.G.Th. See the *Report from the Select Committee on Dramatic Literature* (1832), pp. 16–17, 37–39, for the validity of these patents and for the suggestion that the Killigrew patent was abrogated in the reign of Anne.

[1] Moore prints, 'The interest in the building will in that case be the property of the Proposers.' This sentence, in slightly different draft form, is in W.T.

[2] W.T. and Moore add, 'The Proposers will, in this case, conducting the business under the dormant Patent

any profit they can make of their Building employ'd in purposes distinct from the Business of the Theatres and towards which the Privilege of the Patent does not contribute.[1]

The Proposers undertaking the management of the New Theatre shall be entitled to a Sum to be settled by the Proprietors at large or by an equitable arbitration.

Then it is proposed that all the Proprietors of the two Present Theatres Royal of Drury Lane and Covent Garden shall share all profits from the Dramatic entertainments as above specified exhibited at the New Theatre—that is each shall be entitled to receive a Dividend in proportion to the shares he or she shall possess of the present Theatres— First only deducting a certain nightly sum to be paid to the Proprietors of Covent Garden Theatre, as a Consideration for the licence furnished by the exercise of their present dormant Patent.[2]

Should the above Plan be carried into execution it is evident that there will be a more extensive Field for the encouraging and rewarding of Theatrical Performers as well as greater scope for the Talents of Dramatic Writers—so that the Proprietors instead of being compell'd to lower the Drama by diminishing their present establishments, (which they are sensible must be the case) will be enabled by enlarging the circle of Audiences, to support all their entertainments with additional Lustre.

The Proposers have only to add that they are so entirely convinced of the general Advantage and Equity of the Plan now offered that they do not hesitate to join the following Proposition to the execution of it viz. They will severally undertake to any Proprietor with whom they are now in Partnership who shall be apprehensive that his or her Present Property may be impaired instead of benefited by the

above mentioned, bind themselves, that no theatrical entertainments, as plays, farces, pantomimes, or English operas, shall at any time be exhibited in this Theatre but for the general advantage of the Proprietors of the other two Theatres.'

[1] W.T. ends here.
[2] Moore brings the letter to a close at

this point, adding only the following whimsical conclusion: "Fore Heaven! the Plan's a good Plan! I shall add a little Epilogue tomorrow.

R. B. S.

'Tis now too late, and I've a letter to write
Before I go to bed,—and then, Good Night.'

establishment of the New Theatre,[1] they will with such Proprietor undertake to Purchase at a Proper Notice his or her share any time within the period of two Years from the commencement of the Plan—The Price to be fix'd at the full present Value and estimation of their Property—Or if any Proprietor shall prefer a certain Dividend from the whole they are ready in manner as before to Rent the share of such Proprietor for any desired Term at an Estimated Sum to be fix'd on an Average Profit of any number of past Seasons— But if the Proprietors of Covent Garden Theatre do not think it expedient to Prefer the exercise of their present[2] Dormant Patent in the Proposed Theatre—The Proposers are ready to listen to any other Plan which they or any other Proprietor shall think more for the advantage and security of both Theatres. | T. Harris[3] | R B Sheridan[3] exd.

25 November 1777.[4]

51. To David Garrick

Roe-Byron MS. C.68/232, Newstead Abbey (Nottingham Corporation). *Pub.*: *Garrick Corr.*, ii. 348. *Address*: David Garrick Esq. *Dock.*: Sheridan.

10 Jan. [*1778*][5]

Dear Sir,

I have been *about finishing* the Verses which were to have follow'd you to Althorp[6] every day since you left Town, and as idle as such an employment is I have been diverted from it by one thing or other still more idle even than Rhyming: I believe I shall give up all attempts to versifying in future, for my Efforts in that way always bring me into some foolish

---

[1] For the later history of the 'third' theatre, see Ian Donaldson, 'New Papers of Henry Holland and R. B. Sheridan', *Theatre Notebook*, xvi (1962), 118–22.

[2] 'Present' is inserted in the same hand as that of the date.

[3] His signature.

[4] In the hand, probably, of a solicitor. It differs from that of the transcriber as well as those of S. and of Harris.

[5] Dated from the reference to Cumberland's 'Battles', for this must surely refer to the coming performance of

Richard Cumberland's *Battle of Hastings*, acted on 24 Jan. 1778. Cumberland (1732–1811) wrote two letters to Garrick that were docketed 'To me at Althorp Dec 77 abt B of Hastings'. See *Garrick Corr.* ii. 286; E. M. Graham, *The Beautiful Mrs. Graham* (1927), pp. 130–2.

[6] Garrick was on terms of intimate friendship with John, 1st Earl Spencer (1734–83), and his wife Georgiana (1737–1814), and visited them at their Northamptonshire seat.

Predicament. What I write in a Hurry I always feel to be not worth reading, and what I try to take Pains with, I am sure never to finish: However such as it is the Poem[1] shall salute your return, and it will then have the advantage of finding you less at Leisure to be critical—tho' indeed but that I am not sure of your even receiving this at Althorp I would endeavour to acquit myself of my Promise tho' something after the Time.—I mean to be vastly civil to Female Talent of all sort, and even to the affectation of it where the Person is very handsome (—for the Grace of Venus which passes all understanding, atones for an abundance of Frailty—) and my Bards shall be *very easily* recompensed.

> —In due Proportion *She* rewards their Toils,
> —*Bows* for a *Distich*—for a *Stanza*—smiles;
> *Familiar Nods* an *Epigram* attend,—
> An *Ode* will almost rank you as a *Friend*;
> A *softer Name*—fond *Elegy* bestows,
> But *nearest to her Heart*— a *Sonnet* flows:

I need not attempt to write you any News—I hear everywhere how valiantly you are fighting Cumberland's Battles for him—I hope the Bugle meets with due Honor—I must send this away or I shall be too late for the Post— | your most sincere | and obedient | R B Sheridan.

Great-Queen-Street
 Jan 10th:

52. [To the Licencer of Plays]

Huntington MS. LA 457. Only the signature is in S.'s hand. *Dock.*:
R 7th Novr. 1778. but approved by the Lord Chamberlain in Octr.

13 Oct 1778

Sir,
 If the following New Entertainment in Two Acts call'd

[1] Not found. It may be the one mentioned by Garrick in a letter of 6 Jan. 1777 to Lady Spencer: 'I have lately seen part of [a] Poem that is to make it's appearance this winter—the chief subject is the *Characters of Women . . .*' (*Letters of David Garrick and Georgiana Countess Spencer* (ed. Earl Spencer and C. Dobson, Cambridge, 1960), p. 81).

The Camp[1] meets the Approbation of The Lord Chamberlain We shall have it perform'd at the Theatre Royal in Drury Lane. | R B Sheridan

13 Octobr. 1778.

53. To David Garrick

Folger MS. Copy.

26 Nov. 1778

Messrs Harris and Sheridan present their Compliments to Mr. Garrick and desire his acceptance of the enclosed Ticket.[2] They have likewise put down the names of all his family upon their free list.

Kings Theatre
Nov. 26. 1778

54. To Bray[3]

Hyde MS. [Ph.] *Address*: Mr. Bray | Great Russel-Street.

[1778–81?]
Wednesday

Sir,

I was in hopes before this to have been able to have brought Mr. Ewart with me in order to settle Mr. Heaviside's annuity.[4]—Which in the course of a week will I think be effected. And this occasion'd my delaying to pay you the expences lately incurr'd, which certainly should also be discharged by Mr. Ewart. But as I cannot positively fix the Day I enclose a Note to pay them and shall be obliged to you to give the Bearer the Receipt. | I am, Sir, | Your humble Servant | R B Sheridan

---

[1] Performed at D.L.Th. on 15 Oct. 1778.

[2] Probably for Bertoni's opera, *Demoofonte*, given at the King's Theatre on 28 Nov., when Pacchierotti made his début in England.

[3] William Bray of Great Russell Street is noted in *Browne's General Law List* (1777) as an attorney.

[4] Probably in connexion with the King's Theatre. A statement of its accounts in the Salt MSS. shows that T. Heaviside was paid £161. 7s. 0d. on 27 May 1779, and £100. 2s. 3d. on 15 Sept. 1780.

55. To Samuel Ireland[1]

Folger MS. D. a. 82, no. 13. *Address*: – Ireland Esqr. *Dock.*: Mr. Sheridan | Rec'd Jan. 2 79

1 Jan. 1779

Dear Sir,

I have been for some time taken up by some particular Matters of Business which have prevented my having the Pleasure of seeing you. You must give me leave to keep your Piece for a few Days longer[2]—when you shall certainly receive it and my sentiments as far as they are worth while communicating to you. | Your very obedient Servant | R B Sheridan

Friday Evening.

56. To Willoughby Lacy

Shuttleworth MS.

[26 Jan. 1779]

Dear Sir,

I have nothing to do with the arrangement of Persons at Mr. G——'s[3] Funeral—I suppose they have ask'd you as a private Friend[4]—in which Light I intended to have gone— 'till I was ask'd to go as mourner, for I believe nobody has an Idea of attending in a Theatrical capacity but the actual Performers[5]— | Yours sincerely | R B Sheridan

Tuesday

W. Lacy Esq.

[1] Father of William Henry Ireland, the forger, and himself an author and engraver. A drawing by him of Mrs. S. is listed in an undated catalogue of Francis Harvey (item 287) in my possession.

[2] Thomas King told Ireland on 6 Jan. 1778 that although S. had promised to read Ireland's opera, *The Flitch of Bacon*, he had not done so. Ireland asked for its return, and after some delay obtained the work. He submitted it again on 19 Sept., on the understanding that S. would pass an opinion as 'from one Gentleman to another'. He sent S. reminders on 25 Nov.

and 29 Dec. See Folger MS. D. a. 82, nos. 6, 11, 12.

[3] Garrick died on 20 Jan. and was buried on 1 Feb. S. was chief mourner.

[4] A copy of the printed invitation to mourners is in the Folger Shakespeare Library, and shows a woman (Melpomene weeping ?) by the side of an hour glass.

[5] Twelve actors from D.L.Th., and twelve from C.G.Th., represented the patent theatres at the funeral. After it was over, S. spent the rest of the day in silence: see J. T. Smith, *Nollekens and his Times* (ed. Whitten, 1920), i. 184.

57. To Richard Rigby[1]

Earl Spencer MS. *Dock.*: Mr. Sheridan | to Mr. Rigby | March 25 1779

24 Mar. 1779[2]

Dear Sir,

I have attempted two or three Dedications to Lady Spencer without being able to please myself in the least.

Scarcely having the Honor of more than a mere Introduction to her Ladyship I don't feel that I have a Right to say much, and I don't believe that she would approve of it if I did. However I had effected a Page or two, when all my Ideas on the subject were put out of sorts by reading Mr. Cumberlands Dedication of *Calypso* to the Duchess of Manchester.[3] On the first impulse of doing something as *unlike* that as possible, I thought it safest to say as little as I could.—Accordingly I have merely inscribed The Verses to *Lady Spencer*; and have put my Prose Compliments into the Fire: which after all I believe is best as the odds are that they were inadequate to the Subject, as the Verses are to the Object they attempt.[4]—Otherwise the Poem should not have been printed without my first shewing you what I had intended to precede it, as you desired.—But I find that if I dont publish it someone else will, and I should lose the opportunity of paying even the slight Tribute I have attempted of my Respect for Lady Spencer.[5] | I have the Honor to be, |

[1] Richard Rigby (1722–88), politician, was Paymaster to the Forces. His letter accompanying the above is still at Althorp. It is dated 'Pay Office, 25th March 1779', and reads: 'Mr. Rigby presents his respects to Lady Spencer, and takes the liberty of sending her Ladyship a letter He has receiv'd this morning from Sheridan. He thinks it but a lame excuse for idleness, as want of Genius must not be supposed to be the real cause.'

[2] I assume that S. wrote the night (Wed.) before Rigby's note was sent.

[3] *Calypso*, a Masque in three acts, was played at C.G.Th. on 20 Mar. 1779, and was by Richard Cumberland. The dedication is laboured, and its attempted compliments are pedantic and tasteless.

[4] *Verses to the Memory of Garrick* consisted of three parts: 'An Exordium or Exhortation to praise Garrick; a most laboured and heavy Description of the Fates of Painters, Sculptors, Poets, and Actors; and an Application or Inference (in the Pulpit Style) that Garrick should have a better Fate than any of them' (*St. James's Chronicle*, 11–13 Mar. 1779). This tribute was presented at D.L.Th. on 11 Mar.

[5] The dedication to Lady Spencer appears before the printed versions of the monody; it runs to forty-seven words, and is dated 25 Mar. 1779.

Dear Sir, | Your very faithful | and obedient Servant |
R B Sheridan

Great Queen-Street
Wednesday Night.

58. To Joseph Cradock[1]

T. S. Blakeney MS. Text from Mr. Blakeney's transcription. *Pub.*:
Cradock, iv. 183. *Address:* – Craddock, Esq. | Gumley, | Leicester-shire.

5 June 1779

My dear Sir,
    If it is in your Power and you will either vote for or not
vote against J. Townshend[2] at this Cambridge Election[3] you
cannot conceive how good-natured a thing you will do—and
how much many People as well as myself will be obliged to
you. | Yours sincerely, | R B Sheridan.

June 5th, 79.

59. To Samuel Ireland

Folger MS. D. a. 82, no. 18. *Address*: Saml. Ireland Esqr. | No 9,
Arundel-Street | Strand *Dock.*: Aug. 29 79

Heston[4]
Aug. 29th. *1779*

Sir,
    There appears to me to be some mistake relative to the
Dramatic Piece of yours in my Hands—at least I am led to
think so from a letter of yours which by some mistake I

[1] (1742–1826). He is best remembered
for his memoirs and his epilogue to *She
Stoops to Conquer*; but he also wrote and
adapted plays.
[2] John Townshend (1757–1833),
second son of George Townshend, was
an intimate friend of S.
[3] James Mansfield gained a narrow
victory over Townshend in the Cambridge University parliamentary election. 'More voters than has been often
known were drawn together from all
quarters' (J. H. Jesse, *George Selwyn and
his Contemporaries* (1844), iv. 187).
[4] S. occupied a large house there
between 1779 and 1781.

had not seen 'till yesterday.—When I met you some time since I mentioned to you that the Piece should certainly be performed—and I do not recollect that you wish'd to have it returned. Since then I believe Mr. King spoke to me on the subject—and I said the same to him. So that I am really at a loss whether I have got hold of a former letter of yours— or not.[1] But if you have changed your intention about the Piece or wish to have it back to do anything to it I'll trouble you for a Line—and it shall be left as you shall appoint, | I am, Sir | Your obedient Servant | R B Sheridan

60. To ——[2]

Pub.: Sichel, i. 609.

[*29 Oct. 1779*]

Let Chaplin know he is to do the Player King to-morrow.[3] What's to be done about sending the copy to the Licenser?[4] It's all ready as soon as I have got it. Who must be put in the farce in Parker's[5] room? Ask if Mr. Davies[6] must be sent to get ready in Lodovico in 'Othello' if Parker should not be able to play on Monday. Get the copy signed by Mrs. Sheridan for the Licence.

Make the principal tragedians rcd: it's a black bill. Put Wright's[7] name in. He does the Beefeater. I must have all the chorus at dinner, etc., to-morrow at five. | R. B. S.

You need not call Parsons.[8] Scratch out Grove.[9]

[1] On 8 Feb. 1779, Ireland asked for the return of his piece, and repeated the request on 16 Mar. He happened to meet S. on 15 Apr. and was told that 'the piece shou'd certainly be brought out next season'. The above letter was a reply to Ireland's note of 16 Mar.: see Folger MS. D. a. 18, nos. 14, 16.

[2] To the prompter or secretary of the company. The first paragraph of the message appears on the verso of one page of the manuscript version of *The Critic*. The second paragraph appears on another.

[3] Henry Chaplin took this part in *Hamlet* on 30 Oct., when *The Critic* (acted for the first time) was also given.

[4] See Letter 61.

[5] Sichel's mistake? Packer usually played Lodovico. He had the part of a justice in *The Critic*.

[6] He played Lodovico for the first time on 1 Nov. 1779.

[7] Roger Wright (d. 1786)?

[8] William Parsons (1736–95) played Sir Fretful Plagiary.

[9] Groves, a minor actor?

61. [To the Licencer of Plays]

Huntington MS. LA 494. [Ph.] Subscription only in S.'s hand.

29 Oct. 1779

Sir

If the following Dramatic Piece of two Acts[1] call'd *The Critic* or a Tragedy Rehears'd meets the Approbation of the Lord Chamberlain We shall have it perform'd at the Theatre Royal Drury Lane | R B Sheridan | For self and Partners.[2]

29th of October
1779

62. To Richard Fitzpatrick[3]

Add. MS. 47582, ff. 177–8. *Address*: Honble | Richd. Fitzpatrick.

Queen-Street [*25 Oct. or 1 Nov. 1779*][4]
Monday Night—

Dear Fitzpatrick—

I have just heard that you are in Town. Gen. Burgoyne[5] will sup here tomorrow Night, after the *Farce*—which I want you to come and abuse with him and Wyndham[6] who are all that will be here.—But the case is this—Wyndham can come better on Wednesday—and when I saw Gen. Burgoyne it was the same to him. Now for some theatrical Reasons Wednesday is much better for me, and if I can then have the Pleasure of your Company I will try if it continues equal to Burgoyne—but if not it must be tomorrow and I wish you

[1] It was advertised as 'a Dramatic Piece in three acts' (*Pub. Adv.*, 30 Oct. 1779). It was printed (1781) in three acts.

[2] For other applications to the licencer by S., see *Catalogue of the Larpent Plays in the Huntington Library* (comp. D. MacMillan, San Marino, 1939), pp. 71–73, 76, 78, 80, 81, 83–88, 90–93, 96–99, 216; and *Theatre Notebook*, xii (1958), 82.

[3] Richard Fitzpatrick (1748–1813) was the second son of John, 1st Earl of Upper Ossory. He was M.P. for Tavi-

stock, 1774–1807, and Secretary at War 1783 and 1806–7. He was also a well-known wit, author of the prologue to *The Critic*, and a lifelong friend of Fox.

[4] George Tufnell (1723–98) withdrew from the Middlesex election on 25 Oct.: see *Pub. Adv.*, 26 Oct. 1779. For S.'s delay in completing his 'farce' (*The Critic*), see *Morn. Chron.*, 2 Oct. 1779, and Kelly, ii. 308–9.

[5] General John Burgoyne (1722–92), soldier and playwright.

[6] William Windham.

would come exceedingly—for I say with my own Author—
'Nothing is so pleasant as a judicious Critic who—'[1] etc. |
Yours sincer[e]ly | R B Sheridan.

Will you direct my Servant whether or not he shall leave a
Note he will have for Burgoyne—to be determined by you
as above—

Tufnel you see gives up—see what exertion does!

63. To Samuel Ireland

Folger MS. D. a. 82, no. 21. *Dock.*: Mr. Sheridan | Jan. 5. 1780

5 Jan. 1780

Mr. Sheridan's Compliments to Mr. Ireland. He will
be glad to see him if convenient to Mr. Ireland on Friday
at one.—

Mr. Sheridan mentioned to Mr. Ireland that He would
write to him as soon as [he] could put his Piece in a course of
Representation and sooner it could be to no purpose. The
Piece is now in his Father's[2] hands and will very soon be
preparing for Rehearsal unless Mr. Ireland wishes to do
anything more to it.[3]

Wednesday Evening

64. To Samuel Ireland

Folger MS. D. a. 82, no. 23. *Address*: S. Ireland Esqr. | Arundel-
Street | Strand *Dock.*: Mr. Sheridan | March 23. 80

23 Mar. 1780
Thursday Night

Dear Sir,

Immediately after the Holydays we *will* go to work.[4] I

[1] Sir Fretful Plagiary says, in *The
Critic*, I. i, 'I am never so well pleased
as when a judicious critic points out any
defect to me; for what is the purpose of
showing a work to a friend, if you don't
mean to profit by his opinion.'

[2] Thomas Sheridan was acting manager at D.L.Th. for the season, 1779–80.

[3] This is S.'s reply to Ireland's letter
of 9 Dec. 1779, in which Ireland had
repeated what he had written in a letter
to S. of 1 Sept. 1779: that his play had
been completed some three years earlier
and might be in need of revision. See
Folger MS. D. a. 82, nos. 19–20.

[4] This is a reply to Ireland's letter of

1780

am really ashamed of the Delay—but the Fact is I must take the Liberty of doing something to the Piece and if the whole Theatre had depended on it I have not yet had it in my Power. | Yours very truly | R B Sheridan

65. To Joseph Cradock

Alec Clunes MS. *Pub.*: Cradock, iii. 80.

July 12th: —80
Great-Queen-Street.

Dear Sir,

After so many Delays, however unavoidable, I hope we shall yet have the satisfaction of giving your Piece[1] to the Public without doing it the injustice which it must have experienced had it been performed at a time when our tragic Heroines[2] were of such small estimation. I trouble you therefore at present only to beg you will not conceive me to be negligent or forgetful in the matter. Tho the Business which has rather hasten'd my writing to you at present relates to a Letter which our Friend Mr. Townshend[3] has this morning shewn me, and which I understand he received from you some time since at Cambridge. You here,[4] in promising him your Vote, make a reserve as referring to and waiting to be decided by my Conduct with regard to the Tragedy. I am sorry I confess that you should think the reserve necessary, but in justice to Townshend[5] I cannot delay reassuring that you yourself shall be the only arbiter as to the time of bringing out the Play in Question, and whenever you think the Company able to do it justice (which in

16 Mar. 1780, reminding S. of his broken promises. A year later (7 Mar. 1781), Ireland sent S. a cutting letter and asked him to return the piece. It was not acted at D.L.Th. See Folger MS. D. a. 82, nos. 22, 24.

[1] *The Czar*. As far back as 14 Sept. 1778 Garrick had written to Cradock to apologize for being unable to attend the first night: see C. Oman, *David Garrick* (1958), p. 367.

[2] The leading tragic actresses at D.L.Th. were Mary Ann Yates (1728–87) and Elizabeth Younge (1744 ?–97).

[3] He was again a parliamentary candidate for Cambridge University, and was duly returned.

[4] Possibly 'have'.

[5] The passage, 'which our friend . . . justice to Townshend', is not printed by Cradock for obvious reasons.

my Judgement it will be next winter) it shall immediately be put into Rehearsal. | your's sincerely | R B Sheridan

I am at present endeavouring to engage Mrs. Siddons,[1] of the Bath Theatre, which if I effect I will inform you.

66. To Joseph Cradock

R. G. E. Sandbach MS. Text from Mr. Sandbach's transcription.

[*1780?*]
St. James's [?]
Monday ——

Mr. Sheridan's Compliments to Mr. Craddock and will be very happy to see Mr. Craddock if he will do him the favour to call at this office[?] tomorrow before twelve.

67. To Joseph Cradock

Pub.: Cradock, iii. 80. *Address*: J. Cradock, Esq., Royal Hotel Pall Mall.

[*1780–4*]
Tuesday.

Dear Sir,
If I had known you had been in town, I should have applied for your determination about the Tragedy,[2] which I had put into Mr. Younger's[3] hands, to be ready, if you had no objection to be performed now. | Your ever sincere and obedient, | R. B. Sheridan.

[1] Sarah Siddons (1755–1831) had been unsuccessful when she played at D.L.Th. under Garrick in 1775–6. She acted in the provinces for some years, joining the Bath Theatre in 1778. Lefanu, p. 380, says that Thomas Sheridan brought her to S.'s notice. She did not return to D.L.Th. until 1782.
[2] *The Czar* was not acted at D.L.Th. but was printed in 1824.
[3] Joseph Younger died on 4 Sept. 1784, after being deputy manager at D.L.Th. 'about three or four years' (*Gent. Mag.* liv (1784), 717).

68. To Ozias Humphry[1]

Osborn MS. Text from Mr. Alastair Wood's transcription. *Pub.*: Watkins, i. 253–4. *Dock.*: Mr. Humphries from Mr. Sheridan.

[*Aug. 1780*]

My dear Sir,

I am very much obliged to you for the trouble you have taken and for your letter.[2] I assure you I am the farthest in the world from being indifferent in this matter—for something has happened since I saw you to make me think still more of it.—Do you think it would be impolitic if I were to talk a little with our Friend Crispin? If you were to send him to me I could do it without letting him conceive that I was the Person in question. They are damn'd Fellows if they think to mend themselves by choosing a Scotsman and a *Mac* too! —But let me see, you will be at Honiton on wednesday and I may have a Letter from you on Friday and I assure you I shall be most seriously obliged to you if you will get the best intelligence you can immediately—my reason for wishing to be so quick in it is that if there appears a tolerable Probability I would get Sir G. Young[3] applied to immediately not to engage his interest, if he has not done it,—I have been looking at the account of the Voters of Honiton and I find that Sir G. Young had them almost all for him and it must be bad if he supports this Scot,— | yours faithfully | R B Sheridan.

---

[1] Ozias Humphry, R.A. (1742–1810), lodged as a young man with the Linleys at Bath. He was a native of Honiton, and S. was exploring the possibility of becoming its member of parliament. Honiton was a corrupt borough with a long allegiance to the Yonges.

[2] Humphry wrote to S. from Exeter on 13 Aug. 1780 (Harvard MS.) to report on two of the candidates for Honiton: 'Mr. McLeod is a nephew to Mr. Bacon who was formerly an unsuccessful Candidate to represent the Borough. Mr. Cox is in Treaty for a considerable estate . . . if he make the purchase it will give him a command of near fifty additional voters. . . . tis understood that beside the present candidates two or three others hold themselves ready to propose.' At the election, Alexander Macleod was returned with Sir George Yonge; the unsuccessful candidate was Lawrence Cox. See *Bath Chronicle*, 13 Sept. 1780. Macleod was unseated in 1781.

[3] 5th baronet (1733–1812), M.P. for Honiton, 1754–61, 1763–96.

Monday

Mrs. Crewe who is now home, hearing I was writing to you, sends her Compliments and says you were one of her oldest acquaintance.[1]—If you find any good in having one or two of these at H[oniton] do.[2]

69. To Ozias Humphry

Pub.: Partly in P. & S.C., 19 Dec. 1850, lot 601; and in *A.P.C.* (1917–18), p. 215.

18 August 1780

[Refers to some purchase that is being negotiated[3] and the possibility of his going to Bridgwater with Fox.]

70. To Ozias Humphry

Salt MS. *Pub.*: Watkins, i. 251–2. *Address*: Mr. Humphry | Newman-Street | Oxford Road

[*July–Sept. 1780*]

My dear Sir,

Upon my soul I believe you were wrong about Honeton—as I have been close to it—but tho' wanted was obliged to go to another Place I am after.[4] Therefore now do two things—1st: write a Letter to Honiton (by express better) and tell them that before the election yet a good man and true may offer and pay them too, and that they should act accordingly[5]

---

[1] Frances Anne (d. 1818), wife of John, later 1st Lord, Crewe (1742–1829). Humphry's account book (Add MS. 22948, f. 9) notes his receiving eight guineas from Crewe 'for a small portrait of Mrs. Crew leaning on her Hand'. This entry is dated 21 June 1768.

[2] Watkins does not print the postscript.

[3] Payment for the Honiton burgesses ? Or those of Stafford ? He had to raise £1,000 to secure election at Stafford: see the *Cyclopaedian Magazine*, ii

(Dublin, 1808), 68; and Watkins, i. 255.

[4] The *Bath Chronicle*, 27 July 1780, noted the arrival at Bath of 'the Hon. C. J. Fox; . . . Mr. and Mrs. Sheridan'. The *Morn. Post*, 6 Sept. 1780, reported that S. had gone to Stafford to offer himself as a candidate. Sichel, i. 614, suggests that some noblemen wanted S. to stand for Wootton Bassett.

[5] This is possibly Humphry's letter of 3 Sept. 1780 'To the revd. Mr. Tucker' (Royal Academy Library,

1780

—2dly send me a Letter to the Post office Bridgewater which will certify that I am the Person and puff me too—all this is in case on my return from where I am going, if unsuccessful, I should want to try Honiton—having an offer of very strong support. Do these two things. | Yours in real haste | R B Sheridan.

71. [To His Stafford Supporters]

Pub.: Morn. Chron., 18 Sept. 1780.

[*13 Sept. 1780*]

Gentlemen,
Having had no opportunity yesterday after the close of the poll to return you our thanks, as we wished to do, for the steady and independent support which we have so successfully received from you, we take this most expeditious method of expressing our grateful and hearty acknowledgment, for the manly confidence you have reposed in us, and the high honour you have done us, in chusing us your Representatives in Parliament, for the *free*[1] Borough of Stafford.

We have found you men of your words—we will deserve the continuance of your friendship by serving you faithfully, *as you have served us*—if we deceive you, you will have no difficulty in turning us out again, as we shall deserve; independent candidates will no more be afraid to offer themselves, for you have now made it appear that you are the *masters of your own rights*, and that you are determined to hold them in your own hands, and to keep your Borough free. | We have the honour to be, | Gentlemen, | Your faithful servants, | Ed. Monckton,[2] | Rich. Brinsley Sheridan.

Humphry Corr., ii, no. 112). Watkins, i. 252–3, omits the postscript: 'Mr. Baker particularly Interests himself for Mr. Sheridan and the moment he is determin'd to come will exert himself to the utmost in his favor.' But this letter does not mention payment.
[1] Free from the taint of belonging to one wealthy man. On 19 Mar. 1781

John Kenderdine and three other Stafford burgesses wrote to S. (Harvard MS.) to say, 'we propose to have a feast on the 12th September it being the day of the Election which day we look upon to be the Day of our deliverance from Slavery'.
[2] Edward Monckton (1744–1832), son of John, Viscount Galway.

72. To the Duchess of Devonshire[1]

The Duke of Devonshire MS. *Pub.*: 'Selections from the Letters of Georgiana, Duchess of Devonshire', ed. the Duchess of Devonshire, *The Anglo-Saxon Review*, ii (1899), 46–47.

London, Sept. 19, 1780.

Madam,

I am entirely at a loss how to thank Your Grace for the Honor and service which Your Grace's condescending to interest yourself in my election at Stafford has been of to me. Having sent the Recommendation which I had the Honor to receive from Lady Spencer to his Lordship's Agent, I profited by the Permission allow'd to me to make use of your Grace's Letter as my first and best introduction to Lord Spencer's Interest in the Town. I assure Your Grace that I found good effects from it even out of the circle of influence which Lord Spencers Property and Character so justly maintain in Stafford. It is no Flattery to say that the Duchess of Devonshire's name commands an implicit admiration whenever it is mentioned, and I found some that had had opportunities of often seeing and of hearing more of your Grace who were so proud of the Distinction as to require no other motive to support anyone who appear'd honor'd with Your Graces recommendation.

Having written to Lady Spencer I need not intrude on Your Grace to express how highly obliged I feel to Lord Spencer. And I have avoided asking Mr. Fox[2] to thank your Grace on my account, because I am perhaps even unfairly ambitious to owe all the Gratitude myself. | I have the Honor to be | with the greatest Respect | your Grace's | most devoted humble Servant | R B Sheridan

I ought to mention to your Grace That there is not a Doubt of Mr. Fox carrying his Election here tho' the matter is not likely to be very soon over. He canvasses with the greatest

[1] Georgiana Cavendish, Duchess of Devonshire (1757–1806), was the eldest daughter of the 1st Earl Spencer, and wife of William, 5th Duke of Devonshire. She was a woman of many talents, and great sweetness of manner. In the next twenty years, S. was on terms of close friendship with her.

[2] Charles James Fox (1749–1806), second son of Henry, 1st Lord Holland. He stood for Westminster at this election and was returned with Rodney.

industry and treats his good Friends with a Speech every Day besides.

73. [To Thomas Dudley]

The Historical Society of Pennsylvania MS.

London Oct 16th: 80

My dear Sir,

Among Those Friends whom I have returned my Thanks to by Letter since I left Stafford it is true you are the last I write to, but it is with the greatest sincerity I declare that it has not been from my thinking that I owe more to any Person's Friendship or Assistance than I do to Mr. Dudley's.[1] I was in hopes since I have been in Town to have had the Pleasure of seeing or hearing from your Brother, with whom from what you mention'd to me at Stafford, I had the expectation of having the pleasure to be acquainted before my return. On this Idea I delay'd writing to you, but tho' I have been disappointed in this hope, and tho' this comes very late yet I cannot reconcile it to myself to see you again without having endeavor'd to remove any appearance of neglect or omission on my Part since the time of my receiving such kind assistance from your Friendship and Support.

As I shall be at Somerford[2] on Wednesday I shall shortly have the Pleasure of personally acknowledging this to you— till when | believe me, dear Sir, | with great esteem | your obliged and sincere Friend | R B Sheridan.

74. To Mrs. Thrale

Public Library of Victoria MS., Melbourne. [Ph.]

9 Nov. [1780]

Mr. Sheridan presents his Compliments to Mrs. Thrale.[3]

[1] Presumably Thomas Dudley, one of S.'s strongest supporters at Stafford in the next thirty years. In 1788 he was listed in the number of Staffordshire gentlemen paying Game duty, as of 'Shut End, Esq.' (*Birmingham Gazette*, 22 Sept. 1788).

[2] Edward Monckton's house, Somerford Hall, seven miles north of Wolverhampton.

[3] Hester Lynch Thrale, afterwards Piozzi (1741–1821).

He is extremely sorry that at the Time He received Dr.
Delap's[1] Tragedy He did not perceive that it was accompanied by a Card from Mrs. Thrale desiring him to acknowledge its coming safe, or Mr. Sheridan would have
executed Mrs. Thrale's commands before. Dr. Delap's
Friends may be assured that the Tragedy shall have every
attention paid to it in Mr. Sheridan's Power and as speedily
as possible.

Great Queen Street.
Nov. 9th.

75. To Frances Greville[2]

Pub.: *The Critic* (1781), as epistle dedicatory.

1781

Madam,
    In requesting your permission to address the following
pages to you, which as they aim themselves to be critical,
require every protection and allowance that approving taste
or friendly prejudice can give them, I yet ventured to mention no other motive than the gratification of private friendship and esteem. Had I suggested a hope that your implied
approbation would give a sanction to their defects, your
particular reserve, and dislike to the reputation of critical
taste, as well as of poetical talent, would have made you
refuse the protection of your name to such a purpose. However, I am not so ungrateful as now to attempt to combat
this disposition in you. I shall not here presume to argue
that the present state of poetry claims and expects every
assistance that taste and example can afford it; nor endeavor
to prove that a fastidious concealment of the most elegant

---

[1] The Rev. John Delap (1725–1812)
was rector of Lewes, Sussex. His tragedy,
The Royal Suppliants, was performed at
D.L.Th. on 17 Feb. 1781, with a prologue by Mrs. Thrale. See J. L. Clifford, *Hester Lynch Piozzi* (Oxford,
1941), p. 195; *Thraliana* (ed. K. C.
Balderston, Oxford, 1942), i. 484–5;
J. Hemlow, *The History of Fanny*

Burney (Oxford, 1958), p. 133.
    [2] Frances Greville (born Macartney)
was the wife of Richard Fulke Greville
of Wilbury House. She was a literary
lady, well known for her 'Ode to Indifference'. She died in 1789. S. probably
knew her through his friendship with
her daughter, Frances Crewe.

productions of judgment and fancy is an ill return for the possession of those endowments.—Continue to deceive yourself in the idea that you are known only to be eminently admired and regarded for the valuable qualities that attach private friendships, and the graceful talents that adorn conversation. Enough of what you have written, has stolen into full public notice to answer my purpose: and you will, perhaps, be the only person, conversant in elegant literature, who shall read this address and not perceive that by publishing your particular approbation of the following drama, I have a more interested object than to boast the true respect and regard with which | I have the honour to be, | Madam, | Your very sincere, | And obedient humble servant | R. B. Sheridan.

76. To His Brother

W.T. *Pub.*: Rae, i. 382–4.

April 2nd. 1782.

Dear Charles,

Tho' I have time only to send you a very few lines to Night I will not omit to convince you how very much a man of Business I am become, by acknowledging the receipt of a Letter from you[1] this Day—

I take it for granted that you know from our Newspapers that it is *The Under secretary of State*[2] who is become thus punctual.—Whether you may think I have chosen prudently or not I can't tell, but it is the situation of all others that I have thought the rightest for me to take—I wanted to force myself into Business Punctuality and information:—and when I resolved to be in their[3] way I resolved also to sacrifice every other object.—The want of attention or knowledge

---

[1] Charles Sheridan became M.P. for Belturbet, in the Irish Parliament, in 1776, and was called to the Bar in 1780. He was, at this period, counsel to the Barrack Board. His letter is probably the one printed by Moore, i. 370, as from Dublin, on 27 Mar. 1782. He begged S. to use his influence on his behalf.

[2] With the fall of North's ministry, a new administration under Shelburne and Rockingham took office. S. obtained the post of Under-Secretary of State for the Northern Department, an office that brought him into close contact with the Secretary, Charles Fox. [3] Rae reads 'this'.

of Business shall not positively be an objection to me in anything I may aim at hereafter—as you shall see and hear—
and so also will you hear of Mr. Secretary Fox—

But to the Point you wish to know so much.—Lord Carlisle[1] is certainly to come home immediately—and The Duke
of Portland[2] to go over to you.—My very particular Friend,[3]
next to Fox himself, will be his secretary—under these
circumstances I need not add that now France[4] is not likely to
be forgotten—but I should wish to know from you immediately somewhat that you wish to post[5] for or the kind of
Line.—As for the Letter to Lord Carlisle no one was to
blame and I not in the least[6]—for the matter was, that when
Fox came to write the awkwardness of it struck him more
forcibly than when he promised—and the event shews[7]—
but if they will do a good thing at posting, it will be no harm.[8]
You will have a new commander-in-chief—a Friend of
mine too[9]—but tho' there[10] will be no secrets in a few Days,
you will see that they had better not be publish'd by you—

I wish you would have (if you are intimate enough) a full
and friendly talk with Mr. Grattan[11]—and tell me what the
effect would be of repealing the Declaratory term[12] here,
suppos[e] moved by the new secretary I mean the Irish one,
and whether it would not be judged right on both sides afterwards to settle in some kind of convention a sort of union, of
commercial regulation, and a security of future agreement

---

[1] Frederick Howard, 5th Earl of
Carlisle (1748–1825), was viceroy of
Ireland, 1780–2. He was an intimate
friend of Fox.

[2] William Cavendish Bentinck, 3rd
Duke of Portland (1738–1809).

[3] Richard Fitzpatrick.

[4] Rae reads 'that man Foine is',
which seems even less satisfactory than
W.T. The allusion, surely, is to Charles
Sheridan's letter of 27 Mar., where he
hopes that Carlisle's administration will
remain in office in Ireland and that Fox
will write Carlisle a letter to obtain a
government post for Charles Sheridan.
'Francis', his brother's second name,
would fit the sense, if S. were being
whimsical.

[5] Rae reads 'push for'.

[6] That it was not written and sent.

[7] Change of viceroy.

[8] Rae reads 'at parting, it will do no
harm'.

[9] Burgoyne.   [10] Rae reads 'these'.

[11] Henry Grattan (1746–1820) pressed
strongly at this time for legislative independence for Ireland. See his letter to
Fox of 18 April (*Fox Corr.* i. 403–9).

[12] Rae reads 'Declaratory Law'. In
the debate in the Irish parliament of
13 June, on Yelverton's bill to repeal
Poynings's law, Grattan said 'he wished
to avoid moving for an Act here declaratory of our rights until after the repeal
of the 6th Geo. I. . . . . Mr. Fitzpatrick
opposed the idea, said a simple repeal
came up to our demand, and was sufficient' (*Beresford Corr.* i. 207–8).

and co-operation in great matters by which some wider bond of connexion[1] than merely the having the first magistrate in common!—you know my sentiments and all I mean about it. I have pressed[2] extremely this repeal—but it is wonderful how little any People here have thought or enquired about Ireland—it seems to me now the precise time for it.[3]

God bless you Dear Charles and if you have any good in you write me a long letter and if you can get the direct and candid[4] sentiments and views of the real acting People on your side, I don't mean the Government side, but such men as Grattan and Lord Charlemont,[5] it may be of service both to you and the cause to furnish me with them and I should think that under the new system here they would have no repugnance to speak out and really say what they think had best be done here— | Yours ever sincerely, | R. B. Sheridan

I shall write to Liley[6] in a Day or two.

77. To the Earl of Surrey[7]

The Duke of Norfolk, Arundel Castle MS. Text from Mr. F. W. Steer's transcription. *Pub.*: Rhodes, p. 97.

April 4th, 82

My dear Lord,
    The Truth is that what you desire[8] (tho in my opinion it is a compliment from you to ask it) is a matter that does not rest wholly with me, and it is a point about which I have had some bickering with my Partners, who talk of *general Rules* being broken, *Partialities* etc. etc.—however I hope I am settling it to your satisfaction, the committee have never

[1] Rae reads 'union'.
[2] W.T. 'peopl'd'. Possibly an error by S. I follow Rae.
[3] On 25 Apr. Portland wrote to Buckingham from Dublin: 'Unless large concessions are made *there will be an end of all Government. . . .*' (Fitzwilliam MS. (Sheffield)).
[4] Rae reads 'cordial'.
[5] James Caulfield, 1st Earl of Charlemont (1728–99).

[6] Possibly Thomas Liley, 'an ingenious schoolmaster at Enfield' (*Gent. Mag.* xlix (1779), 138.
[7] Charles Howard (1746–1815), who succeeded his father in 1786 as 11th Duke of Norfolk. He was a Protestant, and a Whig.
[8] He sought the freedom of the greenroom. The *Pocket Magazine*, iii (1795), 205, stated: 'It has been said, that Mr. Sheridan could never refuse any one.'

given any formal leave but to those who claim a right, others drop in as private Friends and your Lordship will do me the honor to use that claim: and when I abandon my Power there[1] I will do my best to leave it as a Priviledge.—I shall certainly be obliged to give up my Theatrical administration, and I am even at present holding it, like Lord North on the Day of your Lordships motion,[2] 'till a new and I hope a better government is fix'd.

For my own Part I have taken a resolution, which I have confidence enough in myself to know I can keep, to give myself up thoroughly and diligently to a Business and a Pursuit[3] which whether I am right or not is more to my fancy and Feelings— | I have the honor to be | my dear Lord | Your's sincerely | R B Sheridan.

78. To Edmund Burke[4]

Fitzwilliam MS. (Sheffield). *Dock.*: Mr. Sheridan

St. James's
Sunday Evening—April 7th. [1782]

My dear Sir,

On tuesday or wednesday next it is proposed to send an address from the Common-Council to his Majesty on his changing his ministry,[5] and professing confidence etc. etc. There are two or three Gentlemen who have sent us Performances of their own penning for this Purpose, but which

---

[1] It was reported that S. would give up his share in D.L.Th. at the end of the season, and that 'the gentlemen in treaty with him for the purchase of it, are said to be Mr. Colman, and Captain Thompson' (*Morn. Her.*, 6 Apr. 1782). Nothing came of this. Instead, Thomas King was offered the management, with the option of purchasing a share within two years. See *Lond. Chron.*, 25–27 July 1782.

[2] Surrey had given notice in 8 Mar. 1782, that North's government no longer possessed the confidence of the country, when North himself entered the Commons and announced the King's intention to change the administration.

[3] Politics.

[4] Edmund Burke (1729–97), statesman and writer.

[5] On Apr. 9 1782, J. Adair wrote to Rockingham: '. . . the business of this day in the City terminated very agreeably . . . the Address to the King passing at length *without one dissentient voice*. Everybody vied with each other in expressions of confidence in, and approbation of our new administration' (Fitzwilliam MS. (Sheffield)). The Corporation of London went in procession to St. James's and presented their address on Friday, 12 Apr.

appear very objectionable. Mr. Fox has desired me to trouble you on the subject, and to endeavour to perswade you to give them something as short as you please which I am sure would at once put an end to the competition of these gentlemen who appear extremely tenacious at present of their several pretensions—and nothing that they have written would be right, or proper to be adopted by any other Place—if this finds you too busy I beg you will excuse the interruption and | believe me Dear Sir, | your very sincere | and faithful Servant | R B Sheridan

79. To His Brother

Harvard MS.

Monday Night
April 8th. [*1782*]

Dear Charles,

I have just received your's—which of course was written before you had heard from me. When you receive those [you] will understand our state here and my telling you very shortly (which is all I have time to do) our News of to Day. Eden[1] to the astonishment of every body came down to the house to day and after some odd talk move[d] for leave to bring in a bill to repeal Part of the 6th. of George 1st.—He has acted like a man without any understanding. Lord Carlisle writes that he is sent over to give the new administration all assistance and intelligence in his Power, he took wrath at something, or pretended it about Lord Carlisle, and most imprudently declines giving any information whatever, and even wrote this in a Letter to Lord Shelburne.[2] Then comes down without any communication and throws this Question

[1] William Eden, later 1st Lord Auckland (1744–1814), had been Irish Secretary under Carlisle. He returned to England and tried to embarrass the new administration by proposing the repeal of the hated act of 6th Geo. I ('for the better securing the dependency of Ireland upon the Crown of Great Britain') without prior discussion. Fox charged him with giving the new government no time to frame its policy, and Eden withdrew his motion.

[2] Sir William Petty, 2nd Earl of Shelburne, later 1st Marquis of Lansdowne (1737–1805), was Secretary for the Southern Department in Rockingham's administration.

into the house, telling them how shocking it will be if they think to evade it—and that he shall go off to Ireland to-morrow and report if they do. I never saw a man so baited or his conduct so universally reprobated.—It was rather an auk[w]ard situation for me, however I managed to declare I would vote with him if he divided, but was obliged to abuse his conduct as upon my soul I think it merited. He at last with a very ill grace withdrew his motion—he has entirely lost all credit here by this maneuvre—. There is a Cabinet now sitting about Ireland and tomorrow there will be a message from the King to the Commons—saying there are jealousies etc. in Ireland and deserving their considera-tion etc.—

It would be a right and spirited thing for some member with you immediately on Edens appearance in your house to call on him to state the information (which you have a right to *suppose*) he gave to ministers here of the state of Ireland.— If you mean to do well use all your interest that your house may adjourn a little from the sixteenth,[1] and you will find every thing is meant here that Irish heart can wish.— | your ever | R B Sheridan

I find I can send this by express, but I have time to add no more.

80. To His Brother

Osborn MS.

London
Saturday April 20th: 1782.

No News, so but one Line and that is to beg you will not be so lazy as only to answer my Letters[2] but let me know about things as I will you—without waiting to hear. When I write next I'll answer your others | your's Dear Charles ever | R B Sheridan

---

[1] After a long speech by Grattan on 16 Apr. the Irish House of Commons adjourned until 22 Apr.

[2] C. F. Sheridan replied on 26 Apr. 1782: '. . . I have written twice for your once . . .' (Widener MS.).

81. To Richard Fitzpatrick

Add. MS. 47582, ff. 90–94. *Address*: Right Honble. | Richd: Fitz-
patrick *Fr.*: R B Sheridan *Dock.*: Sheridan | May 20th, 1782

Monday Night
May 20th: 1782.

Dear Richard,

I intended this evening to have written you a very long
Letter—but it will be a very short one, as it is late and
I am to send it to Lord Clermont's.[1] My not having written
before you are to attribute entirely to the ill character you
gave your Post-office, and you are not to recollect that I
might have sent by the Messengers. But now that Ireland
has got her Rights and your administration is so well entitled to prosper I shall write with Pleasure, and I only
beg you to imitate my Punctuality. If this was to be the
long Letter, which it is not to be, I should endeavour to
state to you what appears to me to be the general situation
of internal Politics here, which probably Charles has not
time to do very fully, but on this subject I really will send
you some Pages, and then I will communicate regularly.—
At present I must not omit giving an opinion (which
Charles agrees in entirely, and which indeed he means to
write to you upon particularly and has desired me to mention
it if I wrote to Night) on the style and tenour, as they strike
me at least, of THE *Secretary's*[2] Dispatches to the Duke of P.[3]
It is impossible not to see a reserve and a disingenuous
management in them that cannot be very pleasing to you
who are to act under them. There is a caution of fixing the
Duke of P.'s representations of the State of Ireland as the
sole responsible Ground for the concessions which have
been made. He is to be the Person answerable for the consequences, and every acquiescence to the arrangements which
he has thought necessary to the carrying on the Government
is dwelt on as a particular Grace and grant of Power to him.

---

[1] William Fortescue, 1st Earl Clermont (1722–1806).
[2] Extracts from Shelburne's dispatches to Portland and Fitzpatrick are
printed in Lord Fitzmaurice's *Life of
William Earl of Shelburne* (1912), ii.
95–103.
[3] Portland.

All this must strike you, and I can only say that if it did not you would think so at once were you to connect it with the whole of the conduct of that Person in every other article here, but if there is any use in remarking on it, it is in saying what Charles finds the best method of counteracting a similar conduct here, and that appears to be *not giving way* or *conceding in the least*.—If Lord S.[1] does not feel that a Person in the Duke of P.'s situation undertaking the Government of Ireland in such a situation as the country was and is, can scarcely claim too much, either of support or respect, it would perhaps prevent future Difficulties to tell him so at once. And now observe you, I have Charles's authority, independent of my own opinion, for believing that you are a Brother-in-Law[2] void of irrational prejudices or I should not write so, but if I am to tell you truly how things are going on, and likely to go on here I must say a good deal on this subject, which is the horrible Part of the Business here, and which, tho' things are pretty quiet now, will I doubt overturn all and in the worst way—and so of that hereafter. In the mean [time] take care that you teach Godliness to the Bishops, and do you in particular set them a good example by the purity of your conduct and the strictness of your Life, in order that they may set a good example to others and so the Land become sanctified and your government approved in the eyes of a pious Prince and a pious Minister.

Now as for news. You know all there is of course, and from Burgoyne what is thought of it—I wish Pigott[3] was not now let to go and supersede Rodney,[4] because Ministers make themselves a Party against Fortune and unnecessarily take a responsiblity off her shoulders on their own. You however are a strict politician and I dare say think otherwise.— No News of Howe.[5]

But we have had this Night news of a private nature as good as possible from Russia—by a messenger—the Empress seeming in a bloody rage against the Dutch and re-

[1] Shelburne.
[2] Fox's brother Stephen married Fitzpatrick's sister Mary.
[3] Hugh Pigot (1722–92), admiral, was appointed commander-in-chief in the West Indies, in place of Rodney.
[4] George Rodney, later 1st Lord Rodney (1719–92), admiral. See p. 148.
[5] Richard, 4th Viscount, later Earl, Howe (1726–99), admiral. Commander in the Channel.

1782

solving either to force them to make Peace or to help us—
which is thought very good.—In the East things are bad
notwithstanding the supplement to the Gazette,[1]—Full
Powers are going to Grenville,[2] tho' it is not expected the
Treaty will come to anything now. Why won't you give
honest Irishmen your good Places there? and here after I
had heard a fine report about my Brother is Charles[3] at the
Duke of P.'s instance canvassing and entreating and almost
advertising for *anyone* who is an Englishman and willing to
suceed Lees![4] I have been ask'd much to write to you about
this—and I did not for two reasons one because I understood you were very good about it, and the other a foolish
one, but it really looks as if any Person in the world might
have it, for neither Charles nor I of course, nor *Fraser*[5] when
applied to to Day could think of one to send to you.

I ought now to finish with sending you any private news
I could collect—but how should I know what is going on in
the idle and dissipated world!—

You have heard the Fate of our Parliamentary reform.—
About which we took a good deal of Pains, but we were
bullied outrageously[6]—however whatever you may hear
depend on it the thing gets strength. Burke on this subject
acquitted himself on Friday last with a most magnanimous
Indiscretion, attack'd W. Pitt in a scream of Passion, and
swore Parliament was and always had been precisely what it
ought to be, and that all people who thought of reforming it
wanted to overturn the constitution.[7] I have written five

[1] The capture of Ceylon from the Dutch was described in the *London Gazette*, 18 May 1782, in Admiral Hughes's dispatch concerning the attack on Nengapatam, and the articles of capitulation.

[2] See p. 147.

[3] Fox.

[4] Charles Sheridan was appointed Under-Secretary for Military Affairs (vice John Lees) on 6 June 1782.

[5] Possibly W. Fraser, Under-Secretary of State for the Northern Department.

[6] Pitt's motion 'to enquire into the state of the representation' of 7 May, was defeated by 161 to 141. Burgoyne

said of S.'s speech for the motion: 'Sheridan much above anything he has yet done in the House. I think I never heard more acute wit than part of his reply to the advocate . . .' (Add. MS. 47582, f. 76).

[7] On Sawbridge's motion to shorten the length of parliaments. Pitt supported it, saying that those who governed by corruption always voted against the motion. 'Mr. Burke caught fire at his friend's remark and warmly asserted his own purity in always opposing it [i.e. the motion]. Mr. Burke defended his conduct, . . . in one of the most able speeches we ever heard in Parliament' (*Morn. Chron.*, 18 May 1782).

146

times as much as I meant. | Your's ever sincer[e]ly | R B Sheridan.

tell me if one may send you word carelessly by the Post of anything that occurs—as I conceive Charles must grow Lazy when the warm weather comes, if ever it does come, and then I mean to put in for all the Punctuality

82. To Thomas Grenville

Pub.: *Court and Cabinets*, i. 27–28.

St. James's, May 21st, 1782.

Dear Grenville,

You are certainly one of the best negotiators that ever negotiated;[1] and so says the King, your royal master, who is going to send you the fine silver box[2] which you receive with this, and which, with great envy, I learn is your property; and which, if the serious modesty of your former despatch could have been seriously construed, you would not have been entitled to. Though I have not written before, have not my punctuality and remembrance appeared conspicuous in the newspapers you receive? These tell you all the private news, and all that is important of public you will have heard before you receive this; so this must be a very short letter, and indeed the messenger is almost going; and Charles has been writing to you, which is another reason for my saying very little. Mr. Oswald[3] talks very sanguinely

[1] Fox nominated Grenville as envoy to the French government, to tell Vergennes that Britain was prepared to negotiate a general peace on the basis of independence for America, and a return to the position of 1763.

[2] On 8 June, Grenville wrote to S.: 'The silver box which you say you looked at with envy I no sooner saw than I heartily wished back at His Majesty's Silversmith's, and in the answer I wrote to Charles I made an early protest against any ministerial establishment, nor has a ten days' possession made me more enamoured of the King's Sign Manual or the parchment that hangs to

it' (Add. MS. 47563, f. 22).

[3] Richard Oswald of Auchencruive (1705–84), a business man sent by Shelburne to Benjamin Franklin in Paris to say that the new administration wished for peace but would continue the war if the French terms were excessive. He returned to England with a message from Franklin to Shelburne; on 23 April, the Cabinet decided to give him authority to settle preliminaries with Franklin. Grenville was afterwards nominated to discuss terms with Vergennes. George III saw Oswald as 'a useful check' on the negotiations carried on by Grenville for Fox; but Fox himself saw in Oswald's

about Franklin, and says he is more open to you than he has been to any one; but he is a Scotsman, and belonging to Lord Shelburne. If the business of an American treaty seemed likely to prosper in your hands, I should not think it improbable that Lord Shelburne would try to thwart it. Oswald has not yet seen Lord Shelburne; and by his cajoling manner to *our secretary*[1] and eagerness to come to him, I do not feel much prejudiced in his favour; but probably I judge wrongly whenever the other secretary is concerned, for I grow suspicious of him in every respect, the more I see of every transaction of his.[2]

I am just told that the messenger is ready, so more in my next. There is no particular news. The Dutch are got back to the Texel. Lord Howe still off there, but nothing likely to come of it. Sir G. Rodney, notwithstanding his victory, is to be recalled, and Pigott is sailed.[3] This I think very magnanimous in the Ministers or very impolitic;[4] events must justify, but it is putting themselves too much in their power.

We had a good illumination for this news.[5] You see how we go on in Parliament by the papers; we were bullied outrageously about our poor Parliamentary Reform; but it will do at last, in spite of you all. | Yours ever sincerely, | R. B. Sheridan.

83. To Thomas Grenville

Pub.: *Court and Cabinets*, i. 30–32.

St. James's, May 26th, 1782.

My Dear Grenville,
    Charles not being well, I write to you at his desire, that

work an attempt by Shelburne to conduct the negotiations with France as well as America. See Fitzmaurice, op. cit. ii. 117–28; and G. Stourzh, *Benjamin Franklin and American Foreign Policy* (Chicago, 1954), pp. 169–73.
    [1] Fox.
    [2] Shelburne had a reputation for disingenuousness. Note *Fox Corr.* i. 366 for S.'s 'spirit of prophecy'.
    [3] The Whigs blamed Rodney for pillaging St. Eustatia; he also was

thought to be a favourite of George III. He was recalled, and Pigot was sent to take his place. News of Rodney's victory over De Grasse on 12 April arrived in London on 18 May, and an express was sent to Plymouth to stop Pigot sailing, but it arrived too late. See H.M.C., *Various Collections* (1909), vi. 334.
    [4] The recall certainly made the ministry unpopular.
    [5] London was illuminated on 18 May to celebrate Rodney's victory.

you may not be surprized at having no private letter from him with the despatch which Mr. Oswald brings you.[1] There is not room, I believe, for much communication of any very private nature on the subject of your instructions and situation, as his public letter, you will see, is very sincerely to the purpose. If anything in it admits of modification, or is not to be very literally taken, I should conceive it to be the recommendation of explicitness with Oswald; on which subject I own I have suggested doubts; and Charles wishes you to have a caution for your own discretion to make use of.[2]

I perceive uniformly (from our intercepted information) that all these *city* negotiators—Mr. Wentworths,[3] Bourdeaux,[4] etc.—insinuate themselves into these sort of affairs merely for private advantages, and make their trust principally subservient to stock-jobbing views, on which subject there appears to be a surprising communication with Paris. Mr. Oswald's officiousness in bringing over your despatch and other things I have been told since by those who know him, lead me to form this kind of opinion of him; but you will judge where this will apply to any confidence that should be placed in him.

Surely, whatever the preliminaries of a treaty for peace with France may be, it would be our interest, if we could, to drop even mentioning the Americans in them; at least the seeming to grant anything to them as at the requisition of France.[5] France now denies our ceding Independence to America to be anything given to them, and declines to allow anything for it. In my opinion it would be wiser in them to insist ostentatiously (and even to make a point of allowing

[1] Oswald arrived in Paris on 31 May (*Fox Corr.* iv. 213) with Fox's dispatch (ibid., pp. 206–9).

[2] The intrigues of the rival negotiators and their masters are obvious in the *Fox Corr.* i. 344, 359–66; iv. 200–6, 245–6; Fitzmaurice, op. cit. ii. 135–47.

[3] Paul Wentworth (d. 1793), stockbroker and political agent.

[4] Bourdieu and Chollet, merchants, 45 Lime Street, is the only firm in *The London Directory* (15th ed., 1780), that resembles this one.

[5] In his dispatch to Grenville of 26 May, Fox declared: 'you should lose no time in taking all the advantage possible of the concession which his Majesty has . . . been induced to make, with respect to the independency of the Thirteen States; . . . to authorise you to make the offer of the said independency in the first instance, instead of making it a conditional article of a general treaty' (*Fox Corr.* iv. 206).

something for it) on the Independence of America being as the first article of their treating; and this would for ever furnish them with a claim on the friendship and confidence of the Americans after the peace. But since they do not do this, surely it would not be bad policy, even it we gave up more to France in other respects, to prevent her appearing in the treaty as in any respect the champion of America, or as having made any claims for her; we giving her up everything she wants equally, and her future confidence and alliance being such an object to us. Were I the Minister, I would give France an island or two to choose, if it would expose her selfishness, sooner than let her gain the *esteem of the Americans* by claiming anything essential for them in apparent preference to her own interest and ambition. All people, of all descriptions, in America, will read the treaty of peace, whenever it comes, which France shall make with this country; and if they should see there that she has claimed and got a good deal for herself, but has not appeared to have thought of them, however they may have profited in fact, it would certainly give us a great advantage in those sort of arguments and competitions which will arise after a peace; whereas if it appears as a stipulated demand on the part of France that America should be independent, it will for ever be a most handy record and argument for the French party in that country to work with; and this, as things stand now, and as far as my poor judgment goes, appears not to be a very difficult thing to have either way. And so these are my politics on that subject for you.

You will find Rodney has taken some more ships. The unluckiness of his recal[l], I think, appears to increase in its ill effect;[1] and people don't seem to fancy Pigott. Rolle[2] has given notice that he will move on Thursday to know who advised His Majesty to recal[l] Rodney; and out of doors

---

[1] 'This step of recalling Rodney has displeased many people and raised something like an opposition to the ministry. . . . A motion of censure was offered in the House, but not made, and the speakers against the Ministry were very few. Governor Johnstone was the most violent . . .' (*Memoirs of Sir S. Romilly* (2nd ed., 1840), i. 229). See the letter of 'Tom Catt-Call' in the *Morn. Chron.*, 27 May 1782.

[2] John, afterwards Lord Rolle of Stevenstone (1750–1842), M.P. for Devonshire and 'hero' of *The Rolliad*.

the talk is the same. Charles[1] gave Johnson,[2] who had been very violent on this subject the other day, an excellent trimming; but there was a good deal of coy with the other.

The arming plan don't seem to take at all.[3] We have not yet heard from Ireland since Burgoyne took them over a constitution.[4]

There is nothing odd or new to tell you, but that here is a most untimely strange sort of an influenza which every creature catches. You must not mind the badness of my scrawl:[5] and let me hear from you. Does Lafayette[6] join your consultation dinners with Franklin, as some of our Roupell intelligence sets forth? I take it for granted the French Ministers will think it a point of spirit to seem rather less desirous of peace since your defeat in the West?

Howe is still off the Texel, and the Dutch safe within.[7]

What mere politics I write to you! One might as well be a newspaper editor at once, I believe, as anything that politics can make one: but all other pursuits are as idle and unsatisfactory, and that's a comfort. | Yours ever, | R. B. Sheridan.

84. To Thomas Harris

Add. MS. 27925, ff. 5–6. *Address*: T. Harris Esq. | Knightsbridge *Dock.*: Mr. Sheridan | July 2d 1782.

2 July 1782
Saturday 4 o clock

Dear H.

I'll get these six two hundred and fiftys, exchanged directly

[1] Fox was angry at Johnstone's claim that Fox was an improper person to move the thanks of the House to Rodney, and retorted that he would move the thanks of the House even to Johnstone, if ever Johnstone should render any service to his country.

[2] George Johnstone (1730–87) was Governor of West Florida, 1763–7, and a commissioner to treat with the Americans, 1778.

[3] Shelburne's plan of a military association in every town and wapentake. See the *Morn. Her.*, 25 May 1782.

[4] Burgoyne left England on 16 May: see *Morn. Her.*, 17 May 1782.

[5] Grenville replied on 8 June, expressing mock astonishment at having received two letters from S.: 'I am however at length convinced of it, for certainly your hand is not easily counterfeited' (Add. MS. 47563, f. 21).

[6] Marquis de Lafayette (1757–1834), soldier and revolutionary. In later years, S. said he 'united the spirit of a Hampden to the loyalty of a Falkland' (Watkins, ii. 353). Grenville had written to Fox (*Fox Corr.* i. 350) to say that he would breakfast with Lafayette at Franklin's.

[7] A Dutch attack on the north coast of England was feared: see the *Morn. Chron.*, 21 May 1782.

for 12. of £150. and more if I can. Garton[1] has also one of [£] 250, and another of £150 besides those he gave me the Receipt for. Which will make £2200. In the mean time I have no possible way to pay Pacchierotti,[2] but by Garton's accepting a Note for his last Payment—which Pacchierotti will take at 2 months—and he wants to leave England to-morrow. Garton has no objection but desires me to write to you first. The Case is you see that He may be sure at least of this money from the above securities before the Note can be due—for Johnson is quite positive that Stone etc. will lend even back to the £300, when once the subscriptions are paid up—and then Garton may have as much of the money as he likes, and I'll empower him to receive it of Stone,[3] but from this Delay I have no other possible way of satisfying Pacchierotti, and it will be the Devil and all to detain him. I have paid Pozzi[?][4] and another who are going directly to Day. Pray send me a line for Garton. | yours truly | R B Sheridan.

85. To Thomas Grenville

Pub.: Court and Cabinets, i. 53–54.

Thursday, July 4th, 1782.

My Dear Grenville,
    Knowing that you very much dislike your situation, I don't know how to call ill news what I am now going to inform you of. Charles has this day resigned the seals; as he is much engaged, I have undertaken to let you know this event, and make the last exercise of our office the sending a messenger to you, as it would certainly be unfair to lose a

[1] Jonathan Garton was Treasurer of C.G.Th. from 1767.
[2] Gasparo Pacchierotti (d. 1821), Italian castrato singer. He found it very difficult to obtain money due to him from S., and wrote him an 'incendiary' letter but never sent it. See Constance Hill, *The House in St. Martin's Street* 1907), pp. 224–6.
[3] Richard Stone, William Brummell, Albany Wallis, and Robert Burton were named as trustees for securing the payment of £12,000 to Andrea Gallini, on behalf of S. and William Taylor, who are named as 'Proprietors of the King's Theatre'. This document (Widener MS.) seems to belong to early in 1781.
[4] Possibly Signora Pozzi, who sang at the King's Theatre in 1778, or Rossi, who sang at the Haymarket in June 1782.

single hour in assisting you in your release. I understand you cannot leave Paris without leave from hence, as you have the King's commission; but by sending this to you directly, it will be in your own hands to require that leave in as peremptory terms as you please.[1]

What relates to Lord Rockingham's death you are informed of. The day before it happened Charles made a question in the Cabinet on the policy of not reserving the Independence of America as a matter of treaty and the price of a peace, but to grant it at once unconditionally; on which he was beat.[2] And immediately on Lord Rockingham's death, Lord Shelburne informs them that he is to be First Lord of the Treasury and the King's Minister, though *against his wish*, etc., etc. They proposed the Duke of Portland, which the King refused; and after a great deal of idle negotiation, in which it was evident there was no power left with our friends, the measure of to-day was determined on. Lord John Cavendish[3] goes out with Charles, Keppel[4] follows; but, to his shame, in my opinion, the *Duke of Richmond*,[5] I believe, will remain. Mr. Pitt[6] joins Shelburne, and will be either Chancellor of the Exchequer or Secretary of State. For the rest, it is not known whether they will make up out of the old set, or take all new. Conway also will stay.[7] But still, those who go are right; for there is really no other question but whether, having lost their power, they ought to stay and lose their characters. And so begins a new Opposition; but wofully thinned and disconcerted, I fear. I am sure, however, that you will think what has been

[1] Grenville wrote to Fox on 9 July, to say that he had written to Shelburne to ask for his own recall (Add. MS. 47563, ff. 33–34).

[2] A few days earlier Fox had made 'an open avowal of his inclination to allow independence to America, and spoke of it as a measure agreeable to the ministry; that upon the question being proposed in the Cabinet it was carried against him, and that he thought himself so far pledg'd on that subject as to render his continuance in office totally improper' (*Leeds' Mem.*, p. 73).

[3] Lord John Cavendish (1732–96),

Chancellor of the Exchequer.

[4] Augustus, 1st Viscount Keppel (1725–86), First Lord of the Admiralty.

[5] Charles Lennox, 3rd Duke of Richmond (1735–1806), Master-General of the Ordnance. He retained this post and his seat in the Cabinet until 1795.

[6] William Pitt (1759–1806) had declined office in Rockingham's Government, and now became Chancellor of the Exchequer.

[7] Henry Seymour Conway (1721–95) was commander-in-chief under both the Rockingham and Shelburne administrations.

done was right. Fitzpatrick is here, but returning to Ireland; where, however, neither he nor the Duke will remain.

I write in great haste, which you must excuse. | Yours ever truly, | R. B. Sheridan

What you hear of Cornwallis[1] having lost some transports, is a matter of no magnitude.

86. To the Earl of Surrey

The Duke of Norfolk, Arundel Castle MS. Text from Mr. F. W. Steer's transcription. *Pub.*: Rhodes, pp. 262–3.

London
April 23d: [*1783*]

My Dear Lord,
    The Board is strong in numbers at present, so that a stray member is less miss'd[2]—and now nothing is thought of but the Taxes to provide for the unfortunate Loan,[3] which gets abused more and more every Day. There is no chance of Cyder I conceive being meddled with, so your Lordship and the Whigs of Hereford[4] may toast the Defeat of Harley with safe consciences. I am afraid no talking will make the Coalition a popular measure, we must do something to convince People that we are not the worse for it.

    Here is no news. Threats to attack the Loan again from Day to Day, but nothing attempted.

    Lord Northington[5] goes to Ireland, and Wyndham[6] Secretary. | Your's my Dear Lord | most faithfully | R B Sheridan.

I am to thank you for your royal Present.

---

[1] Charles, 2nd Earl, and afterwards Marquis, Cornwallis (1738–1805), second in command of Loyalist forces in North America.

[2] Surrey was a Lord of the Treasury in the coalition government of Fox and North, which came into office at the beginning of April.

[3] On 23 Apr. S. (as a Secretary to the Treasury) brought in a bill for raising £12,000,000 by a loan. See *Parl. Reg.* ix (1783), 642.

[4] Surrey had a strong political interest in Herefordshire through his second wife, Frances Scudamore of Holme Lacy. In June 1783, 'when he was somewhat inebriated', he rode into Hereford on a cider cask: see H. Twiss, *Life of . . . Eldon* (1844), i. 145–6.

[5] Robert Henley, 2nd Earl of Northington (1747–86), Lord-Lieutenant of Ireland, 1783–4.

[6] William Windham.

87. To William Brummell[1]

Add. MS. 36593, f. 199.

Treasury Chambers
June 6th [*1783*][2]

Dear Brummell,

I did not answer your Letters sooner being in expectation of having something more decisive to communicate to you relative to Mr. Whiteford's[3] claim. I have stated it to the Duke of Portland[4] and urged more than once the evident injustice with which he has been treated. I have no doubt but that it will now be settled to your Friend's satisfaction and most probably in the mode which you have pointed out— of which I will immediately inform you.— | Your's ever | R B Sheridan

W. Brummell Esq.

88. To Caleb Whitefoord

Add. MS. 36595, f. 212.

[*1783*][5]
Tuesday
Albemarle St.

Mr. Sheridan presents his Compliments to Mr. Whiteford, and will be glad of the Pleasure of seeing him at the Treasury tomorrow at twelve.

Mr. S. having been out of Town had not the Favor of Mr. Whiteford's Note 'till this morning.

[1] William Brummell (d. 1794) was private secretary to Lord North during the whole of North's administration.

[2] Dated from Brummell's letter to Whitefoord of the same day: 'I have just received the Inclosed from Sheridan, which I send to You, that your own Diffidence may not lead you to think that your Friends forget you. . . . If I have not soon some other and more explicit Answer from the same Quarter I shall renew my Attacks. . . .' (Add. MS. 36593, f. 198.)

[3] Caleb Whitefoord (1734–1810), diplomatist. For his friendship with Brummell, see *The Whitefoord Papers* (ed. Hewins, 1898), pp. 171–2.

[4] First Lord of the Treasury in this administration.

[5] Dated from a letter by S.'s wife to his sister Alicia, of 6 Feb. [1783]: 'We are now settled in a very comfortable ready furnish'd House in Albemarle St. for this Winter, when if Matters turn out as we hope we shall have an opportunity of suiting ourselves at our leisure for next year.' (LeFanu MS.)

89. To Edmund Burke

Fitzwilliam MS. (Sheffield). *Dock.*: 1783. | Mr. Sheridan. *Pub.*: E. Burke, *Correspondence between 1744 and 1797* (ed. Fitzwilliam and Bourke, 1844), iii. 11–12.

[*1783*]
Friday morning

My dear Sir,
    I protest to you nothing could mortify me more than to think that you can for a moment believe me such a coxcomb as to receive any advice or hint of any sort from you with any other feeling than the most serious and grateful Attention. I did not express what I meant last night or you would not think otherwise, which I am afraid by your Note you do: and I shall not be set right in my opinion untill I find that you do not continue to judge so of me by your again taking the trouble to give me that advice and council which I must be an Ideot not to know the value of, and which I declare, without a particle of compliment, I shall always feel as the truest act of Friendship and condescension you can honor me with. | Believe me, Dear Sir, | with the greatest esteem and respect | your sincere and obedient | R B Sheridan

90. To Sir Henry Clinton[1]

Clements MS. [Ph.] Only the signature is in S.'s hand. *Dock.*: R B Sheridan Esq | to | Sir Henry Clinton K.B. | Octr. 17th 1783.

17 Oct. 1783

Sir,
    Earl Cornwallis in his Letter of the 4th of August last,[2]

[1] The elder (1730–95). He was commander-in-chief of the Loyalist forces in North America, 1778–81, and took Charleston in Jan. 1780.
    [2] The Clements MSS. include Clinton's reply from Harley Street, 6 Nov. 1783, in draft and fair copy. He remarks,

'As I did not judge it becoming for a Person in the high Station I was honored with to take any Share in, or Emoluments resulting from, Prizes captured in such a War; I left it entirely to the Army to appoint their own Agents.' He had heard that one of them, Hay, mentioned to the Lords Commissioners of his Majesty's Treasury, that he believes there is a Sum of Money unappropriated, and which was called Prize Money, in the Hands of the Commissaries of Captures who were appointed by You at the Reduction of Charles Town: I am commanded by their Lordships to desire you will acquaint this Board with the Names of the Commissaries, and what Money you think is in their Hands | I am | Sir | Your most Obedient | humble Servant | R B Sheridan

Treasury Chambers[1]
17 October 1783
Sir Henry Clinton etc. etc. etc.

91. To Thomas Orde[2]

The Lord Bolton MS. *Dock.*: Feby. 1784 | Mr. R. B. Sheridan | N.B.

Feb. 1784[3]
Bruton-St:
Wednesday Night

Dear Sir,
    I beg leave to trouble you with the enclosed Letter.[4] I dare say my Brother will have the Pleasure of your acquaintance, and tho' it should not be a Political connexion I am

had remitted 'to England about ten thousand Pounds of the Money arising from the Sale of Captures made in Charles Town; And that Mr. Green (Secretary to Admiral Arbuthnot) who was employed on the Part of the Navy, received a very considerable Sum more.' The Army report, dated 'Charles Town June 1st 1780', also accompanies these papers and shows that Major James Moncrief and Lieut. Gratton (of the 64th Regiment) with two merchants, R. H. Powell and William Greenwood, were appointed trustees for the prizes. S. has written at the foot of the report: 'the above have since been disposed of as I understand by order of Col. Balfour, and the commander viz. £800 payed

into the Treasury, by Mr. Gratton as appears by their letter in 84.'
    [1] For other Departmental letters of 1783, see iii. 282.
    [2] Thomas Orde, afterwards 1st Lord Bolton (1746–1807), was now chief secretary for Ireland under the Duke of Rutland.
    [3] Dated from C. F. Sheridan's letter to S. from Dublin Castle on 10 Mar. 1784. It begins: 'I am much obliged to you for the letter you sent me by Orde . . .' (Moore, i. 409). Orde appears to have set out from London about 19 Feb.; see *Beresford Corr.* i. 249.
    [4] From S. to his brother. See Letter 92.

sure He will shew every attention in his Power to your commands in any other respect.

I wish you a safe and pleasant journey, tho' I can't wish your Friends here a prosperous political Voyage. | I have the Honor | to be Dear Sir, your's very faithfully, | R B Sheridan

92. To His Brother

Pub.: Moore, i. 409.

[Feb. 1784]

. . . But you are all so void of principle, in Ireland, that you cannot enter into our situation.[1]

93. 'To the People of England'[2]

Pub.: *Morn. Chron.*, 2 Mar. 1784.

18 Feb. 1784

My Worthy Countrymen,

I sincerely believe we are all agreed upon one point, which is, that we love liberty, and that we hate to be treated like tools or slaves. And taking this for granted, I wish much to have an opportunity of explaining to you the nature of these quarrels and disputes which have lately arisen in Parliament, and which I verily believe have been strangely misrepresented to you, and unless a story is plainly told, I do not see that any person can be supposed to understand it.

I am no parliament man myself, but am one of the people, and a most sincere lover of liberty, who having with great

[1] For C. F. Sheridan's long reply, see Moore, i. 409–17. S. had resigned, with the administration, after the rejection of Fox's India Bill on 17 Dec. 1783.

[2] W. Windham wrote to S. from Norwich (Widener MS., bearing the questionable date of 5 Mar. 1784), to say that a letter 'which I conceive to be written by you' was to be inserted, in the following week, in the 'morning chronicle, of the 2d. I think'. I accept his guess as accurate because the letter 'to the people of England' is written in the manner of *The Drapier's Letters*, and S. was fond of taking his models from the early eighteenth century. It is also headed 'Letter I', and since I have found no other, I conclude that S., characteristically, did not complete the series.

attention, watched the motions of all the parties, think, I can perceive to what points they tend, and will lay before you my ideas upon this subject, as shortly and as plainly as I can. And first, I must mention what you may perhaps know already, that it is the peculiar privilege and inestimable blessing of British subjects to choose their own Representatives in Parliament, and these Representatives have the power of raising by taxes, etc. all the money that is found necessary for carrying on the government of this great Country.—Nor can the King or the House of Lords raise a farthing, without the consent and approbation of our Representatives.—Our Representatives, therefore, undoubtedly hold the purse of the Nation, and that being the case and seeing that they represent us, a great and powerful people, I really think they are entitled to much respect, both from the Crown and the House of Lords, and this respect has always been shewn to them, since the glorious revolution, till the present times.[1] Since that great event, our Sovereigns have been extremely desirous to keep on a friendly footing with our Representatives, and have always been particularly careful to appoint Ministers that were agreeable to them, and who had their confidence. Unhappily for the Crown, unhappily for the People, that is not the case at present; for the House of Commons, who are our Representatives, have declared, by a solemn Resolution, that the present Ministry have not their confidence, and the consequence is, that the whole public business of the Nation stands still. Now supposing the House of Commons to be ill founded, in their opinion of the present Ministers (which subject I intend to examine hereafter) do not you think it would be a very wise thing in the Crown, out of respect and friendship to our Representatives, to lay aside the absurd obstinate dispute and say, 'Well gentlemen, as you cannot put your confidence in the present Ministers, rather than stop important business, and risk more misfortunes, after those we have already suffered, from a similar obstinacy, we will name new ones, who we hope shall have your confidence, as there is nothing we hate so much as a quarrel with the Representatives of our People.'

[1] Over Pitt's India Bill, which had been rejected on 23 Jan. 1784. See *Speeches*, i. 81–86, for S.'s views on 'minions of the Crown'.

In a future letter I shall explain the supposed cause of the dispute, and lay before you my observations upon it, being with great regard and affection, | Your faithful friend and servant, | MENTOR

Feb. 18, 1784.

94. To Joseph Cradock

Pub.: Cradock, iv. 184.

Bruton-street, March 23, 1784.

Dear Sir,

I am very happy to hear of your return to England, though I must beg you to excuse my so soon addressing you after your arrival, to request a favour; but your obliging conduct in this matter upon a former occasion encourages me. You will easily perceive that I am going to renew my application to you in favour of our friend Mr. Townshend;[1] and, as the embarrassment of a different political connexion on your part does not now exist, I have the more reason to flatter myself that he will be honoured with the continuance of your interest and support. I have the honour to be, dear sir, your's very truly, | R. B. Sheridan.

95. To Evan Nepean[2]

Osborn MS. *Pub.*: *Morrison Cat.* vi. 126. *Dock.*: Wedy. 25. August 1784 | R. B. Sheridan Esqr. | E N.

Wednesday Augt. 25th: *1784*

Dear Sir,

Will you excuse my requesting your attention to the Case of a man condemn'd at Norwich,[3] on whose account I have

[1] William Pitt became a candidate at this Cambridge University election, and was returned with Lord Euston. S.'s friend Townshend and the Solicitor-General, Mansfield, were unsuccessful.

[2] 1751–1822. He was a professional administrator, and was at this period Under-Secretary for the Home Department.

[3] Matthew Parker was condemned to death at the Summer assizes of 1784, for house-breaking. Parr petitioned the King and, through the Bishop of Winchester, obtained the support of Pitt for a reprieve. See Parr, *Works*, i. 150.

received a Letter to be laid before Lord Loughborough[1] who is unfortunately out of Town. The Gentleman who interests himself in this matter at Norwich, is Dr: Parr,[2] Clergyman of a most respectable Character and great Learning who I am confident would not interfere in a case wholly unworthy of the clemency he solicits, if Lord Sidney[3] therefore has the goodness to take the matter into consideration I should hope that notwithstanding Lord Loughboroughs unfortunate absence the poor man might be saved or at least respited. | I have the Honor | to be, Dear Sir, | Your very obedient Servant | R B Sheridan

E. Nepean Esq.

96. To Thomas Graham[4]

N.L.S. MS. 3591, f. 142. *Pub.*: E. M. Graham, *The Beautiful Mrs. Graham and the Cathcart Circle* (1927), pp. 187–8. *Dock.*: Sheridan London | Octr. 1784.

23 Oct. 1784
Octr: 23d: 1783[5]

Sir,
I am very glad that I happen'd to be in Town to receive the Favor of your communication relative to the Meeting at Perth.[6] Nothing can be more judicious or better drawn than the Resolutions you inclosed, and as I think it may be of consequence to circulate them I have had them inserted into most of the London Papers, one of which I enclose.
I will look at the Act as you desire and I have no doubt of finding it like most of the revenue Laws of last session a

[1] Alexander Wedderburn, afterwards 1st Earl of Rosslyn (1733–1805), was Lord Chief Justice.

[2] Samuel Parr (1745–1825), classical scholar, was Headmaster of Norwich Grammar School. He had been at Harrow in S.'s day.

[3] Thomas, Lord Townshend, later 1st Viscount Sydney (1733–1800), was Home Secretary.

[4] Thomas Graham, afterwards Lord Lynedoch (1748–1843), soldier.

[5] S.'s error.

[6] The magistrates and commissioners of supply of Perthshire met at their annual general meeting on 5 Oct. 1784, and drew up eleven resolutions on the licensing of small stills in the Highlands. The gist of these is to be found in the fourth: 'the 46th act of the last session of Parliament has imposed on a great part of the gentlemen of this county the degrading office of acting as spies and assistants to the inferior officers of Excise . . .' (*Caledonian Mercury*, 6 Oct. 1784).

composition of absurdity and oppression. I will take the earliest opportunity of conveying your ideas[1] on this matter to Mr. Fox, and shall be extremely happy to receive information and your instructions on the other subject.

We have reason to believe that the Taxes are working extremely to the discredit of Administration throughout the Country. The Window Tax is certainly becoming every Day more odious for People find their Tax worse or dearer than before. I rather think it may be a measure of ours to procure Petitions and instructions on this subject against the meeting of Parliament. In this case they should come from all quarters possible.—

Here is no news but what the Newspapers have. But on the whole we think the state of Politics mending fast. | I have the Honor to be | Sir, with great Truth | your very sincere | and obedient Servant | R B Sheridan

T. Graham Esq.

97. To Stratford Canning[2]

W.T.

[*20 July 1785*]
Wednesday[3]

Dear Canning,

What a sad correspondent you are! waiting to answer Letters,[4]—why anyone will do that—an Irish correspondent should write all himself, but really and truly there has been nothing here but what the newspapers know. And we look entirely to Ireland for anything like an event about the propositions.[5] The Battle has been fought on our side very ably

[1] See A. M. Delavoye, *The Life of Thomas Graham, Lord Lynedoch* (1880), p. 19.

[2] A Whig banker and London merchant, who was visiting Ireland with his wife, Mehitabel. On 11 July, Mrs. S. wrote to her: 'S—— sends all the Politics to Mr. C—— I suppose. I am tired of thinking of them.' (Canning MS.)

[3] Dated from the references to the end of the debate on the Irish Resolutions.

[4] Canning wrote to S. on 30 June 1785 (Harvard MS.), and complained that he had sent him three letters without receiving one reply.

[5] Pitt's Irish Resolutions were intended to give Ireland some trading advantages in return for help with the defence of the Empire. They were introduced in the Irish parliament on 7 Feb. 1785, and at Westminster, on 22 Feb. They were so bitterly attacked by Opposition and manufacturing

in the House of Lords, what few amendments there are are against Ireland—we shall have done with them on Friday[1] and then Mr. Beresford sets off with them[2]—if they are treated with patience in Ireland you are a herd of Slows and Blockheads[3]—Thurlow said in the Debate on Monday that your *Patriots* were all in the pay of France[4]—We shall be very happy to see you back at our Villa at Putney,[5] and will take care to set all the apricots against you come. C. Fox the Fair[6] is very well and condescends now to be a little acquainted. | Yours ever | R. B. S.

Pray write on. I mean to send you a *Ballad* for the Paddies. I have a cousin (R. Sheridan,[7] named) if you meet him you may talk with him about any confidential mischief—He is a sound man and true—

98. To Stratford Canning

W.T.

[*26 July 1785*]
Tuesday[8]

Dear Canning,
    How do you all do? I have been scolding Mrs. S. for not

interests that Pitt reintroduced them in modified form on 12 May, and they were carried in the Lords on 18 July.
[1] The Commons debated the amendments made by the Lords to the Irish Resolutions, on Friday, 22 July (*Parl. Reg.* xviii (1785), 546).
[2] John Beresford (1738–1805), First Commissioner of the Irish Revenue, waited for them in London. See *Beresford Corr.* i. 269–84.
[3] For S.'s contempt for the Resolutions, see Sichel, ii. 82–84.
[4] Not in his speech of 18 July, as summarized in the *Parl. Reg.* xviii (1785), 115, or *Universal Daily Register*, 20 July 1785. Perhaps it was the sense of one sentence in the latter: 'Protection she [Ireland] must have from some country, in case of a separation from this.'
[5] In a letter of 25 Aug. [1785], Mrs. S. writes to Alicia Lefanu: 'I have been

leading a quiet life lately at Putney in Mrs. Canning's Cottage, which she kindly lent me during her absence.' (W.T.).
[6] Possibly Caroline Fox (1767–1845), daughter of Stephen, 2nd Lord Holland. Or Catharine Fox who married Captain Banbury in 1807 (*Leveson Gower Corr.* ii. 275). For her manuscript copy of *The School for Scandal*, inscribed 'From the Author. Catharine Banbury', see S.C., 9 Nov. 1954, lot 471.
[7] S.'s first cousin, Richard Sheridan (d. 1793), was called to the bar in 1774. He became a King's Counsel and was M.P. for Charlemont. 'A man beloved by all who know him, honourable and upright, of firm Whig principle' (H.M.C., *Charlemont MSS.* (1894), ii. 122).
[8] The Tuesday before Pitt's Bill was presented.

writing more [to] Sister Christian,[1] which is some atonement for not writing myself—There is little to tell you here.[2] The Countries seem playing at Cross Purposes if what I hear from Ireland is true. Pitt's Bill will not make its appearance 'till thursday or Friday—nor the joint address go to the King 'till friday[3]—they mean to try to cajole Paddy out of his notions on the independent Legislature and persuade him that a parcel of fine words on the subject in the Bill as there are in the address are the same thing. How does the Temper of the People stand? we shall adjourn on monday or tuesday 'till october—and then if you have swallow'd this Plan meet and make Law of it—and do nothing else—and then prorogue till January.

When do you return? I think of going to the sea side in a week[4]— | Your's ever | R. B. S.

99. To His Brother

W.T.

[*Early Aug. ?1785*]
Bruton St.
Saturday Night

Dear Charles,

One line, and that you will be surprised to receive—you will have got before this the 3rd Edition[5] of your famous Resolutions—pray take a fit of Industry and let me know what you are to do with them in Ireland—if you accept this settlement in its present Form I hope I shall never hear the name of Ireland again while I live— | Yours ever, | R. B. S.

I will really write to you but for fear you shouldn't answer me directly, or not tell me what is really thought like a Castle Tory I shall try some one else besides—

[1] Mehitabel Canning's moral principles were stricter than those of her friends.

[2] Mrs. S. wrote to Mrs. Canning on 28 July to say ,'there is nothing stirring of an amusing nature in the Political or Gallant world' (W.T.).

[3] The Irish Resolutions were brought in on 2 Aug., and the House adjourned until 27 Oct. Parliament was prorogued to 24 Jan. 1786. The joint address of Lords and Commons was presented to the King on Friday, 29 July 1785.

[4] The visit was postponed to the following year.

[5] The first version was that of Feb. 1785; the second, that of May. The third, embodying amendments by the Lords and Commons, is printed in the *Parl. Reg.*, xviii (1785) 546–54.

100. To William Eden

Add. MS. 34420, f. 76.

[*19 Aug. 1785*][1]
Friday
2 o clock

Dear Eden,

We have a Friend just arrived with the first intelligence that Government has fled the Field in Ireland.—The House met on monday and Orde announced his giving up the Business—desiring only to be permitted to print his Bill for his own justification. This after a long talk was agreed to. Opposition thought it best not to press further, and so the matter finishes. | Yours ever | R B Sheridan.

I wish to god we were to meet here now.

101. [To Willoughby Lacy]

Shuttleworth MS.

[*Nov.1785*]
Herefordshire[2]
Tuesday

Dear Sir,

Owing to my having changed my course from Wynstay[3] I did not get your Letter 'till yesterday. I shall be in Town

[1] The 'Bill for finally regulating the Intercourse and Commerce between Great Britain and Ireland . . .' is printed in the *Gent. Mag.* lv (1785), 645–51. An account of its reception by the Irish House of Commons is also given there (lv. 656–8). S.'s note may be dated from the letter that precedes it in the Auckland Papers (Add. MS. 34420, f. 71): it was written by W. Woodfall to Eden, from Dublin on 16 Aug. 1785 and announces the administration's abandonment of the bill. On 21 Aug., Mary Tickell noted that her husband, 'last night receiv'd a short Letter from S— with the Irish good news' (Folger MS.).

They were at Colchester.
[2] Uvedale Price told Samuel Rogers that S. and his wife passed some time at Price's home at Foxley, Herefordshire: see Clayden, i. 389. This may be dated from a letter to Mrs. S. by Mary Tickell, docketed 'Novr. 25th' [1785], in which she says 'I have no doubt Foxley has its comforts' (Folger MS.).
[3] S. and his wife were at Sir Watkin Williams Wynn's seat, at Wynnstay, near Ruabon, in October 1785: see *The Hamwood Papers* (ed. Mrs. G. H. Bell, 1930), p. 57; and Mary Tickell's letters (Folger MSS.). Cf. iii. 189, n. 3.

1785

in a few Days so it is unnecessary for me to say more than to assure you that it is and always has been my desire to relieve you from the embarrassments which have come on us both since the Purchase of the Theatre[1]—and if in the other article you seem to allude to I have not *yet* been able to accomplish what I wish'd, it has been owing to the obstinacy and unreasonableness of others with whom I ought to have had more weight | Yours very | sincerely | R B Sheridan.

102. [To Albany Wallis?]

Harvard MS. Copy.

[*c. 1783–5*]

Sir,

The Proposal which I communicated to you relative to the application of the money to arise from the renewal of the forty Renters shares[2] did in my opinion contain an arrangement equally for the Interest of all Parties concern'd in the property of Drury Lane Theatre. But as you apprehend that the Legatees of Mr. Garrick[3] may conceive that an undue preference is shewn to the Purchasers of Mr. Lacy's Annuity[4] in the proposed Distribution and that it may not be proper for you on that account to act for us in the renewal of these Shares, I conceive the best method to remove this Difficulty will be for you to do us the favor to communicate the Proposal above mention'd to all parties interested by Mr. Garrick's Will in the Property of Drury Lane Theatre with the substance of the remarks which I mean to make in this Letter on the present state of that Property, and my Idea of

[1] In May 1778, Lacy had sold his moiety to S. for £31,500, and an annuity of £500 for life for his wife and the same sum for life for Robert Langford (Add. MS. 38607, f. 150). Lacy was arrested for debt on several occasions, as a consequence of 'his heedless way of living'.

[2] Granted in 1762, they expired in 1783. The proposed renewal was advertised on 13 Feb. 1783: see Winston, 1782–4.

[3] The will is printed in T. Davies, *Life of Garrick* (1780), ii. 409–16.

[4] S. wanted to use part of the money raised by the grant of renters' shares to buy back Lacy's annuity. On 18 Oct. 1782, the annuitants (named Latter, Nairn, and Turner) had pressed for payment due to them (Harvard MS.), and just before Easter term 1785, S. paid Latter £771. 7s. 0d. (Widener MS.), a sum that included legal costs.

the Measures to be persued for our common Interest. I must premise however that with respect to the power of renewing these Shares the Proprietors alone are to decide, but it is undoubtedly just that the money arising from them should be applied to no other purpose but the reduction of the Debts and Incumbrances of the Theatre, and it is certainly to be wish'd that this may be done in the manner most satisfactory to those who have Priority of Claim. In order however to shew why I conceiv'd that Mr. Garrick's Legatees who are clearly entitled to the preference ought not to insist upon it in the present Instance I must humbly recapitulate the Circumstances which have attended the Mortgage and Security in question, and the grounds on which I conceive that those who are Securities to them are entitled to a particular consideration from the present Mortgagees as to why my Interest should be considered as blended with theirs.

Purchas'd from Mr. Garrick at the Price of Thirty five Thousand Pounds for his Moiety Dr. Ford and myself paid the whole of the money for our Shares amounting to Twenty five Thousand Pounds and Mr. Linley gave a perfect security[1] beside[s] having his share in Mortgage for his ten thousand.

The Price was undoubtedly a great one considering the situation of the Patent and that the Property was encumber'd with an annuity of sixteen hundred a year to Renters besides the annuity to Walpole,[2] and that Mr. Garrick had just receiv'd the money for the last forty Shares which were renew'd previous to the Sale. The renewal of the Patent[3] however was spoken of by Mr. Garrick as a matter of course and he in some measure undertook to do it for us. However on our joint application afterwards to Lord Hertford[4] I perceiv'd there was no prospect of it. After our Purchase was compleated we found that Mr. Garrick had a Mortgage to the amount I think of fifteen or sixteen Thousand Pounds upon Mr. Lacy's Share. Mr. Lacy soon after proposed to

[1] 'In security for the mortgage to Garrick Mr. Wallis has . . . Possession of the Title Deeds of all the other Property Mr. Linley possesses' (Folger MS. T. a. 117).   [2] See p. 113, n. 1.
[3] Granted to Garrick and James Lacy on 26 Oct. 1761 for twenty-one years from 2 Sept. 1774.
[4] Francis Seymour Conway, 1st Earl (later Marquis) of Hertford (1719–94), was Lord Chamberlain 1766–82 and Apr.–Dec. 1783.

borrow a further sum from Garrick for the settlement of his affairs and we consented to become Securities with him. Mr. Garrick refusing to lend the additional sum otherwise and representing to us that it would be the means of obliging Mr. Lacy, and Binding us together in harmony, This was accordingly consented to, but from what misunderstanding I know not, when the Deeds came to be executed we found it was proposed that we should be security not merely for the sum then to be advanced to Mr. Lacy but for the preceding Mortgage also, the whole amounting to two and twenty Thousand Pounds and for this we became bound without any indemnity whatever.

Differences soon after arose between us and Mr. Lacy upon subjects which it is needless to recapitulate which ended in an arbitration. Reference to Mr. Garrick and a friend of Mr. Lacy who decided on our side.[1] Mr. Lacey afterwards proposing to sell either his Oxfordshire Estate[2] or his Theatrical Property, various propositions were made which however produced no change in the Property till Mr. Harris and I being extreamly sanguine of the success of a new Plan we then had relative to a third Theatre[3] which did not appear in the same light to Mr. Lacy, we were induced to offer such terms to Mr. Lacy that an agreement was in consequence executed for the Sale of his Moiety to me.

As you drew up this agreement and were acquainted with the whole of the transaction I must beg here the attention of Mr. Garrick's Executors and Legatees to some of these Particulars which I state as a strong ground for that equitable Consideration from them which I now claim for the property under its present Circumstances. It is reasonable to suppose that I could not have undertaken this purchase without the consent and advice of Mr. Garrick and the fact is that I took no one step in it but with his concurrence. If Mr. Garrick had disapprov'd of the measure or of the

---

[1] See p. 108, n. 1.

[2] His trustee, Marriot, states that Lacy's extravagance left him short of money to pay off an encumbrance of £5,000 on the Eynsham estate, and that he resorted to money-lenders. Lacy then sold the estate (worth £22,000) to Lang-ford for £8,000; and agreed to sell his share in D.L.Th. to him also. S., however, promised him £1,000 a year above Langford's offer; and Lacy sold out in May 1778. See Winston, 1801–4.

[3] See Letter 50.

assistance which it was evident the Theatre must give towards accomplishing it, his signifying his intention of calling in his Mortgage would have made it impossible for me to proceed but Mr. Garrick duly considered the circumstances of the Theatre. He had in the whole a stake of two and Thirty Thousand Pounds in it with arrears of Interest. He knew that nothing was so fatal to such a Property, where there is so little real value as division among the proprietors. He had seen it shut up in our dispute whether Mr. Langford and Captain Thompson should manage on the part of Mr. Lacy, and tho we were always engaged to him for Mr. Lacy's Mortgage yet the Circumstances under which we became bound would not have made it a desirable thing to have press'd us personally for so great a sum.[1] Mr. Garrick was aware that while we differ'd among ourselves I cou'd only be attach'd to the Theatre by my connexion with Mr Linley and Dr. Ford. My share was comparatively small and I received no emolument whatever for managing tho I then entirely gave up my whole time to it while from the friendship between Mr. Harris and me I might have had any proposition I wished of his Patents made over to me. Consequently if Mr. Lacy had sold to other persons as Mr. Garrick apprehended he would do or had made over his share in trust to them, he must suppose that we would endeavour to leave the Theatre[2] or that no great agreement could follow in the Government of it. It was natural therefore for him to wish to see it in hands where it was pretty certain there would be no Desertion at least and in Consequence he not only approv'd the reason of my becoming the purchaser of Mr. Lacy's Moiety tho he thought the Price very great but encouraged me to it with the most direct and friendly appearance that he would never suffer his Mortgage to be called in in any way that should embarrass or distress me. The Bargain was accordingly concluded on the following Terms. Thirty one Thousand five hundred Pounds and an

[1] See *Garrick Corr*. ii. 303, for the bond 'in penalty of £44,000 for the payment of £22,000 and interest', endorsed by Garrick, 'my security. . . . 'Tis a thumper!' It is of 3 Jan. 1777.

[2] *Lond. Chron.*, 15–17 July 1777, reported that S., Linley, and Ford were likely to sell their moiety in D.L.Th. to 'Mr. Langford, Mr. Bateman, an attorney of Maiden-lane, and Mr. Duberly, the army taylor'.

annuity of one Thousand Per Ann. redeemable at eight years Purchase etc. Mr. Lacy's to be indemnified from his Moiety of the joint Debts then incurr'd on the Theatre which exceeded six Thousand Pounds. It was afterwards settled that Mr. Lacy should have twenty saleable Privileges of free admission. This taking the Price at which the Annuity is now proposed to be repurchased without mentioning the Box made the sum for this Moiety at the least forty three Thousand Pounds which is eight Thousand Pounds more than Garrick sold [for]. Now Sir, I am perfectly aware that Mr. Garrick's Executors and Legatees are not bound by Mr. Garrick's friendly intentions or promises to me, as no binding provision was made on the subject, yet I cannot but think that they will esteem it not only equitable but conducive to their own Interest to fulfill as far as they conveniently can his intentions and plan in the Business. And I think this more when I am to state what has been since done to strengthen their Security and to place things in a Train to realize the property bequeathed to them. In this light I cannot admit the renewal of the patent as a slight Consideration.[1] This I affirm was done from political Connexion as a personal favor to me, and was consider'd as much so as if I had obtain'd the promise of a place for Life of a Thousand Pound per Ann. For whatever was practised when Theatrical Property was of comparatively inconsiderable value it was evident that there was no Intention in any government to give merely to the claim of the Theatre the renewal of a patent which they were selling with the addition of a few Old Cloathes at the rate of seventy or eighty Thousand Pounds, without at least taking the Patronage of an encreased annuity of a thousand or twelve hundred Pounds a year upon it, and this was distinctly stated to me when it was given with a smaller annuity than is now paid to Mr. Walpole, and Mr. Fox acknowledged the obligation in this light. The Patent so renew'd was immediately lodged in your

[1] The proprietors of D.L.Th. sought at the beginning of the previous winter the renewal of the patent because they wished 'to issue a new set of renters shares' (*Morn. Post.*, 17 Sept. 1783). The grant (New York Public Library MS.) was dated 13 Sept. 1783 and was made for twenty-one years from 2 Sept. 1795. Thurlow refused to affix the Seal because he found that the Crown could not grant a patent for more than one life or twenty-one years.

hands and the theatrical security to the Legatees undoubtedly wore a new face upon it. I do not want to dwell on other services which I think I have done to the Theatre by personal Interest or I should state that my saving this Property from the proposed Tax[1] and not without the greatest exertion as well as good fortune was I sincerely think diverting a Mischief which would in the end have reduced the value of it on a Sale one Third. I might state also that my personal friendship with Mr. Harris is perhaps one of the first reasons that a third Patent is not experienced in a hostile way against us, the ill consequence of which to the property Mr. Garrick was most anxiously aware of. I mention these Circumstances as well because I most sincerely declare that the moderation I now require from Mr. Garrick's Legatees is asked by me as a matter of equity and Justice, as much as favor, as to shew that it never can be the Interest of Persons having a Stake in such a Property to persue measures to detach the minds of the Proprietors from any great anxiety for its prosperity, or to prevent those who have the Controul over it from deriving any present advantage from its success. This has been the case for some years past and in my opinion we should have been much nearer out of Debt if it had been otherwise, but as I think this is the time when a different Line must be persued I will state accurately as I can what the present situation of the theatre is—Of a large Debt exclusive of the Mortgages incurr'd by our inexperience in our outset, and by a most expensive alteration made in the stage and scenery, there remained a sum due exceeding six thousand Pounds, when I purchas'd from Mr. Lacy (the proprietors having up to that time received but a very inconsiderable Dividend). This enabling me however to compleat the purchase (altho' Renters' Shares were granted for this purpose, and to assist the Buying of Mr. Harris's share in the Opera House which was then thought would be an advantage to Drury Lane Theatre) encreased the Debt, from that time the

---

[1] For a discussion of the tax upon theatres, see the *Morn. Post*, 15 Mar. 1782; and the *Parl. Reg.* vi (1782), 423–4, 437, 441–3. S. argued in the House that 'the product of the tax was but a trifle to the public in comparison of the injury it would do to private property, and the oppression with which it must be collected'. He added that he intended to present his objections in writing. The *Morning Post* writer called the tax 'an act of wantonness'.

Proprietors have received no Dividend whatever, Eight hundred Pounds was indeed advanced to me for a piece which it was then my purpose to bring out[1] and five hundred Pounds being due to me by agreement for a year of the Management I remain indebted to the general property in the sum of three hundred Pounds. By our continuing to leave the whole of the Profits for the payment of the Debts and by a more œconomical management this accumulated Debt is reduced[2] to a sum which without applying any of the Money arising from the renewal of the Renters Shares might be discharged with ease in the present season were the demands of so pressing a nature as to make it necessary still to forego a Dividend to ourselves but this is by no means the Case. The greatest part of them being running accounts with Persons where our Credit is good and who would be perfectly satisfied to be paid by installments. In the mean time a most embarrassing demand attended with Law expences has come on my Moiety of the property from Mr. Lacy's Annuitants[3] whose arrears it is evident from the foregoing statement it has been utterly out of my Power to pay. With regard to those Gentlemen who purchased this Annuity from Mr. Lacy it has not been possible for me to persue a fairer line of Conduct towards them while the Theatre did not enable me to pay them than to resist every thing that might tend to depreciate their purchase and to propose the moment it appear'd at all feasible to repurchase the Annuity which they have reason to think so ill secured at the full Price they gave with Interest from the time. Now the Objection you state to this is the Priority of Claim of Mr. Garrick's Mortgage and that if Money is raised upon the Property it should be applied to the payment of the arrear of Interest on that Mortgage or the reduction of the principal. You have also said that the

[1] The D.L.Th. 'Receipts and Payments' ledger for 1777–8 (Folger MS.) reveals that £300 was paid to S. on 1 Jan. 1778 'by Order of the Managers on Account of a new Piece to be produced this Season by him'. The play may not have been written, for the sum was returned on 20 Feb. 1778.

[2] In the season of 1782–3, £9,540. 2s. 9d. was paid towards the old debts of D.L.Th.: see the New M. Mag. (1838), Pt. i, 523.

[3] Presumably Latter, Nairn, and Turner's demand of Oct. 1782. Apart from payment to Latter before Easter term 1785, S. made over £826. 8s. 1d. to 'Mr. Lacy's annuitants' during the 1785–6 season: see the 'Receipts and Payments' ledger (Folger MS.) of D.L.Th. for that season.

Money already paid to Mr. Lacy ought more justly to have
been paid to Mr. Garrick. To that however there was no
objection at the time, the appropriation of that sum to Mr.
Lacy being done with Mr. Garrick's consent who was influenced by the considerations I have before mention'd
and I am convinced independently of his friendship for me,
thought it better for his Mortgage on the whole that the
Purchase should receive that assistance. In my judgment
there are precisely the same reasons to induce the Legatees
to wa[i]ve their Claim (if it is to be consider'd as a Claim) to
payment from these Shares and to be satisfied that I should
apply my part of them to extinguish as much as I can of
this extravagant Annuity which is hourly perplexing and
disgracing the Property and stands in the way of Measures
which might be adopted for the Punctual payment of their
Interest as well as for a temperate but certain reduction of the
principal—but as you seem to think it absolutely necessary
that part of the sum at least should be applied to their use,
I have given up the Idea of repurchasing more of the Annuity
than appears essential to the Credit of the Theatre and to
fulfil offers which I have made on this subject. On this
Idea you will see the proposal relative to the Shares is drawn.
The precise Division of the Sum must be ascertain'd by the
terms to be made with those of the Annuitants who are to be
repaid and this settlement, and application of my part of the
Money to arise from the shares, will, I trust be satisfactory
to Mr. Garrick's Legatees, when they have duly consider'd
the subject, and the whole of the circumstances I have been
led to state at so much length in this Letter. I have now only
very shortly to propose a regular and Systematic mode of
applying the future profits of the Theatre, in which I consult as much as it is in my power the Claims of Mr. Garrick's
Legatees, and I hope that it will be found satisfactory, because it is absolutely and peremptorily the utmost I can, or
will undertake to do.

   After the application of the money arising from the Shares
in the manner above mention'd an exact account of the out-
standing Debt at the commencement of the present season
due from the Proprietors in general, shall be deliver'd to
you, The Treasurer shall furnish you with an exact list and

estimate of our Establishment, and incidental Expences.[1] He shall engage regularly to deliver to you a weekly account of the receipts of the Theatre, and the particulars of the Disburs[e]ments, the Payments to be made in the following order

1st. The Performers, Servants, etc. on the pay list and the Renters.

2nd. Provision to be made for the Rent, Taxes and Mr. Walpole's Annuity.

3rd. All Tradesmen's Bills and other expences incurr'd in carrying on the Business of the Present Season.

4th. The sum of one Thousand Pounds to be taken up by Money set apart weekly for that purpose to be applied to the discharge of the general Debt due from the Proprietors (if a smaller part of Mr. Lacy's Annuity is repurchased by me, one Thousand Pounds from the new Renters' Shares might also be applied to this purpose).

5th. The Years interest on Mr. Garrick's Mortgage to be taken up every night, and to be paid with the account given in at the end of every week.[2]

A similar sum for the other Proprietors to Ballance this. After these payments or full provision made for them, whatever surplus Profit shall remain, shall be a Dividend for the Proprietors [to] be taken Monthly according to their Shares, I charging my own share with what shall remain of Mr. Lacy's Annuity in such manner as shall be agreed between me and the Annuitants—this order of Payment to remain untill the Debt due now from the Proprietors in common shall be wholly extinguish'd then to continue with this variation only, that in lieu of the fourth Article I will engage to charge my Moiety from that time with a further Payment of five hundred Pounds Per. Ann. to be taken up with the Interest from Mr. Garrick's Mortgage and previous to my receiving my Dividend towards the reduction of the Principal and as this reduction can be but gradual, and will not immediately commence, I will agree also, that in all future

[1] Much greater efficiency in keeping the accounts and balancing the books is shown in the D.L.Th. ledger, 'Receipts and Payments, 1785-6' (Folger MS.). Thirty pounds a night was set aside for the renters' interest.

[2] The D.L.Th. ledger, 'Receipts and Payments, 1786-7' (Folger MS.), notes, 'Interest Mr. Sheridan to Executors of David Garrick 1 year—£1100'.

Renters' Shares to be granted or renewed, one half of my proportion of the Money arising from them shall be applied to the same purpose. This I repeat, after fully considering the Subject and my own situation is *all I can do*.

You once drew out a settlement for us, something on the plan of this according to that I was to have receiv'd a thousand Pounds by weekly Payments as my Dividend in the manner the proprietors used formerly to take it and then a certain sum was to be set apart for the reduction of the Debts and Mortgages and the remainder (if any) to be a further Dividend for the Proprietors. In my opinion the settlement now proposed is better for the Creditors and it remains for the Proprietors to take care that it shall not be worse for themselves. The Payment of the Interest of five Per Cent to Mr. Garrick's Legatees will not only be punctual and certain but the whole will be paid in seven Months. And I trust they will find the performance of this so well secured that it may even cease to be desirable to them to call in the Mortgage hastily, and at once were it practicable to pay it off. It is not however my meaning that they are to be tied up from calling in the Mortgage at any future time according to their discretion. I beg again to be understood, as offering here a decisive Settlement on my Part and to the extent of what I can engage to fulfil—were I to offer more my own private embarrassments must either fall upon the Property, or I must in a very short time sell my Interest in it altogether at a time when perhaps it might be in a state of the utmost discredit and confusion. With this alternative before my Eyes, if the Legatees insist on the Mortgage being call'd in, I must either endeavour to get some friends to take it, or gain what time I can till it is in my power to satisfy them. On the other hand, if my proposition is thought reasonable I shall have every motive and inducement to apply all my endeavours, and to give as much attention as I can to the raising the Credit and value of the Property and sharing in the present advantage of its success I shall be anxious on their accounts as well as my own for a time when circumstance may perhaps enable me either to pay off the Principal of this Mortgage at once, or to assign to the Legatees the whole of the Profits for that Purpose.

I have nothing further to add than that I will any day in this week meet any of the legatees, or the other Executors upon this Subject if any further explanation is judg'd necessary. But there are many Circumstances some of which you are apprised of which make it indispensably necessary that no further time should be lost on the subject of the Renters and the Settlement with those of Mr. Lacy's annuitants from whom it is purposed to repurchase.

I shall be much obliged to you therefore to communicate with the Parties concern'd as expeditiously as possible. | I am | Sir | Your Obedient Servant | (sign'd) R B Sheridan[1]

103. [To William Pitt]

Sir Edward Hoare MS. Text from Col. R. P. F. White's transcription.

[3 May 1787][2]

Sir,

The Prince having informed me that His Royal Highness had assured you that nothing would be said in the House of Commons to Day relative to the Question of tomorrow, I took the Liberty of sending a message to you from Downing Street to request your attendance, in which case it was proposed to have moved to adjourn the House to Monday. The notoriety of the circumstance of his Majesty's minister having had an interview with his Royal Highness it is conceived would have made this measure highly proper, and respectful to that interference which it is earnestly hoped may yet prevent the necessity of any Parliamentary Discussion upon the subject. | I have the Honor | to be, | Sir, | Your obedient | Humble Servant | R B Sheridan

Thursday
past 4

---

[1] 'Sign'd' and signature are in S.'s hand.

[2] Alderman Newnham had given notice that he would bring forward a motion on 4 May, for the relief of the Prince of Wales's debts. Pitt saw the Prince on 3 May and 'after a conference of an hour Mr. Pitt went to his Majesty and returned to the Prince between three and four' (*Morn. Chron.*, 5 May 1787). S.'s letter seems to indicate a desire that Pitt should attend the Commons that evening, so that the House might be adjourned and further time given to private negotiation.

104. To William Pitt

P.R.O., Chatham Papers, 30/8, 105, f. 191. *Dock.*: Mr. Sheridan

[*3 May 1787*]

Mr. Sheridan presents his Compliments to Mr. Pitt, and begs leave to inform him that there will be no motion for adjournment made tomorrow, but previous to Mr. Newenham's¹ withdrawing his Question. Mr. Sheridan is commanded by his Royal Highness to deliver Mr. Pitt a message² which He will take an opportunity of doing before four o'clock.

Bruton St.
Thursday Night.

105. To William Pitt

P.R.O., Chatham Papers, 30/8, 105, f. 193. *Dock.*: Mr. Sheridan

[*4 May 1787*]³

Mr. Sheridan presents his Compliments to Mr. Pitt. He

¹ Nathaniel Newnham (*c.* 1742–1809), M.P., London, 1780–90; Ludgershall, 1793–6 (Judd). He is named with another London alderman, Harvey Christian Combe, in the twelfth part of the D.L.Th. indenture of 1793 (P.R.O., Chancery Procs., C 13/2325).

² 'Pitt wrote a letter on Thursday [i.e. 3 May] to the Prince informing him . . . that the King was ready to afford him the relief he desired. The letter was so general and so loose that Pitt added his readiness to give any further verbal explanations . . .; and Fox being out of the way, Sheridan had accordingly a conference with him, in which he said he meant the professions in the letter to be understood in the most extensive and liberal sense. . . . The English of this is an offer to propose, from the King, the payment of his debt and increase of his income' (*Minto Corr.* i. 159–60). For the text of the letter, see *The*

Later Correspondence of George III (ed. A. Aspinall, Cambridge, 1962), i. 281, n. 2.

³ Dated from Pitt's letter to the King on 4 May 1787: 'Mr Pitt received, just as the House was up a note from Mr Sheridan desiring to see him, in consequence of his Royal Highness's commands. Mr. Sheridan brought a letter from the Prince of Wales which Mr. Pitt has the honor of transmitting. He thought it right to decline entirely all verbal communication with Mr. Sheridan on the subject, and has since written a letter to his Royal Highness, which he also submits to your Majesty's perusal' (*The Later Correspondence of George III* (ed. cit.), i. 282). The Prince's letter demanded an explanation of Pitt's statement in the Commons that day, to the effect that no terms for the settlement of the Prince's debts had been agreed. See *Parl. Reg.* xxii (1787), 251.

is commanded by his Royal Highness to wait upon Mr. Pitt this evening, and begs to know whether ten o'clock will be a convenient hour to Mr. Pitt.

Carleton-House
7 o'clock.

106. To Mehitabel Canning

Bath Municipal Library MS.

[*25 July 1787*]
Bristol Hot Wells[1]
Wednesday 25th.

Dear Mrs. Canning,
    I send you only a single Line at Present to say that Betsey[2] is pretty well and I hope and trust will bear the Shock which is impending over her with more fortitude and resignation than I had expected—I expect our poor Mary[3] will scarcely survive the Night. I mean to take Mrs. S. and the little Girl[4] away instantly when it happens. She wishes to go to Town and to see the other Children I will write again to you when I get there. I have not determined on our Course afterwards—but I shall be very happy if we can manage to meet. I will attend to the promise you remind'd me of in your last Letter to Betsey immediately, but I must take another opportunity to ask you something about the manner in which you wish it to be executed. | Yours, my Dear Mrs. C. | most sincerely | R B Sheridan

[1] The Hotwells, near Vincent's Rocks, Clifton, were noted for water that was 'a specifick for the dysentery, spitting of blood, consumptions' (*New Bath Guide* (new ed., 1787), p. 55).
[2] Mrs. S.
[3] Mrs. S.'s favourite sister, and the wife of Richard Tickell (1751–93), man of letters. On 20 June she was taken from her home at Hampton to Clifton, and died there of tuberculosis on 27 July 1787. See Mrs. S.'s letters to Mrs. Canning of 26 June and 22 July 1787 (Bath Municipal Library MSS.).
[4] Elizabeth (*c.* 1781–1860), Mary's daughter. Her other children were boys, Richard and Samuel: see Black, pp. 129–30, 153.

107. [To William Thomson]¹

Bodleian Library, Western MS. 25448, f. 99.

[*23 Aug. 1787*]

Dear Sir,

I enclose the Notes which I have accepted. I wrote to Pearce² who I suppose is out of Town—but I enclose a Line as you desire—I shall see our friend Dr. Parr tomorrow —there is a ridiculous assault upon Ballendenus in the Public Advertiser of to Day by Major Scott³ | Yours very truly | R B Sheridan

108. To Samuel Parr

Pub.: Parr, *Works*, i. 797–8.

Crewe Hall, January 20 [*1788*]⁴

My Dear Sir,

I have twenty times meant to write to you since I saw you, and at times when I should have had more to say. At present I only take a pen to say that we threaten, Mrs. Crewe⁵ being of our party, to call at Hatton⁶ in our way to town the third or fourth of next month. You are not however to make any provision for us, for our party is such that we must sleep at Warwick, and we must not separate. I hope Spencer⁷ is with

¹ In Aug. 1787 S. gave Thomson (1746–1817) two notes of £50 each for his first year's service as political writer for the Foxites. See Moore, ii. 70; and Parr, *Works*, i. 744.

² Probably William Pearce (1751–1842), miscellaneous writer and Chief Clerk of the Admiralty; but possibly John Pearse (*c.* 1760–1836).

³ John Scott-Waring (1747–1819) was Warren Hastings's over-zealous agent. In a letter printed in the *Pub. Adv.*, 23 Aug. 1787, Scott mocked Parr's 'high-flown panegyric . . . upon the god of his idolatry, Mr. Sheridan', which had appeared in the Latin preface

to Parr's edition of the work of William Bellenden (*c.* 1533–87). A further letter by Scott on the same subject is in the *Pub. Adv.*, 3 Sept. 1787.

⁴ Mr. Warren Derry dates the letter 1788, from internal evidence.

⁵ She was a beauty but was (according to Mrs. S.) of an unhappy disposition.

⁶ Parr held the perpetual curacy of Hatton, Warwickshire, from 1783, and lived there from Apr. 1786. Tom S. was one of his pupils.

⁷ William Robert Spencer (1769–1834), poet and wit, was also one of Parr's pupils. He was at Hatton in Jan. 1788: see Parr, *Works*, viii. 295.

you; he will get a letter from me which he ought to have had long since. Tom is in great disgrace with his mother. I hope he can plead diligence in other respects to atone for his neglect towards her: there was some trial or argument or speech which you pointed out to me at Crewe, and advised me to read with a view to Hastings'[1] Trial. I have forgot what it was, pray if you recollect, favour me with a line while I am at this place. I was very busy about other matters while in town, and have been a little idle since I have been here, so that I have a truant's feeling about my India task.[2] Have you seen a Latin poem abusing us all, which I see mentioned in the papers?[3] All here desire to be particularly remembered to you, and we hope Mrs. Parr[4] and your daughter are well. | Dear Sir, yours most sincerely, | R. B. Sheridan.

109. To Edmund Burke

Fitzwilliam MS. (Sheffield).

Crewe-Hall
Feb: 3d [*1788*]

My Dear Sir,
    I must rely upon your Indulgence to pardon my being such a Truant from the Committee.[5] But I found Mrs. Sheridan's remaining in the country so very necesssary for the Re-establishing her Health that I have been induced to defer our returning to Town as long as I could.[6] I shall have the Pleasure however of joining you on thursday or Friday,

---

[1] Warren Hastings (1732–1812), Governor-General of India, 1773–85.
[2] In a letter to Alicia Lefanu from Crewe Hall on 19 Jan. [1788], Mrs. S. writes: 'Dick sends his kindest love to you . . . he is very busy preparing for this great Trial in Westminster Hall' (LeFanu MS.).
[3] Probably the anonymous 'Carmen Antamœbæum, in olentem Bellendeni Editorem', published by Bell in 1788. For this attack on Parr's Latin preface to Bellendenus, see Parr, *Works*, i. 209, 211.
[4] Parr's first wife, Jane Morsingale

of Carleton, Yorkshire, whom he married in Nov. 1771. In 1788 he had two daughters, Sarah Anne (1772–1810) and Catherine Jane (1782–1805).
[5] The Commons Committee of Management of Hastings's Impeachment.
[6] In her letter to Alicia Lefanu from Crewe Hall on 19 Jan. [1788], Mrs. S. described how the shock of her sister Mary's death had badly affected her own health. She also mentioned that she and S. had fixed to go to London 'about the first or second of next month' (LeFanu MS.).

and I only write a Line to make my Peace and my apologies before we meet, and to assure you that I will work very hard afterwards. | I am most sincerely | and faithfully | Your's | R B Sheridan

110. [To Sir Peter Burrell]¹

Pierpont Morgan Library MS. *Dock.*: Mr. Sheridan had probably been in the river Shannon more than once, P.B.²

[*1788?*]³

My Dear Sir
    Will you be so kind to send me my Trial Tickets by the Bearer | Your's ever | R B Sheridan

Monday

111. [To Sir Peter Burrell]

Pierpont Morgan Library MS.

[*1788?*]

My Dear Sir,
    I have really lost the Tickets you gave me—will you give me leave to trouble you for two tomorrow⁴ | Your's truly | R B Sheridan

¹ Sir Peter Burrell, 2nd baronet (1754–1820), afterwards 1st Lord Gwydir, was in charge (as Deputy Great Chamberlain) of the arrangements for the trial of Warren Hastings.
² This appears to refer to the next letter.
³ Hastings's trial began on 13 Feb. 1788. S.'s famous oration (*Speeches*, ii. 55) commenced on Tuesday, 3 June. The letter seems to belong to the pre-vious day, but what appears to be a contemporary hand has dated it 'April 20th 1787'.
⁴ The Morgan Library also possesses a letter from Mrs. S. to Burrell, dated 'Thursday morn'. She asks for two tickets for her mother and sister and adds 'she shall only trouble Sir Peter once more on the day Mr. Sheridan speaks'.

112. To H. S. Woodfall, Junr.[1]

Princeton University Library MS. *Address*: Mr. H. S. Woodfall junr.
| Dorset-St. | Salisbury-Court. *Dock.*: 1788.[2]

[*1788?*]

Dear Sir,

I am very much obliged to you for the Pamphlet, which
I read with curiosity, and I assure you with very great Pleasure—and whenever it is convenient to you to give me a call
I shall be glad to say more to you on the subject. I must call
too on your father the first moment I have and among other
exhortations charge him not to attempt to pervert your Poli-
tics. | I am, Dear Sir, your very sincere | and obedient Ser-
vant | R B Sheridan.

Bruton-St.
Wednesday Evening

113. To His Brother

Pub.: Rae, ii. 28.

[*12 Aug. 1788*][3]

It is to no purpose to use many words in communicating to you the melancholy situation in which I have found
my father at this place. He is I fear past all hope. I have re-
quested Dr. Morris[4] to write you a more particular account;
but be prepared every hour to hear the worst. No view of
sickness or decay while death is at a distance gives an idea

[1] Henry Sampson Woodfall had two sons. This is probably addressed to the elder, George (1767–1844), who was in partnership with his father until 1793. The younger son, Henry, was later secretary of the London Assurance Company.

[2] In pencil, and possibly is not contemporary with S.

[3] Thomas Sheridan was now so ill that he could 'scarce walk across the room for feebleness and disease', and he determined to leave Ireland and go to Lisbon to improve his health. With his daughter Betsy, he came to London and saw S. He went on to Margate, where a hot salt-water bath brought on a fever. S. was summoned to the bedside. Rae (ii. 28) says that the letter was written two days before Thomas Sheridan's death.

[4] Michael Morris, M.D., F.R.S., physician to Westminster Hospital. See Lefanu, p. 428.

of the frightful scene of being present at the last moments of such a person and so circumstanced. You will prepare and inform my sister[1] in the properest manner. Poor Betsy[2] is almost laid up.

114. To Daniel Jarvis[3]

Harvard MS. *Pub.*: Moore, ii. 15.

[*15 Aug. 1788*]
Friday morning

Sir,

I wished to have seen you this morning before I went to thank you for your Attention and trouble. You will be so good to give the account to Mr. Thompson who will settle it—and I must further beg your acceptance of the enclosed[4] from myself. | I am, Sir, | Your obedient Servant, | R B Sheridan.

I have explained to Dr. Morris who has informed me that you will recommend a proper Person, that it is my desire to have the Hearse and the manner of coming to Town[5] as respectful as possible.

115. To the Duchess of Devonshire

Dufferin MS. *Pub.*: Sichel, ii. 430–1.

[*Oct. 1788?*][6]

As for the other charge—my 'wanting to make *a great*

[1] Alicia, in Dublin.

[2] S.'s sister. Cf. *Betsy Sheridan's Journal* (ed. W. LeFanu, 1960), p. 116.

[3] A Margate physician who had attended Thomas Sheridan. His description (Harvard MS.) of what happened then is printed by Moore, ii. 14–16.

[4] William Thompson, S.'s father's servant, was to settle the account, but S. also gave Jarvis ten pounds, 'a most liberal remuneration'.

[5] Thomas Sheridan died on 14 Aug., and S. left Margate next morning, intending that his father should be buried

in London, only to find later that his father had given instructions that he was to be buried in the parish 'next to that in which he should happen to die'. So he was buried at Margate.

[6] I date this from the only allusion to Bridgeman that I have found in Georgiana's correspondence at this time. It occurs in Chatsworth MS. 908 [28 Sept. 1788], where the Duchess describes the entertainment she has prepared for the Calonnes when they reach Chatsworth in the following week. Bridgeman married Lucy Byng on 29 May 1788.

deal of some *very slight* and *natural* treachery of *poor* Tamphosbine's[1]—never was anything so unjust! I did not even know to what flagitious and unheard of lengths *poor* Tamphosbine had attempted to proceed 'till you told me! and now I shudder to think there can be such treachery in the world natural or acquired!!! I am clear such men can have no Peace of mind! But was I malicious or unfair about this? Pray remember that what I wrote was on the table at D² House and left for Bess[3] to finish—at least I left the Story in safe hands. But I should not be in the least surprised to hear of some sort of jocose tale of this sort being made even about me: for it is a world alas! in which *Propriety* of *conduct*, and Purity and decorum of sentiment are only taunted at and reviled! I must certainly seek some *Cavity*, and there pass my disappointed Life in praying for all your amendment, and deprecating the heavy retribution which I fear is in store for you.

And now after all I will admit that it was very good natured in you to write to me again, and very wrong in me not to write before—but the truth is that I had got at one time so compleatly bewilder'd in every possible scrape of every description, that the obvious thing to many People would have been to lie down and die. And I could not write to you with Pleasure then, tho' I always wish to hear from you.— I had a letter from Cheshire when I received yours from Leicester—very curious.—But why should you make any particular restraint for yourself if C. Greville comes with your Bridgemans?[4] I shall never think, let it come in whatever shape to me, that you have violated our League in anything you say, and it should be understood that you might talk of me in any way you like for any purpose, or I of you— only keeping faith to each other. As for C. G. tho' I think he would abuse me, I believe him to be very well-meaning— if his meaning was of a sort that signified.

[1] Unidentified. Possibly this was the Duchess's *cavaliere servente*, John Craufurd; or Charles Grey, who on 13 Jan. 1789 was said to be (with Lambton) the object of 'the old attack of Sheridan' (Sichel, ii. 425).

[2] Devonshire House.

[3] Lady Elizabeth Foster (1759–1824), mistress of the 5th Duke of Devonshire and, after Georgiana's death, his wife.

[4] Charles Greville (1762–1832), brother of Mrs. Crewe. For his 'incessant chattering', see *Leveson Gower Corr.*, i. 106. Orlando Bridgeman (1762–1825) became Earl of Bradford in 1815.

You ask me about Canning[1] and I must not forget to tell you, which I was nearly doing, that I have both had a Letter and seen him since—I brought his Letter one day to Town meaning to send it to you, but I did not write—but I will write again from Deepden and send you that and another. I am not satisfied about W. Spencer—but you may rely on my never thinking more of it as far as relates to him. What you will think odd is that I have had a Letter also from *him*, but nothing about this, but what is odder it is accompanied by one from his mother,[2] and what is odder still she wants to see me, and her motive still odder than all. I left these letters too at Deepden or I would send them to you and if by the blessing of God you had been wise in the Times I would have ask'd you what I ought to do.

I ought also to tell you a Piece of a Political secret, but after such a volume Ma'am! I think you will dispense with my telling anything more—or even mentioning the Eclogue I have written for her you called Callonius[3] and Tamphosbine—in which there are some very pretty verses[4] I assure you. The character of the Shepherds well discriminated—their community of woe and hope, the brisk despondency of the one, and the discriminating mirth of the other, the broken sighs and broken English, the apostrophe to Necker[5] and the quotations from Tully, The State Papers, the Garter and the state Arcade, all are naturally introduced and are even ornamental without violating the simplicity of Pastoral responses. The Character of Bess too—but this reminds me of the unextinguishable enmity which at this moment rages in my breast against *her*.—never to be explain'd —never to be appeased!—God bless *you* . . . T.L.[6]

---

[1] George Canning (1770–1827) was Mehitabel Canning's nephew, and was frequently in the company of the Sheridans. He was at Deepdene with Mrs. S. and Tickell on 11 Aug. 1788 (W.T.).

[2] W. R. Spencer's mother was Mary, daughter of Lord Vere.

[3] Charles Alexandre de Calonne (1734–1802)? Soon after his dismissal in 1787 by Louis XVI, Calonne came to England. On 5 July 1788 the Duchess wrote to her mother, 'I ring the changes on Calonne and Crawford' (Chatsworth MS. 878).

[4] Not found.

[5] Jacques Necker (1732–1804) was reappointed Director General of Finance in France, in Aug. 1788.

[6] S.'s unexplained pet-name for the Duchess of Devonshire.

116. To J. W. Payne[1]

Brotherton Collection MS., Leeds University.

[*6 Nov. 1788?*]

My Dear Payne,

It is very much wish'd for reasons which I will explain to you that you would come to Town *immediately*. I send this by express, and pray send to me in Bruton St. the moment you arrive. Lord Loughborough desires me to add his wishes that you would come to us directly[2]—| yours sincerely | R B Sheridan.

Thursday
3 o'clock.

117. To the Prince of Wales

Windsor MSS. 41915–6. *Dock.*: From Sheridan to the Prince.

[*6 Nov.? 1788*]

Sir

I entreat your Royal Highness to pardon my intruding for a moment on your attention at a time when your Royal Highness's mind must be so wholly engaged in the most distressful and embarrassing occupations,[3] and I trust your Royal Highness will believe that nothing but the sincerest zeal and Devotion to your service could have induced me to it. There are circumstances, which I will not now presume to detain your Royal Highness's attention by relating, which

[1] John Willett Payne (c. 1752–1803), naval captain, was keeper of the Privy Seal and Private Secretary to the Prince of Wales.

[2] George III was seriously ill of 'a palsy on the brain' and was thought to be in imminent danger of death: see *Particulars of the Royal Indisposition* (1804), pp. 1 and 3. Payne was needed as an intermediary between the Prince of Wales and his advisers, S. and Loughborough.

[3] The *Lond. Chron.*, 6–8 Nov. 1788, reported that 'the Prince of Wales has discovered the most endearing sensibility and solicitude on account of his Royal Parent's alarming situation. His own health has been affected by his watchfulness and anxiety; he was let blood on Thursday night....'

made me think it an indespensible Duty to endeavour at this moment to have that species of communication with the Chancellor[1] which under your Royal Highness's sanction was before proposed, and that I should not answer the service I owe your Royal Highness if I omitted it. Your Royal Highness will perceive by the Notes I have the Honor to enclose that this evening was fix'd for my seeing the C. but that your Royal Highness's command has call'd him to Windsor.[2] Lord Loughborough was equally convinced of the Propriety of the measure[3] and I thought myself bound to venture on it without further instructions from your Royal Highness at present so delicately and affectingly circumstanced. But certain considerations now induce me most humbly to request your Royal Highness would be graciously pleased to think a moment on the subject, for tho' according to my poor Judgement, most sincerely directed to your Royal Highness's service, it appears a measure *most conducive* to your Royal Highness's just and worthy Objects, yet I dread at such a Juncture taking the smallest step that may not meet your Royal Highness's approbation. I trust I need not assure your Royal Highness that whatever commands I am honour'd with will be received and executed with the most sacred confidence. Your Royal Highness will perceive that it is probable the C. will send to me immediately on his return, which has compell'd me to this abrupt intrusion. I have taken the Liberty to desire Weltje[4] to send this in the most proper manner, and perhaps your Royal

[1] Edward, 1st Lord Thurlow (1731–1806), claimed to have counselled the Prince to follow the advice of the physicians: 'Everything must flow to him of itself; he could only interrupt its course by impatience to receive it. . . . The Prince appeared convinced and expressed great obligation to me, but after he saw Sheridan he adopted the contrary course' (H.M.C., *Various Collections* (1909), vi. 278–9). His opponents thought he was trying to ensure a place for himself in any new government formed under the Prince's auspices; his friends thought he wished to achieve a compromise in a coalition government.

[2] The Lord Chancellor went to Windsor on 6 Nov. The avowed purpose was to discuss a way of treating the King, who had been ungovernable that night. See Rose, i. 87.

[3] Payne wrote to Loughborough on 7 Nov., stressing the Prince's friendship for and high opinion of Loughborough and adding, significantly, 'He [the Prince] has this morning talked to me of rejecting any rule, where somebody was not united to him' (Campbell, vi. 189).

[4] Louis Weltje was Clerk-Cook to the Prince, and acted as his factotum. He died 23 Oct. 1800.

Highness will be pleased to return to him whatever commands I am to be guided by.

I shall endeavour peremptorily to enforce your Royal Highness's commands respecting the Public Papers,[1] or any wish on the subject signified by your Royal Highness.

I have only again to implore your Royal Highness to forgive my trespassing on your Patience at such a moment, and to attribute it to the earnest zeal and attachment with which I have the Honor to be | Your Royal Highness's | most dutiful and devoted Servant | R B Sheridan

Thursday Night

118. J. W. Payne

Windsor MSS. Addl. Geo. 3. *Dock.*: From Sheridan

[7 Nov. 1788?]
Friday past six

Dear Payne,

I have the Honor of the Prince's Letter[2] safely, and have detained the Messenger awhile in expectation of having a Note from the Chancellor—but there is none yet come—

[1] For the Prince's letter of 5 Nov. 1788, threatening to prosecute any editor who published unauthorized accounts of the King's health, see S.C., 2 July 1935, lot 385. The *Morn. Post*, 14 Nov. 1788, reported that 'one of the leaders of Opposition made use of all his influence, to induce the Conductors of the Public Prints not to mention the illness of the KING.—This being in some measure disregarded, a circular letter was sent to the same persons, stating, that it was the *Command* of — —— — that nothing should appear on the subject of his Majesty's indisposition'. Cf., also, S.C., 27 Nov. 1945, lot 514, for S.'s letter 'to Almon the publisher on suppressing news about the King's health'.

[2] There is a draft (Windsor MS. 41912) and a fair copy (Windsor MS. 41905) of this. The fair copy reads: 'My dear Sheridan, I have just receiv'd your Packet and return the two notes it enclos'd, I think the best way you can act at present, is to proceed with the same overtures as if nothing had happen'd, to say that I was thoroughly appriz'd that it was probable you would have an Interview with the C—— and what was most likely to be the Subject of conversation, but not take any notice of your having sent to me to wish to know, in what manner I was desirous you should act *at the present moment*; Let me know the result of your meeting, and if you think proper (which in my opinion will be the best and most candid way) acquaint him with your intentions of doing so. You may suppose that I write in the utmost hurry; and therefore must conclude with assuring you *of my friendship*.' The draft is dated 'Novr. 7th. 1788'.

and I will not stop the Man's return. I beg you will present my Duty to his Royal Highness and as I perfectly comprehend the Distinction his Royal Highness has suggested in conversing with the Chancellor, I will be careful to attend to it. I will immediately acquaint his Royal Highness with the Result.

The Town is full of Consternation and strange Reports—and these are encreased by the silence of the Papers. I have taken measures to have the best information that can be had of the motions of certain Persons, and their Probable intentions. The Chancellor yesterday after parting with the Duke, wrote immediately to Pitt.[1] I am not sure whether he saw him or not, but Messengers were instantly dispatch'd to the Duke of Richmond, Lord Stafford etc. to bring them to Town.[2] I sent an Express to you yesterday at Brighton understanding that you were there, to beg you to come to Town, as there are some most important considerations which can only be treated of *in conversation*, but which it is of the utmost consequence should be submitted to the Prince's early attention, and I conceived the possessing you with the circumstances would answer every Purpose to the Princes service, without the indelicacy of solicitating his Royal Highness's direct attention to them. And if now his Royal Highness could spare you for a few hours—I think it would be of *essential advantage* that his Royal Highness should have the means of being so confidentially apprized of certain matters.

We have been anxious also about his Royal Highness's Health as we heard he was blooded[3] and very much indisposed. I will detain the Messenger no longer—I am Dear Payne | ever yours | R B Sheridan

[1] Pitt received a note from Thurlow on 7 Nov., saying that the Prince desired Pitt to come to Windsor the next day at eleven (*Court and Cabinets*, i. 435–6).

[2] Charles Lennox, 3rd Duke of Richmond (1735–1806), Master-General of the Ordnance; and Granville Leveson Gower, 1st Marquis of Stafford (1721–1803), Lord Privy Seal. Pitt's message to Stafford, headed 'Secret' and dated 6 Nov. 6 p.m., is given in full by Rose, i. 92–93. The King's symptoms, he wrote, 'proceed from a fever which has settled on the brain, and which may produce immediate danger to His Majesty's life'.

[3] See p. 186, n. 3, and cf. *Court and Cabinets*, i. 437: 'Nov. 7th . . . The Prince seems frightened, and was blooded yesterday.'

119. To J. W. Payne

Windsor MS. 42267. *Dock.*: From Sheridan

[*8 Nov. 1788?*]
Saturday Evening

My Dear Payne,

I send a Man who will call on you very quietly, and with-out causing any Reports which the motion of a Finger does at present. I had reason to believe that I should have heard the result of a meeting which was to have been in *Downing-Street* this evening but it is put off.—

Lord Brudenell's[1] intelligence and its consequences are *in full circulation*—and great Pains seem to be taken to make People believe it. It appears to me that the interdiction in the Papers should *in Part* be taken off.[2] And a general line of intelligence, omitting every hint which respect requires should be omitted, be permitted. I think in justice to the Prince it ought to be so.

After you went I informed Mrs. Fitzherbert[3] that I should have a Person at Windsor to Night to learn whether there was anything essential to the Prince's Service to be com-municated, and she express'd great anxiety to have a Line to be inform'd how His Royal Highness was, etc. | Your's ever sincerely, | R B S.

There is a Mail from the Continent in which there is ru-mour'd to be news of importance, but I have heard no Particulars.

---

[1] James, Lord Brudenell (1725–1811) succeeded as 5th Earl of Cardigan in 1790. He attended the King during his illness, but was also on intimate terms with the Prince. Duchess Georgiana noted, on 2 Dec., that the Prince, Thurlow, and Brudenell went to Windsor to 'look for some private jewels and money of the King's' (Sichel, ii. 410).

[2] They mentioned the King's illness again on 10 Nov.

[3] Maria Anne Fitzherbert (1756–1837) was born Smythe and had been married to Edward Weld and Thomas Fitzherbert. Her marriage to the Prince of Wales on 21 Dec. 1785 is disputed. Rose (i. 88) notes an evening before 17 Nov. 1788 when 'Mr. Sheridan, Mr. Payne, and Mrs. Fitzherbert went to the Prince at Bagshot'. S. was on very good terms with her at this period, and went to Rolle in Dec. 1788 to ask him 'in the Prince's name to desist from any enquiry about Mrs. Fitzherbert' (Add. MS. 41579, f. 12). In January, S. took refuge from bailiffs at her house.

1788

120. To J. W. Payne

Windsor MSS. 41924–5. *Dock.*: From Sheridan.

[*9 Nov. 1788?*]
Sunday: past twelve

My Dear Payne,
  Lord Loughborough call'd on me this morning, after
having sent to Weltje for a servant to take the enclosed. It
contains *the Sketch* Ld. L. mentioned.[1] Something of the
kind ought undoubtedly to be ready to be submitted to the
Prince's consideration, tho' there is as little Doubt that if his
Royal Highness was composed enough He would dictate
it better himself. Every syllable of *the Declaration* will be
canvass'd and all sort of *meaning* discovered in every syllable.
I think the Prince if He adopts the enclosed, will alter
Parts and perhaps something might be added. Lord Loughborough has not only the best intentions and the greatest
zeal for the Prince's service, and certainly no one can advise
with better judgement in such matters—but I own I think
the wording of this stiff, and not in the style which would
answer what may be expected from the Feelings which will
be in the Princes mind. At the same time it cannot be too
general and safe. The mention of *agriculture* etc. is not usual
nor good. Lord L. made some alterations at my suggestion,
but I am sure you will understand how unpleasant a thing
it is to find many faults in such a matter, and as it was before
a third Person I did not care to do it, at the same time I cannot help observing thus much to you, as I really think it
of the *utmost consequence*, that this *first Royal Communication*

---

[1] In an undated letter to Payne,
Loughborough advocated 'a declaration
to be made and entered at the first meeting of council; the substance of which
should be well considered and digested,
because it would be taken as an indication of the spirit of the future Government. It should be short, general, and
at the same time satisfactory to the
public on the great lines of policy'
(Campbell, vi. 193–4). This may well
be part of the letter that Payne replied
to on Monday, 10 Nov. (Campbell, vi.
191–2). If this is so (and the allusion to
'this first Royal communication' seems
to support an early date), the previous
day would be a suitable one for the
meeting of S. and Loughborough. The
references to 'the Prince's being composed enough' and to this later 'certain
event' also suggest that the above letter
belongs to the first week of the King's
illness. Cf. Letter 122.

should be as correct and perfect as possible—and I wish when the necessity comes the Prince's own attention could be drawn to it. You see my Dear Payne, I write without reserve to you, and I am sure no caution is necessary.

I am very much obliged to you for the fulness of your communication last night. I purposely avoid being in the way of People that my name may not be entangled in any Reports.

I have certain intelligence, that measures are *already taking* to give a *particular complexion* to the address which would immediately come from the City of London in case of a certain event,[1] and I suppose the same Game is preparing elsewhere— | Yours most sincerely | R B S

121. To J. W. Payne

Windsor MS. 41918. *Dock.*: From Sheridan.

[*10 Nov.? 1788*][2]

My Dear Payne,

I find there is a messenger going directly by whom I have only time to acknowledge the receipt of yours. If the State continues to be such that a *Regency* is to be thought of, The most early as the well as best formed Judgements must be obtain'd—for in all the Discussions we have had on the subject I perceive new reason to find the Prospect full of Delicacy and embarrassment.—I will prepare a digested statement of the most authoritative opinions that can be collected on this Point. | ever Yours | R B Sheridan

½ past 4. Monday

---

[1] I read this as referring to the King's death, expected at any time in the first week of the illness. The City strongly supported Pitt, and the *Pub. Adv.* (22 Dec. 1788) stated that a meeting at the Royal Exchange was to be held to consider an address to the Prince 'not to dismiss from his Councils those servants of his Majesty, under whose Administration the nation has been restored from the brink of ruin to a state of prosperity . . .'. Cf. Add. MS. 41579, f. 15.

[2] As early as 8 Nov. W. W. Grenville discussed a Regency in a letter to his brother (Dropmore Papers, i. 364); and on 17 Nov. the *Morn. Chron.* printed 'A History of Regencies'. The most suitable Monday is, therefore, 10 Nov., a fitting date for S. to receive the letter (Moore, ii. 24–28) Payne had written to him on 9 [?] Nov.

122. To J. W. Payne

Windsor MS. 41911. *Dock.*: From Sheridan

[*14–15 Nov.? 1788*]

My Dear Payne,
Tho' I have nothing material to communicate to the
Prince, I am too anxious not to wish to hear from you, and
the State of Things to Night. Here *reports* have made a
total Revolution both in opinions of the *future*, and even
of what *has been* the *past* state of the K.'s situation.[1] The
Prince will of course govern his communication to the council if his Royal Highness has call'd them,[2] by the state of
things tomorrow. I shall be happy to hear that the Prince is
well himself. It is true that Letters[3] are sent to all members
of Parliament etc. and these[4] Letters as you will observe
even suppose a *possibility* of the K. being well enough to
prorogue Parliament between this and *thursday*![5] a curious
piece of Deception truly— | Yours ever | R B S.

123. [To Lord Loughborough]

Pub.: Campbell, vi. 192–3.

[*19 Nov.? 1788*]

My Dear Lord,
Every thing remained late last night at Windsor without

[1] '13 November . . . A palsy on the
brain was said to be the cause . . . which
no medical skill could reach; and an
opinion universally prevailed, that it
would be necessary immediately to form
a Regency' (*Particulars of the Royal
Indisposition* (1804), p. 3). By 15 Nov.
Pitt thought that the King might recover completely: see J. H. Rose,
William Pitt and National Revival
(1911), p. 412.

[2] A meeting of the Privy Council
had been arranged for either 17 or 18
Nov. See *Court and Cabinets*, i. 446.

[3] Dated 14 and 15 Nov., and informing members of a probable meeting of
parliament on 20 Nov. See Fitzwilliam
MSS. (Sheffield), and the *Lond. Chron.*,
15–18 Nov. 1788.

[4] Possibly 'those'.

[5] The actual clause reads: '. . . it is
doubtful whether there will be a possibility of receiving his Majesty's commands for the further prorogation of
Parliament; and if there should not, the
two Houses must of necessity as-
semble . . .' (*Lond. Chron.*, 15–18 Nov.
1788).

the least amendment, and in consequence of a consultation of the physicians, they are, I believe, ready to give a decided opinion.[1]

The Prince sends Payne to town this morning. I shall make an attempt at setting his head a little to rights,[2] if possible, for he is growing worse and worse, but a few words from your Lordship will have more weight. Among other things, he tells me he has suggested to the Prince to write directly to the Chancellor, and he tells me that the letter shall be so worded that either he or I may deliver it, so that I suppose his notion is to bring this negotiation into the same train and footing as Lord Sandwich's.[3] It is really intolerable, and I mean to speak very plainly to him. I will endeavour to have the honour of seeing your Lordship this morning; if not, at Lord North's in the evening.[4] | I have the honour to be, with great truth and respect, | Your Lordship's most sincere and obedient, | R. B. Sheridan.

Wednesday morning.

124. To J. W. Payne

Windsor MS. 41704. *Address*: Mr. Payne.

[*1788?*]

Dear Payne,
    We are waiting for you. I have sent my Coach | Yrs | R B S

[1] On 9 Nov. the King's physicians asked Pitt to be allowed a fortnight before they made their declaration; and on 27 Nov. they were examined by the Privy Council at Windsor.

[2] See Payne's letters (belonging, probably, to 8–24 Nov. 1788) in Moore, ii. 21–30, and Campbell, vi. 189–92.

[3] The Prince promised Sandwich that he should be appointed First Lord of the Admiralty when the opposition came into office. This annoyed Fox and Portland intensely, and S. had to persuade the Prince to give up the idea. Presumably S. means that any similar promise of office to Thurlow by the Prince would split the opposition asunder. See Add. MS. 41579, f. 11.

[4] A meeting of 'about 20 Lords and Commoners' of the Opposition was held at Lord North's on Wednesday, 19 Nov. See *Minto Corr*. i. 234.

125. To J. W. Payne

Windsor MSS. 41705–6. *Address*: J. W. Payne Esq. *Dock.*: From Sheridan.

[*20 Nov. 1788*]
6 o'clock

My Dear Payne,
   I have just received the Princes commands to meet him very early in the morn at Backshot.[1] | Yours most sincerely | R B S.

126. To the Prince of Wales

Windsor MSS. 41921–2. *Dock.*: From Sheridan

[*23 Nov. 1788*]

Sir,
   Altho' the message I was honor'd with makes it probable that your Royal Highness's commands may give me an early opportunity of personally submitting to your Royal Highness's Judgement whatever information or idea I have for your Royal Highness's service,[2] yet I cannot refrain from entreating your Royal Highness to pardon my intruding now for a moment on your Royal Highness' Attention, convinced as I am that your Royal Highness's situation is the most arduous, the most delicate, and difficult that can be conceived in the History of any country. Your Royal Highness I am confident will not doubt my sincerity, and I only hope you will pardon the Liberty I take, in saying that your Royal Highness can want no counsel where you have time and opportunity to turn to the suggestions of your own clear understanding, all my apprehension is that the magnitude of many of the Objects which must present them-

---

[1] The Duchess of Devonshire noted on 20 Nov. that the Prince of Wales asked Sheridan, that evening, to meet him at Bagshot next day. See Sichel, ii. 405; and cf. Campbell, vi. 192; *Betsy Sheridan's Journal*, p. 131; and P. Fitzgerald, *Life of George the Fourth* (1881), i. 93.

[2] 'During the whole of the [Regency] contest, Mr. Sheridan was at infinite pains to make himself master of the subject' (*Annual Biography and Obituary . . . 1817*, p. 173). Cf. Sichel, ii. 419, for his 'studying precedents'.

selves to your R. Highness's mind, may render it impossible to advert to lesser Points, which may appear of slight import but which in the event may be of the last importance.—I probably may be too precipitate in my anxiety but the Rumours of the Day urge me with all humility but with the utmost earnestness to implore your Royal Highness, to suspend giving authority or countenance either to the idea of calling in a *different medical opinion*[1] on his Majesty's case, or to the *removal of his Majesty*, or even to the removal of any *Part of the Royal Family*,[2] on the ground of amendment being despair'd of, *untill* by your Royal Highness's command a meeting of his Majesty's Cabinet Ministers shall have been held at Windsor, and they shall have given, upon deliberate and solemn enquiry, an opinion which may bring responsibility where it ought to rest, and prevent the misconstruction of malice in every possible event.[3]

I have again to entreat your Royal Highness to pardon a Caution which may probably be needless, but as it is with the sincerest satisfaction that I hear a universal sentiment of warm and respectful approbation of the whole of your Royal Highness's conduct during this critical and arduous Trial, prevail thro' all ranks and descriptions of People, I cannot help feeling a proportion'd anxiety that no possible ground should be afforded to any, whose malignity or disappointment might hereafter lead them to misrepresent the best actions.

I will not *now* venture to detain your Royal Highness by stating the particular Reasons which have induced me to be so urgent on this Head, nor add more than to repeat the Duty and | Attachment with which | I have the Honor to remain | Your Royal Highness's devoted Servant | R B Sheridan

Sunday Evening

[1] See p. 197.

[2] This was mentioned as early as 20 Nov. in the *Pub. Adv.*: 'Should His Majesty not recover soon, there is a rumour of removing the Royal Family Kew. Some late alarms have made a separation very necessary.' When the proposal to move George III was made, Pitt's supporters claimed that a change of surroundings would be beneficial and that the King could take the air at Kew without being seen by the public: see *Court and Cabinets*, ii. 20–21.

[3] This advice was accepted by the Prince, and the Cabinet met at Windsor on 27 Nov. The King was removed to Kew on 29 Nov.

1788

127. To J. W. Payne

Windsor MS. 41923. *Dock.*: From Sheridan

[*23 Nov.? 1788*]
7 o'clock

My Dear Payne,

I have just got your Letter,[1] just as I had finish'd a Letter to his Royal Highness.[2] I will not stop to tell you the reasons which had induced me [to] trouble him—but if what I heard to Day, and it was said on the authority of Warren,[3] that there is any idea of calling in Dr. *M.*[4] or of the King or Queen's moving, before there has been a Council at Windsor for God sake second my entreaties that it may be suspended and I am sure my reasons, will not be disapproved of when I explain them.—The Man is to wait for a Line from you. | yours ever | R B S.

I have a good deal to tell you

128. To J. W. Payne

Windsor MSS. 41919–20. *Dock.*: From Sheridan

[*23 Nov.? 1788*]
Bagshot
Sunday Night
past 7

My Dear Payne,

I think the Prince cannot avoid seeing any of the Ministers if they desire it, but I own I think the *safe Line* is his Royal Highness having them there in a Body.[5] Which I suppose

[1] See Moore, ii. 29–30.
[2] Letter 126 ?
[3] Richard Warren (1731–97) had been the Prince's physician since 1787.
[4] This is plainly 'M', and cannot represent Anthony Addington (1713–90) who was called in now, or Francis Willis (1718–1807), who saw the King on 8 Dec. Possibly it refers to Donald

Monro (1727–1802): the *Pub. Adv.*, 14 Nov. 1788, noted, 'Dr. Monro is now at Windsor, an assistant to the other medical advisers'; but this was denied in the *Morn. Chron.*, 15 Nov.
[5] S. saw the Duchess of Devonshire on 23 Nov. and said he wished the new government to be 'a true Rockingham administration' (Sichel, ii. 406).

197

will still be his Determination. The D of R.'s[1] duplicity is quite diverting. But I think Pitt's pretending to convey to the Prince any Idea of what ought or ought not to be done *in Parliament*, on the first Day's meeting is evidently a Snare, and depend on it some advantage would be taken of any sanction or any opinion even, which they could draw from the Prince on such subjects. We should square our conduct on that Day of course to the Princes Wishes—but to do it with effect whether by Silence or speaking, the Prince should stand clear of their having the least pretence to insinuate that any interference or wish of his had govern'd our Proceedings.—Possibly the Prince will think it advisable to speak a little more plainly to the Chancellor about Pitt: for I think it a thing much to be avoided to give the least ground to old Thurlow to imagine that the Duke of R. or P[2] can ever Practice any successful maneuvres either with the Prince or with us. I say this because He (the C.) threw out to me a suspicion that Pitt and we should come together,[3] which I told him I thought utterly impossible for many reasons—and the Principal one the Princes own Feelings[4] —at which he seem'd much satisfied.

I scribble this just as I am going—I will send to Windsor in the morn—with whatever news I hear in Town. | Yours ever | R B S.

---

[1] Richmond was thought to favour a coalition (*Dropmore Papers*, i. 368), but the Marquis of Carmarthen noted his saying in the Cabinet of 28 Nov., 'some proposal might be made for a coalition, which he thought would be a fortunate circumstance, as by rejecting any junction with men who were personally obnoxious to the King, we should do ourselves honour, as H.M.'s servants' (*Leeds' Mem.*, p. 124-5).

[2] S. was clearly opposed to any form of coalition with Pitt.

[3] This appears to support the idea that Thurlow wanted a coalition, but when Pitt asked him about the propriety or expediency of joining the Opposition under any circumstances,

he refused to give a direct answer (Rose, i. 90). S. told Lady Elizabeth Foster on 24 Nov., 'they talk of the Chancellor's being President of the Council and Lord Loughborough Chancellor' (Add. MS. 41579, f. 5).

[4] W. W. Grenville wrote, on 20 Nov.: 'On the question of coalition, no offers have as yet been made. The language of Opposition inclines one to think that their idea is *to that*, but the conduct of the Prince of Wales marks a desire of avoiding Pitt' (*Court and Cabinets*, ii. 7-8). The Prince had possession of the King's papers and some of them proved that Pitt had drafted George's rebukes to the Prince.

129. To J. W. Payne

Windsor MSS. 41830–1. *Dock.*: From Sheridan

[*24 Nov. 1788*]

My Dear Payne,

I came to this Place¹ very late last Night to pass one Day and Charles's Groom is come after me—to fetch me back. He arrived at 7 this morning—and as the man says He was going to lie down devilishly tired² it may be that you will not hear of his arrival sooner than by me sending from this Place. I am going to Town directly. The Bearer will wait for any Letter from you³ or commands from the Prince—to whom I also enclose a Letter from Lord L. which I did not get 'till after my return from Bagshot,⁴ and I thought it probable I might have an opportunity of giving it to you in Town—as I am sure his intention was that the Prince should see it—tho' I have not see[n] Lord L. since. I have not myself a Doubt of anything being done or even attempted against the Prince in the House of Commons. I assure you, if they were rash enough to try their utmost our Strength there would be beyond what you could conceive.—Something must be done about the Reports which are raised and circulated in Town and sent into the Country—the malice and impudence of some of them is intolerable.⁵ I hope by

¹ Deepdene, Dorking. The Duke of Norfolk lent the Sheridans this house for the summer of 1788. Mrs. S. wrote to Mrs. Canning on 20 May: 'the House is large enough to accommodate Solomon and all his Wives they say—it is not beautiful in itself, but the Country is charming about it' (W.T.).

² In Aug. 1788 Fox set off with his mistress, Mrs. Armitstead, for a holiday abroad. The Prince asked (about 7 Nov.) for him to be recalled; and he was overtaken at Bologna on 14 Nov.

³ Payne's reply is printed in Moore, ii. 29–30.

⁴ An undated letter by Loughborough to S. is among the Windsor MSS. (38242–4). It was written on 'Thursday night' and may possibly belong to 20 Nov. In it, Loughborough states that he has heard of a 'Project seriously entertained to deny the P.'s right and to form a government either under his name as an elected Regent with limitations, or in the King's name by issuing Commissions and orders by authority delegated from the two Houses to the Ministers'. He recognized that the Prince could not put himself forward at this point, but suggested that he give his friends authority to say that he would not submit 'to any encroachment of his just rights'. A canvass for support of the Prince should then be made.

⁵ See *The Hamwood Papers* (ed. Bell, 1930), pp. 155–6, for a report that Fox had poisoned the King.

this time the truth will have been forced in a formal way into the ears of the Cabinet. | Yours ever, | R B S
Dipden
12 o'clock Monday

130. To the Prince of Wales

Windsor MSS. 41832-3. *Dock.*: From Sheridan to the Prince.

[24 Nov. 1788]

Sir,
    I think it my Duty to inform your Royal Highness, lest your Royal Highness should not be immediately apprized of it from Town that Mr. Fox arrived at seven o'clock this morning. His Servant is this moment come to me at this Place where I meant to have stay'd the Day—but I shall go directly to Town and remain in the way to execute any commands from your Royal Highness. I also take this opportunity of submitting to your Royal Highness's Perusal a Letter I received from Lord Loughborough. I take the Liberty of doing this from a Perswasion that it was Lord Loughborough's intention that I should do so, and that he thought it of consequence that your Royal Highness should be apprized of what it contains. I confess however that I have not myself the slightest apprehension that any of the Efforts Lord Loughborough alludes to can have the smallest success. At the same time it is undoubtedly Prudent to be provided against all possible machinations, and it is with great Pleasure I can venture to assure your Royal Highness from a direct communication with many neutral and moderate People, and with some who might from connexion be supposed to be adverse, that there would *even at present* be a great and decided majority in favour of that Plan of settlement which alone would do justice to your Royal Highness's Right[1] or suit the Principles of the Constitution. | I have the Honor,

[1] The *Lond. Chron.*, a Pittite newspaper, cautioned its readers in its issue of 13-15 Nov. not to accept paragraphs in other papers suggesting that the Prince would be sole Regent with all the Royal prerogatives because he was Heir Apparent. Such discussions, it added, were premature, and could only be settled by the consent of Parliament.

Sir, | to remain with the truest Devotion | Your Royal Highness's | most dutiful and faithful Servant | R B Sheridan.
Deepden
12 o'clock Monday.

131. [To Lord Loughborough?]

Windsor MS. 38245.

[26–27 Nov. 1788?][1]

The Prince wishes your Lordship to inform his Majesty's confidential Servants that it is with the deepest concern and regret that the Family have received communications from the Physicians attending on his Majesty upon which The Prince must decline giving any opinion untill the whole of his Majesty's situation has been fully examined into by his Majesty['s] confidential Servants and such Persons as they shall chuse to join in their Deliberations, and the Opinions and Proceedings of the Physicians have been laid for them.

132. To the Prince of Wales

Windsor MS. 38373.

[Nov.–Dec. 1788?][2]

Sir,

In obedience to your Royal Highness's wishes I have been with the Chancellor this morning and stay'd with him near two Hours. I have taken the Liberty of communicating

[1] I assume that this is the message (*Leeds' Mem.*, pp. 121–4) that Lord Carmarthen described the Prince as sending late at night on 26 Nov., desiring the attendance of the King's confidential servants at Windsor next day at two. When the Cabinet arrived at Windsor, its members examined the physicians to decide if it was necessary to remove the King to Kew. S. and Fox were with the Prince on the morning of 26 Nov.: see Add. MS. 41579, f. 5.

[2] This may refer to negotiations with Thurlow either before or after the return of Fox. Four letters from Thurlow to S., concerning interviews in the first week of Dec. 1788, were among the Frampton MSS.; and S. 'had been with the Chancellor from ten to three' (Add. MS. 41579, f. 13) on 14 Dec. Thurlow said, 'On my conscience I think the King will recover'. He saw the Prince on 19 or 20 Dec. and S. afterwards reported that there were 'no hopes of good from the Chancellor—a shilly shally shabby fellow' (Add. MS. 41579, f. 15). For Thurlow's views on the Regency, see Maggs Catalogue 659 (1938), item 122.

the most material Points to Payne as the shorter method of submitting the Result to your Royal Highness's considera- tion: It is with the greatest satisfaction that I have the Honor to assure your Royal Highness that the Business appears to be precisely in the Train your Royal Highness would wish it—and to promise under your Royal Highness's approbation an essential advantage to your Royal Highness's Service.

I am to hear again from the Chancellor, and I will im- mediately transmit to your Royal Highness an accurate account of the Results | I have the Honor to be | with every sentiment of | Duty and attachment | Your Royal Highness's | most grateful and | Devoted Servant | R B Sheridan Saturday.

133. To Lord Palmerston[1]

Price MS. *Pub.*: B. Connell, *Portrait of a Whig Peer* (1957), p. 185. *Dock.*: Mr. Sheridan | Novr. 1788

[*1 Dec.? 1788*]

My Dear Lord,
The news as far as relates to the Kings health has con- tinued so much the same that there has been nothing worth telling. The case of our Politics is that the Prince has really behaved in the fairest and noblest manner possible. He has very steadily turned aside from all the Practices of the ministers and those employ'd by them, and has now in an open and avow'd manner employ'd the Duke of Portland and Fox to make their own arrangements in case events give him the Power. His conduct to the Duke of Portland,[2] whom he saw at Burlington House on saturday, has been everything thats right—desiring him to shake hands and that they would never again think of the Dispute they had about the motion for paying his Debts etc.—The King is *certainly* worse than ever. Pitt and the Chancellor have both

---

1 Henry Temple, 2nd Viscount Pal- merston (1739–1802).

2 'The Prince said he certainly had been angry with the Duke of Portland for his conduct about the payment of his debts [in 1787].' On 26 Nov. 1788 he 'commissioned Mr. Fox to shake hands with him in his name; and [said] that he would come to Burlington House Saturday [30 Nov.]'. See Add. MS. 41579, f. 5.

seen him. He abused Pitt like a Dog.[1] I believe there will
be no more adjournments and that the measure will be to
propose a previous enquiry into the King's state. | I have the
Honor to be | my Dear Lord | your's most faithfully | R B
Sheridan
Monday

134. To the Prince of Wales

Windsor MSS. 41913–14. *Pub.*: Moore, ii, 19–21, from a draft
version, the manuscript of which is at Yale. *Dock.*: From Sheridan to
the Prince

[*2 Dec. 1788?*][2]

Sir,

From the intelligence of to Day we are led to think that Pitt
will make something more of a speech in moving to adjourn
on thursday than was at first imagined. In this case I humbly
presume your Royal Highness will be of opinion that we
must not remain wholly silent.[3] I possess'd Payne yesterday
with my sentiments on the line of conduct which appear'd
to me best to be adopted on this occasion[4] that they might
be submitted to your Royal Highness's consideration, and
I took the Liberty of repeating my firm conviction that it
will greatly advance your Royal Highness's credit, and, in
case of Events, lay the strongest ground for baffling every
attempt at opposition to your Royal Highness's just claims
and *Right*,[5] that the *Language of Those* who may be in any-
way suspected of acting with a due Deference to your Royal

[1] Sir Gilbert Elliot's letter to Pal-
merston of 1 Dec. gives further details
of this. See Connell, op. cit., pp. 186–7.

[2] Moore (ii. 19) assigns the letter to
the interval between the meetings of
parliament on 20 Nov. and 4 Dec. I
assume that S., in the above, puts his
first request to the Prince for 'uncon-
ditional acquiescence' and that he repeated this in a lost letter to the Prince,
written on the following day. See the
next Letter.

[3] As the Foxites had been on 20
Nov.

[4] Lady Elizabeth Foster noted that S.

said, in the evening of 3 Dec., that 'there
would be warm doings tomorrow in the
House'; and that it was believed 'the
Ministry means to propose a Regency
for a year or a joint Regency' (Add.
MS. 41579, f. 7).

[5] This became the theme of the great
debates of 10 Dec. onwards, but as early
as 26 Nov. we find S.'s wife writing to
Alicia Lefanu, 'it is reported that
Ministry mean to oppose the Prince of
Wales's right to be sole Regent but the
attempt will only disgrace them for
there is but one Voice on the Subject'
(LeFanu MS.).

Highness's wishes and Feelings should be that of great moderation, disclaiming all Party views, and avowing the *utmost readiness* to acquiesce in every reasonable Delay.

At the same time, Sir, I am perfectly aware of the arts which will be resorted to, and the kind of advantages which some People will attempt to gain from *Time*;[1] but I am equally convinced that we should advance their evil views by shewing the least impatience or suspicion at present.[2]

I am also convinced that a third Party will *soon appear* whose interference may in a decisive manner prevent this sort of situation and Proceeding from continuing long. Payne will probably have submitted to your Royal Highness more fully my idea on this subject, towards which I have already taken some successful steps.[3]

Your Royal Highness will I trust have the goodness to pardon the Freedom with which I give my opinion, after which I have only to add that whatever your Royal Highness's Judgement decides shall be the guide of my conduct. — | I have the Honor to be | with the sincerest attachment | Your Royal Highness's | most dutiful and devoted Servant | R B Sheridan

Tuesday evening.

135. To J. W. Payne

Windsor MS. 41834. *Dock.*: From Sheridan

[*18 Nov. or 3 Dec. 1788?*]

near six

My Dear Payne,

I was in great hopes to have heard from you before this—

[1] As Pitt did by a full discussion of the Prince's 'right'.

[2] This had been their attitude on 20 Nov.: 'Opposition had resolv'd to be very moderate to agree to the adjournment should it be proposed, and not to hurry anything' (Add. MS. 41579, f. 3).

[3] The 'Armed Neutrality' was a group of independents, led by the northern magnates, Northumberland and Rawdon. From two letters owned by Mr. F. W. Hilles, it appears that S.'s approaches were made to Northumberland and Sir John Sinclair, with a view to obtaining the support of 'about thirty in the Commons and twenty in the Lords' (*Auckland Corr*. ii. 258–9). Lady Elizabeth Foster noted that S. gave her on 18 Dec., 'the secret news . . . that the arm'd neutrality would be for us—that there had been a meeting at Lord Rawdon's' (Add. MS. 41579, f. 15). Cf. H.M.C., *Various Collections*, vi. 203–7; Sichel, ii. 419.

there will be a meeting in the morn¹ before which I wish to be possess'd of his sentiments—everyone says Pitt is to make a prancing Harangue but I don't have to believe it. I have been at home all Day, not being well. I have really a very bad pain in my head and have had for some Days. I don't know whose sins are visited upon me.—Pray let me hear to Night or early in the morn—I write to the Prince, repeating my extreme Desire for unconditional acquiescence on thursday *on our Parts*.² | your's ever | R B S.

Pray look at a Letter to Day in the M. Chronicle sign'd etc.³ B. Amicus. It is written by Horne Tooke.⁴

136. To Lord Lonsdale⁵

Text from Sir Shane Leslie's transcription, made at Lowther Castle in 1941.

*[Dec. 1788?]*⁶

Mr. Sheridan presents his Respects to Lord Lonsdale, and in obedience to the commands of his Royal Highness the Prince of Wales requests the Honor of waiting upon

¹ The opposition met for consultation on both 19 Nov. and 4 Dec.

² Both times Pitt was expected to propose short adjournments.

³ Badly written. Possibly 'M'.

⁴ A long letter (dated 15 Nov.) by 'M. B. Amicus' was printed in the *Morn. Chron.*, 18 Nov. 1788, under the heading, 'No Regency'. It argued that the Prince had 'no clearer *right*' than the letter-writer himself to 'create a Regency'. The same issue stated that 'the pen of' John Horne Tooke (1736–1812) 'will be vigorously employed upon the occasion of the appointment of a Regency'. 'Magna Britanniae Amicus' wrote on the topic, 'Of Regencies', in the *Morn. Chron.*, 3 Dec. 1788; praised Pitt's administration and condemned 'the folly of appointing a sole Regent'.

⁵ James Lowther, Earl of Lonsdale (1736–1802), commanded nine votes in Parliament and, up to Nov. 1788, had

supported Pitt (H.M.C., *P. V. Smith MSS.* (1891), p. 373).

⁶ On 9 Dec., W. W. Grenville reported that Lonsdale's position was uncertain; but on 17 Dec. he stated: 'Lord Lonsdale's people were against us [i.e. voted against Pitt], in consequence of a letter, written by the Prince of Wales himself, soliciting it as a personal favour' (*Court and Cabinets*, ii. 41, 64). I assume that S. carried the message, possibly on 14 Dec. That he was the intermediary is given some support by a letter written him by the Prince, on what seems to be 16 Dec. The hand is an agitated one and the Prince inquires 'Will the Lonsdales vote sure' (Windsor MS. 41709). For the Prince's letters of 13 and 14 Dec., and Pitt's attempts to win Lonsdale's support, see H.M.C., *Lonsdale MSS.* (1893), pp. 141–3. For the Prince's letter on the question of right, see Appendix G, no. 2.

him tomorrow. If three o'clock is a convenient Hour to Lord Lonsdale Mr. Sheridan will do himself the honor of calling at that time.

Bruton St.   Saturday Night

137. To J. W. Payne

Windsor MS. 38374. *Dock.*: Mr. Sheridan

[*28 Dec. 1788*][1]
Sunday Night.

Dear Payne,

I executed the Princes commission to Night—and left Lord Loughborough highly gratified. He is extremely fair, and I think there are some things he wishes to say which the Prince will be pleased with. He will wait on his Royal Highness tomorrow at two o'clock, pray enquire if that hour is convenient and convey the Princes Pleasure to him if it should not. | Yours Ever | R B Sheridan

There is going to be a ministerial meeting at Manchester[2] which will certainly be defeated.

138. [To C. J. Fox]

Add. MS. 47569, f. 304–5. *Dock.*: Mr. Sheridan

[*1788–9 ?*]
Saturday evening

Dear Charles,

There is nothing in the world I am more convinced of than your Desire to do me any essential service in your Power—but I plague you with this at this time at another Persons instigation, and so I discharge my conscience. If

[1] The Duchess of Devonshire noted in her diary, on Sunday, 28 Dec., that S. informed her that Loughborough was to be Lord Chancellor when the opposition came into power, and was pleased at the idea. On the following day, she noted that S. had been sent by the Prince to Loughborough with this message (Sichel, ii. 421).

[2] On 30 Dec., to thank Pitt.

the appointment you talk'd of *could* take place,[1] it would be happy to me in point of convenience, and in giving me the use of my Time and my mind to a degree which I have found it impossible to say to you; and so I now write it. With regard to executing the Business it is an act of confidence in me which your Friendship must risk in the recommendation and I assure you sincerely if I thought it would now prevent what was likely to turn out a preferable arrangement, putting old Friendship out of the Question, I would not press the matter for a moment. But I think something has occurr'd to me which I'll explain when I see you which might do away [with] the difficulties you mentioned, and in that case I should be vex'd not to have succeeded from never having told you (which might be the case) of how much consequence your interesting yourself decisively in this matter might have been to me.

And now it is ridiculous enough to talk this way in the present state of matters. But if the good Days of opposition are to continue we are all in a Boat,[2] and if the other comes about I have written more to you, than perhaps I should have said, which you will probably think a foolish proceeding, but so it is.— | Your's ever | R B Sheridan.

139. To Lady Duncannon[3]

Brinsley Ford MS. *Pub.*: Sichel, ii. 429.

[*1788–9*]
Tuesday Night.

I must bid *oo*[4] good Night for by the Light passing to

[1] Lady E. Foster noted, as early as 23 Nov. 1788, that the Opposition wished S. to become Treasurer of the Navy and 'head of the Board of Trade' (Add. MS. 41579, f. 4), in the administration that was expected to come into office. In the provisional list made in Feb. 1789, S. was allotted the Treasurership of the Navy, with a stipend of £4,000 p.a. See *Auckland Corr.* ii. 289.

[2] Because the King was considered to

have recovered, the Chancellor moved (on 15 Feb. 1789) the postponement of further consideration of the Regency Bill. The Opposition's chance of taking office had gone.

[3] Henrietta (1761–1821), daughter of John, 1st Earl Spencer, and sister of Georgiana, Duchess of Devonshire. Frederick Ponsonby, Viscount Duncannon (1758–1844) became her husband in 1780 and 3rd Earl of Bessborough in Mar.

[*Footnotes 3 amd 4 continued on p. 208*

and fro near your room I hope you are going to bed, and to sleep happily, with a hundred little cherubs fanning their white wings over you in approbation of your goodness. Yours is the sweet untroubled sleep of purity.

Grace shines around you with serenest beams and whispering Angels prompt your golden dreams and yet and yet— Beware!! Milton will tell you that even in Paradise Serpents found their way to the ear of slumbering innocence.—

Then to be sure poor Eve had no watchful guardian to pace up and down beneath her windows or clear sighted friend to warn her of the sly approaches of T's and F's[1] and W's[2] and a long list of wicked letters. And Adam I suppose was—at Brooke[s]'s!—'fye Mr. S'—I answer 'fye fye Lord D.' Tell him either to come with you or forbid your coming to a House so inhabited.—Now dont look grave. Remember it is my office to speak truth.—

I shall be gone before your Hazel eyes are open tomorrow, but for the sake of the Lord D. that you will not suffer me to blame—do not listen to Jack's[3] Elegies or smile at F's epigrams or tremble at C. W.'s frowns but put on that look of gentle firmness, and pass on in Maiden Meditation fancy free[4]—Now draw the Curtain Sally.[5]

1793. S. was often in Lady Duncannon's company in Mar. and Apr. 1789, and his sister noted her casting many tender looks across the table at him in June 1789: see the Earl of Bessborough and A. Aspinall, *Lady Bessborough and her Family Circle* (1940), pp. 48–52; and *Betsy Sheridan's Journal*, p. 168. On 18 June one of the 'Ladies of Llangollen' heard (*The Hamwood Papers*, p. 214) that S. had been caught with Lady Duncannon and that her husband had begun divorce proceedings. This is confirmed in a letter (Canning MS.; Sadler, pp. 82–83) by Mrs. S. to Mrs. Canning of *c.* 1790, after the Duke of Devonshire had prevailed on Duncannon to forgive his wife.

[4] The Devonshire House ladies were fond of baby-talk. See the satirical description in *Intimate Letters of the Eighteenth Century* (ed. the Duke of Argyll, 1910), i. 314–17.

[1] Sichel, ii. 429, suggests Townshend and Fitzpatrick.

[2] Possibly Charles Wyndham.

[3] Townshend.

[4] *A Midsummer Night's Dream*, II. i. 159–61:
And the imperial votaress passed on,
In maiden meditation fancy free
Yet marked I where the bolt of Cupid fell.

[5] Lady Duncannon's maid. Cf. *Leveson Gower Corr.* i. 115.

140. To J. W. Payne

Windsor MS. 41917. *Address*: J Payne Esqr. *Dock.*: Mr. Sheridan

[*Jan. 1789*]

Dear Payne
    Pray let the Bearer Mr. Jarvis[1] correct Pitts Letter to the Prince[2] by the original— | R B Sheridan
Sunday morn

141. To the Duke of Bedford[3]

Pub.: Sichel, i. 530.

March 29 1789

    I have no scruple, however, of informing your Grace that the sense I have of the hardship of Dr. Ford's being compelled to pay the debt, and the embarrassment the claim[4] has placed him in would at any time decide me to agree to any terms that tended to relieve him.

142. To His Brother

Osborn MS.

[*2 Apr. 1789*]

My Dear Charles,
    It cannot have appeared more unaccountable to you than it does to me that I should not have written to you long since[5]

---

[1] A printer sometimes employed by D.L.Th. He was probably J. Jarvis (of 173 Drury Lane), who printed the 'new political paper', *The Freeholder*, in Mar. 1784.
    [2] Pitt's letter on the limitations of the office of Regent was written on 30 Dec. 1788 (*Leeds' Mem.*, p. 136). It was printed with the Prince's reply in periodicals in Jan. 1789, and was published in pamphlet form by T. Becket

and J. Debrett.
    [3] Francis Russell, 5th Duke of Bedford (1765–1802), ground landlord of D.L.Th.
    [4] For £3,607, arrears of interest claimed by Garrick's solicitors, Wallis and Troward, on the mortgage (originally Lacy's) of £22,000.
    [5] An address to the Prince was passed in the Irish House of Lords on 16 Feb. 1789. Three days later, Charles Sheri-

and very frequently. There was just one period when I avoided it on a principle of Prudence more affecting you than myself and since then the Truth is that I have been daily determining to write you a long Letter, and if it had not been my wish to write so much at Length you would certainly have heard from me. But excuse past omissions and believe me they are never real neglect but proceed from hurry and procrastination.

I wish you joy of your share in the good Deeds of Ireland —and I hope I may wish joy of no ill consequence following to yourself.[1] I hope too that you will continue and sustain the credit you have got as a Speaker. I had your Speech[2] reprinted here—but I found afterwards it was the least correct account of it. It was thought however extremely good, and you have great credit with us and indeed with every one.

I am not now going to write to you on our Politics or yours, but I positively will fully in a few Days.

News there is none—only depend on this—the K. is in a most precarious state, watch'd, but not tried as to intellect.[3] And our adversaries, notwithstanding their seeming exultation, live in the hourly apprehension of Shame and Defeat coming on them by an event which none think more probable than they do.—

I want also to write to you about some private matters— and now I have begun to amend I will not relapse. | Believe me Dear Charles | Yours affectionately | R B Sheridan

dan wrote to S. to say that the Lord Lieutenant, the Marquis of Buckingham, had declined to transmit to London what he called 'an address purporting to invest His Royal Highness with powers to take upon him the Government of this Realm before He shall be enabled by Law so to do'. The two Houses then decided to send a deputation to London to present the address to the Prince himself. Charles Sheridan added that Buckingham was 'more angry with me than any other person who has opposed him' (W.T.).

[1] He lost his post of Under-Secretary of Military Affairs on 8 Aug. 1789, but was consoled with a pension of £1,000 (LeFanu MS.).

[2] S. is probably alluding to his brother's speech of 11 Feb. 1789, when he stated that waiting for England to come to a decision on the Regency would reflect on Irish independence. See *The Parliamentary Register; or, . . . Debates of the House of Commons of Ireland* (2nd ed., Dublin), ix (1790), 42–44.

[3] On 19 Feb. the House of Lords was told that the King was in a state of convalescence. The Opposition could not believe the report.

We lik'd your Delegates extremely.[1] I hope they did us. I got the Duke of York to go to the Irish meeting yesterday and to be President next year which has d[eli]²ghted our Patts.[3]

143. To Edmund Burke

Fitzwilliam MS. (Sheffield). Copy. *Dock.*: Sheridan Respecting a Charge of Hastings Impeachment

[*13 Apr. 1789?*][4]

My dear Sir,
    I will not waste your time by endeavouring to account for my not writing or coming to you before. I really have been endeavouring with the sincerest desire to do any thing you wish me to do—to qualify myself to take a part in opening the *present Charge*,[5] but I find myself as much to seek on the subject as if I had never heard of it, and I should only discredit the cause by attempting it. And I am sure you will make allowance when I say that I have also been necessarily employed about some private affairs of my own[6] which, during the Political occupations of the Winter,[7] I have

---

[1] S. had entertained the Irish deputation and had dined with its members at the Prince's, the Duke of Portland's, and Lord Spencer's (LeFanu MS.).

[2] Manuscript torn.

[3] The Benevolent Society of St. Patrick met at the London Tavern on 1 Apr. The Duke of York was elected President in succession to Lord Rawdon; and the Earl of Cavan, Lord Duncannon, Burke, and Sheridan were chosen as Vice-Presidents: see *Caledonian Mercury*, 6 Apr. 1789.

[4] It is likely that this letter lies between Burke's two undated letters printed by Moore, i. 489–91. The first of them is to Mrs. S., and asks her to prevail on S. to attend the Committee that day, when the Paymaster of Oude, 'Wombell', was to be examined. Dr. Thomas W. Copeland refers me to a note in the Solicitors Accounts (India

Office MS. Eur E. 47, p. 45) which seems to tally with this: it belongs to Thursday, 9 Apr. 1789, when the Committee of Managers of the prosecution of Hastings required the attendance of 'Mr. Wombwell'. S.'s letter may well have been written on the following Monday.

[5] Burke took up the 'Presents Charge' alone on the thirty-sixth day of the Hastings trial, 21 Apr. 1789. The thirty-fifth day had occurred on 13 June 1788, when S. had given one of his most famous speeches, but the trial had then been postponed because of the King's illness.

[6] In Apr. 1789 Franco's executors had filed a long bill against the patentees of D.L.Th. and Garrick's executors. This gave S. much anxiety. See Winston, 1789–93.

[7] The Regency Crisis.

entirely neglected, but which I have been *indispensably obliged* to attend to—I will attend however very constantly, and try to be as useful as I can. I have also another load to discharge my conscience of, the having prevented Mrs. Sheridan answering your Note,[1] which she was more flatter'd with than I ought to avow for her, but I assured her that I would see you the next day and say every thing for her.

Half my excuse I know is unnecessary for I am perfectly confident that in not shewing the Tack[2] of opening this charge with you, I am helping the cause of the Impeachment, which I assure you I have as sincerely at heart as even you yourself, to whom however, as our Leader and General we ought all to be obedient. | I am, my dear Sir, | Yours ever | most sincerely and affectionately, | R. B. Sheridan

Monday Evening—

144. To His Sister Elizabeth

LeFanu MS. *Address*: Miss Sheridan

[Before July 1789][3]

Ma Chère Sœur,

Je suis much disappointed at not having the Pleasure of seeing your fair eyes this morning. I am sure it must be something more than a Hairdressing that has made you break an appointment, tho' possibly my own habit of punctuality, which indeed I carry to a degree of almost ridiculous precision,[4] makes me think more of things than they deserve. I am now going out and if I can I will call on you, of which I apprize you, if not, tomorrow I will wait for you | yours affectionately | R B S.

---

[1] Probably Burke's note in Moore, i. 489–90.

[2] This may be a misreading (and a very understandable one, when S.'s handwriting is examined) by the copyist of 'sharing the task'.

[3] When Elizabeth Sheridan married Henry LeFanu. She refers to S. as

'notre cher Frère' in three letters written between Oct. and Dec. 1788 (*Betsy Sheridan's Journal* (1960), pp. 126, 131, 136). This letter may well belong to one of her London visits of 1784–5, 1786, and July 1788.

[4] S.'s unpunctuality was notorious.

145. To James Ford

Brinsley Ford MS. Copy (in a letter of 21 Nov. by James Ford).

Nov. 17 [*1789*]

My Dear Sir,
Tho I am preparing for You an exact Statement of our accounts and the demands against the Theatre and my means of meeting them—I cannot delay writing you a few Lines, on the Subject of the last letter to inform you that those *Law demands* of Mr. Wallis's shall be satisfied immediately. I have directed Westley not to charge any part of the demand to your Account. It certainly was not understood, nor was it my Intention when I completed the Purchase of your Quarter[1] that any Debts of any sort owing from the Theatre should remain as a demand against You.

The Law swallows up our Profits and returns us Persecution—depend on it I am extracting myself from its Grip and shall release you. I am obliged to make this Effort a joint Business with the Plan of a New Theatre[2] which causes some present Delay but makes the Event more true.

146. To Francis Hargrave[3]

Pub.: *The Annual Biography and Obituary . . . 1817*, pp. 173–4.

10 Dec. 1789

My dear Sir,
I do assure you, that it has given me the sincerest concern, that I have not yet been able to find the manuscripts[4] which

[1] On 18 Oct. 1788, with £18,000; but cf. Moore, i. 264. James Ford's letters (Brinsley Ford MSS.) of 19 Sept. 1789 and 5 Oct. [1789] show that S. and Linley still owed him over £9,000.

[2] S.'s plan to pull down D.L.Th. was checked by the bill filed by Franco's executors in Apr. 1789. The theatre finally closed on 4 June 1791.

[3] (1741 ?–1821), legal antiquary. He had lent S. Hale's 'MSS. concerning the Regency Question' (*Annual Biography*

and Obituary . . . 1823, p. 124). After a vigorous search by S. and Parr, they were later returned to Hargrave.

[4] When reprinted (op. cit., pp. 124–5), S.'s letter contained certain changes: 'manuscript' is found in l. 2; 'many researches' in l. 7; 'no doubt of receiving it' in l. 9; 'to be alluded to' in l. 15; 'the Treasury bills' in l. 15; 'which happens' in l. 16; 'to believe, it will be' in l. 19. These suggest that the 1823 editor misread or tried to improve the text.

you have had the trouble to inquire about so frequently. I know that *it cannot be lost*. But I am most irregular about papers; and, sometimes, in order to be very careful, I hide what I want to secure. I have made many searches when I have come from Richmond;[1] but being now in town for some time, I have no doubt of recovering it, and will immediately have the satisfaction of sending it to you.

The conduct of the Minister in your case[2] is in my opinion the most violent and unjust act, which the vindictive system [adopted][3] since the King's recovery has produced.

When Parliament meets, it is a circumstance very likely to be attended to. The pretence of inattention to their Treasury Bills, circulated by their creatures, is a pretence, which it happens from many circumstances to fall within my experience to be able to place in a proper light. I hope I need not request you to believe, that it will be a satisfaction to me to do you justice; and as far as character is concerned,[4] you need no more, than that the truth should be known. | I have the honour to be, dear Sir, with great esteem, | Your obedient servant, | R. B. Sheridan.

Thursday, Dec. 10,
1789

147. To ――――

Osborn MS.

[*1789–90*]

Sir,

I should think it inconsistent with the anxiety I feel to urge and pursue every just mode of supporting the cause of

---

[1] Writing from Richmond in Aug. 1789, Mrs. S. stated 'I have been leading a solitary Life here till a few days ago when Mrs. B[ouverie] came to settle. As for S―I really do not see him four and twenty Hours in the whole Week― he has lately been most vexatiously harrass'd by Money Matters...' (W.T.). Cf. Horace Walpole, *Letters* (ed. Toynbee, Oxford, 1905), xiv. 196.

[2] He was dismissed from his office of counsel to the Treasury, ostensibly for dilatoriness, but more probably because he had supported the Opposition in the Regency arguments with a pamphlet called *Brief Deductions*.

[3] Inserted in the 1823 version.

[4] Sir Egerton Brydges praised him as a man 'of acute talent, and multifarious reading' (*Autobiography* (1834) i. 190). See also W. Holdsworth, *A History of English Law* (1938), xii. 410–11.

the Tobacco-manufacturers if I did not take the Liberty of requesting the very material support of your evidence on the occasion.[1] I assure you I think it of *the greatest consequence to the cause* both from your Knowledge of the subject and the weight of your Character. Every remark I have heard you make on the Bill and its consequences, has confirmed me in the opinion that your information and judgement given to the House might produce the best Effects, and I have purposely delay'd applying to you 'till the close of the business that your opinion might wind up what is indeed already as strong a case as ever appeal'd to the justice of Parliament.

If you favour us with your assistance I will take care that matters shall be so arranged that you shall not have to wait, or have any trouble [in] attendance and to any Person the least invalid a chair is allow'd. | I am, Sir, | Your very obedient Servant | R B Sheridan

Bruton-St.
Sunday morning

148. To the Duke of Bedford

Gilmore MS. Copy. *Dock.*: Copy of Mr. Sheridans | application to the Duke | of Bedford concerning | Drury lane Theatre

[*1789–90*]

The Proprietors of the royal Patents for Drury Lane Theatre are desirous that the Theatre should be rebuilt.

The Great Sums they have given for the patents would ruin the undertaking unless the exclusive right to exhibit Dramatic Entertainments is maintained and continued to the two Theatres.[2]

[1] At the Commons' committees on the Tobacco Bill, evidence was given by Thomas Gee, William Harrison, and Cosmo Gordon, on 25 June 1789; and by Henry Stone on 6 July 1789. S.'s letter may relate, however, to the agitation for the amendment of the Act of Jan.–Apr. 1790. See *Journals of the House of Commons*, xliv. 494, 522; xlv. 315. The tobacconists showed their appreciation of S.'s strenuous efforts by presenting him with a silver cup.

[2] On 28 Aug. 1788 Harris and S. pledged themselves to maintain their 'just monopoly': see Add. MS. 42720, f. 5.

To secure this the theatres in which these patents are exercised ought to be of such a Nature and so commodious in every respect as to leave the Town no Cause to complain, or to require further Accommodation.

Drury Lane Theatre notwithstanding the great Sums laid out on it is deficient in every essential requisite—

The Ill Effect of this is much aggravated by the Superior Size and Style of Covent Garden Theatre.

In the Year 1776 Messrs Garrick and Lacey expended the Sum of £7000 in enlarging and beautifying the theatre.

The Sum was raised by Renters Shares and left as a Charge on the Theatre Amounting to £560 Per Annum when sold to Messrs Sheridan Ford and Linley.

Since that period the Sum of £7800 has been expended by the present Proprietors for the same Purpose and other necessary Repairs and Alterations—

This Sum has also been raised by Shares making in fact an Addition to the Rent paid to the Duke of Bedford of £1184 Per Annum.—Supposing a considerable Addition to be made to the time of the present Lease and much more if the Lease was not renewed.

In order to erect a new and complete Theatre and to give Security to it when built a Number of the surrounding Houses must be purchased or rented[1] and a considerable Sum employed in the Building, and a further large Sum in the scenery Machinery etc. which must be wholly new to be suited to the new Theatre on the scale necessary to be adopted.

Messrs Sheridan and Linley are at present in Possession of many of those Houses and in Treaty for others not the property of the Duke of Bedford.

But as the Theatre ought to be so constructed as to include all those in or dependent on the Plan and as Embarrassments may arise from the Plan being executed under different Titles—Messrs Sheridan and Linley are ready to convey

[1] In Nov. and Dec. 1789 Henry Holland surveyed premises (in Russell Street and Bridges Street) leased to D.L.Th., and reported that they could be let on a repairing lease but 'as the Theatre Royal might be more conveniently disposed if Rebuilt and as the Duke of Bedford's security would be improved by rebuilding' (Gilmore MS.), Holland valued a building lease on these premises at £88 per annum. For Holland (1746?–1806), see *The Builder*, 15 Sept. 1855, p. 437.

their Property and Interest in the Houses belonging to them on an equitable Valuation to the Duke of Bedford and to hold the whole from him under one Title.

In Case the new Theatre is erected on the present Spot, The Proprietors in addition to what they now hold will have Occasion for the Premises in Russell Street which were offered to Mr. Sheridan and for which the Duke of Bedford is in treaty to purchase.

The Leases under which the Theatre and premises are held to expire in the Year 1795. The Rent paid to the Duke of Bedford during that term amounts annually to the Sum of £379. 1. 0 out of which the Land Tax is allowed.[1] The Premises held of Mr. Wegg[2] (a principal part of which has been lately converted into Scene Rooms and other necessary Appendages to the Theatre) are at an Annual Rent of £114.—The Proprietors also pay Mr. Malthus[3] the Sum of £40 Per Annum for a House in Russel Street through which they have made a Passage to the Boxes. So that the whole Rents now paid for the Theatre and premises belonging thereto (exclusive of the Freeholds purchased by the Proprietors) amount annually to the Sum of £533. 1. 0—besides the Parochial taxes[4] which are extremely heavy.

When the Situation of the present Theatre and the small Extent of the Ground held by the Proprietors are considered, the great Amount of the Rents reserved under their Leases can only be accounted for, from the Circumstance that at the time those Leases were granted a substantial Theatre then supposed to be adequate to all the Purposes required had been previously erected and was standing on the Ground which rendered it unnecessary to lay out any large Sum of Money either in Repairs or otherwise except merely in adding such Ornaments and Embellishments as the Interior part might appear in need of.

The Case is now extremely different, the Proprietors

---

[1] £35. 15s. 11d.

[2] On 26 Feb. 1791 Henry Holland valued 'certain houses in Bridges Street, little Bridges Street and little Russell Court, belonging to Mr. Wegge' at £8,500.

[3] Father of T. R. Malthus. He had let the house to S. as tenant at will.

[4] For water, the watch, the poor, and paving, cleansing, and lighting. The paving, cleansing, and lighting tax came to £23. 18s. 4d. in the 1776-7 season, but was £38. 4s. 4d. by 1789-90.

therefore in their Treaty with the Duke of Bedford hope it will be correctly understood that whether they succeed in this Negociation or not,[1] the greater part if not the whole of the present Building must necessarily be rased to the Ground at the Expiration of the term they now have therein (if not at an earlier Period) and as the old Materials cannot be again used, they will become of very little worth. The Intrinsic Value of the Site[2] alone is all that they apprehend will be calculated in the term, which his Grace may be pleased to offer them.

The Cursory Estimate which has been made of the Expence of the new Building (exclusive of the Ornaments and Embellishments) amounts to upwards of £17,000. The Ornaments Machinery and other necessary Additions which must be made in Consequence of the new Building have also been estimated at the further Sum of £13,000, making together the Sum of £30,000.[3] In this Estimate the Expence of Repairs during the Term which must be borne by the Proprietors is not included.

Having premised this much the Proprietors do now propose to take a Lease of the Premises they at present hold together with the Houses in Russel Street which the Duke is in treaty to purchase[4] for a term of 99 Years commencing at the Expiration of their present Leases, and that it may be referred to two Surveyors one to be appointed by the Duke of Bedford and the other by the Proprietors to ascertain what Rent would be reasonable and proper to reserve in such a Lease.

Secondly As so large a Sum is necessary to be laid out in rebuilding the Premises—The Proprietors further propose that the Sum of ten thousand pounds in part thereof should be advanced by the Duke of Bedford and expended on such

[1] On 30 July 1791 the Duke of Bedford covenanted by deed to grant them a lease of D.L.Th. for 99 years from Christmas 1795.

[2] The *Evening Mail*, 18 Dec. 1789, stated that the Duke would have lost £4,000 a year 'in his Covent Garden rents' had D.L.Th. been moved to a nearby site.

[3] A very cursory estimate. S. later complained that what the architect was 'to finish for £80,000 will not be finished for £160,000' (*Morn. Chron.*, 24 Dec. 1801).

[4] On 26 Feb. 1791 Henry Holland surveyed five houses belonging to Malthus in Little Russell Street, and valued them at £1,800. Three were on leases for thirty-one years from 1790.

Building, and that a proportionate Addition equal to the Expenditure of such Sum for that Term be ascertained and added to the before mentioned Rent and the Theatre and Premises to be erected, be made liable and subject thereto as a Rent Charge.

Thirdly That it be referred to such Surveyors to ascertain the value of the Freehold and Inheritance of the said Ground and Premises and that the Proprietors may be at liberty at any time within five Years to purchase the same at the Price to be settled by such Surveyors and on paying such additional Sum (if any) as shall in the Interim be laid out by the Duke thereon.

Fourthly The Proprietors are willing to retain in their own Hands the freehold Premises belonging to them or to convey the same to the Duke of Bedford on such Terms as shall be deemed fair and reasonable and in the latter Case that they should be leased to the Proprietors for the like term as the other Ground, the Proprietors paying a proportional Additional Rent for the same.

The Proprietors beg to recommend that these Propositions may meet the immediate Attention and Answer of the Duke of Bedford's Agents as from the time . . .[1] the new Theatre will necessarily take in Building every delay that from henceforth may arise will Occasion the Theatre to be shut during the like Interval at the Commencement of the ensuing Season | R B Sheridan[2] | For self and Mr. Linley

149. To the Duchess of Devonshire

Dufferin MS. *Pub.*: Sichel, ii. 431.

[*c. Oct. 1790*]
Bromley—Wednesday evening

I write you a line from hence because since I wrote to you I have heard things from *very good* authority that make me think every thing will look very *warrish* even without news from Spain.[3] The *Empress* certainly is blustering[4]—the K. of

[1] So in manuscript.
[2] The subscription is in S.'s hand.
[3] On 28 Oct. Spain signed a convention that ended the possibility of war with her.

[4] The Russo-Swedish war had ceased in Aug. 1790, but in spite of all Pitt's attempts at further pacification, Catherine went on with her Turkish campaign.

Prussia has actually march'd Troops—and there is very good reason to believe the French Fleet or Part of it has SAILED from Brest.—There is very bad News from India. Lord Cornwallis thinks matters so critical that He does *not* come home—but will probably go to Madras, where he has dismissed and disgraced Holland the Governour, and Taylor one of the Council[1]—for neglecting everything Necessary to oppose Tippoo[2]—who has the country almost at his mercy.—

Our Fleet has come quite home but that goes for nothing. There is more appearance of war at the Admiralty than ever.

Lady M[3] told me you expected to see me—but I had call'd before I wrote. I was very very glad to hear her say that you were in better spirits to Day—and that Lady E.[4] is so much better.—Only *once* get yourself and *her* out of all scrapes and if good Fortune has any good Nature and will do that, let us try her or tempt her no more.

I think if *B*,[5] who is the only one as far as I can judge fit to be trusted or at least the best, was properly spoke to—he would go still farther on good grounds. I will tell you something He told me last Night when I see you. He has now a written authority of yours on this subject in his Desk which *another* Person gave up to him—and which he should give up.

T.L. if you write a Line tomorrow and think I can do any good I will come early on Friday.

---

[1] Cornwallis was Governor-General of India, 1786–93. John Hollond was acting Governor of Madras, Feb. 1789 to Feb. 1790; but left his post when Cornwallis set out to suspend him for corruption. Taylor, another member of the Madras board, was accused of living upon payments of dividends to private creditors of the Nabob of Arcot. See *Cornwallis Corr.* i. 427, 489; ii. 9–13, 20.

[2] Tipu (1748–99) was Sultan of Mysore. He invaded Travancore in 1789 and was not defeated until 1792.

[3] Probably Elizabeth, Viscountess Melbourne (1752–1818), the confidante of the Duchess of Devonshire and of Charles Grey. See Mabell, Countess of Airlie, *In Whig Society* (1921), pp. 13–14.

[4] Lady Elizabeth Foster.

[5] Possibly the Duke of Devonshire's steward, Beard, who is mentioned in Georgiana's correspondence of the period in connexion with her debts. See *Georgiana*, pp. 151–68.

150. To John Harrington

Harvard MS. *Dock.*: Mr. Sheridan to Mr. Harrington Novr. 19. 1790

17 Nov. 1790

Sir,

I some time since express'd to Mr. Holland that I felt something surprised and hurt at the unsatisfactory manner in which the Propositions I transmitted to you had been answer'd. On Mr. Holland's explanation however of the circumstances I should then have renew'd the Application but for a Delay in some preliminary arrangements respecting the Theatre. I [am] now troubling you again on the subject, and shall be much oblig'd by an expeditious statement of the Terms which are proposed to be granted by his Grace[1] for the Rebuilding Drury-Lane Theatre. | I am, Sir, | your obedient Servant | R B Sheridan.
Richmond
Nov 17th:
John Harrington Esqr:

151. To William Adam[2]

Adam MS. *Pub.*: A. Aspinall, *Politics and the Press*, *c. 1780–1850* (1949), p. 447. *Address*: W Adam Esq.

20 Nov. [1790]

Dear Adam,

The Bearer Stuart[3] applies to me for another memorandum to you—and I cannot refuse it to his importunities. Pray give me five minutes to hear all his merits and grievances—and if possible a little Relief | yours ever | R B Sheridan
Nov. 20th.

---

[1] The Duke of Bedford.

[2] 1751–1839. One of the Prince of Wales's advisers, and later a Privy Councillor and Lord Commissary of Scotland.

[3] Charles Stuart offered, on 14 May 1790, to please S. and his friends by 'a few letters on the War, as much as I did by Hampden' (Osborn MS.). On his claim for 143 guineas owing to him for his 'Abridgement of Politics' in the *Morning Herald*, and '£50 for the Excise business', see A. Aspinall, op. cit., pp. 446–8. In what seems to be a later letter (Harvard MS.) to S., Stuart mentions that he has 'endeavoured by trivial but sincere acts, to repay your generosity and friendship'.

152. To the Duchess of Devonshire and Lady Elizabeth Foster

Dufferin MS. *Pub.*: Sichel, ii. 433.

[*1790?*][1]

I don't know whether you are all out giddy gay and chirrip[p]ing like Linnets and yellow-Hammers or sitting at home soberly like pretty Bantams and Peafowl on your Perches. Pray send me Line if you receive this dear T.L. Dear Bess.—I called today.

153. To the Duke of Bedford

Pub.: Kelly, ii. 21–22.

[*Early 1791*]

That he was sorry he could not grant his request,[2] as the carrying on Italian operas at the Pantheon was most unjust and unfair towards the claimants on the Opera House in the Haymarket, as well as to Mr. Taylor,[3] the chief proprietor, who was making every effort to rebuild it;[4] and that, so far from aiding it, he would do every thing in his power to counteract it.

154. To Henry Holland

Gilmore MS. *Address*: Henry Holland Esqr. | Sloane-Street *Dock.:* Mr. Sheridan | March 24th. 91 | concerning Longman

23 Mar. 1791

Dear Sir,
    I have agreed with Longman[5] that he shall take eleven

---

[1] So dated by Sichel.
[2] Bedford asked S. to compel Thompson, Thomas Sheridan's former manservant who owned a piece of ground behind the Pantheon, to sell it to the directors. See Kelly, ii. 21.
[3] William Taylor. See Kelly, ii.

360–5; Farington, i. 210.
[4] Burnt down on 17 June 1789, and reopened 26 Mar. 1791.
[5] He owned premises in Russell Street and Drury Lane occupied by J. M. Bowley.

hundred Pounds for the Houses. I trust our difficulties are all overcome—I should have called on you but that I have been out of Town to get rid of my cold—'Fiery Expedition' must be our Guide[1]— | your's truly | R B Sheridan

Wednesday Evening.

155. [To Lady Duncannon]

Dufferin MS. *Pub.*: Sichel, ii. 432.

[*12 Apr. 1791*]
Tuesday Night

Your letter made me happy and easy—but let me hear of no checks or Relapses[2] do you mind
Fox and Grey are just gone from me
I will speak if there is an opportunity, but I don't think there will be a good one—for Grey and Maitland[3] must say all the obvious things and the other side will say little—so there will be nothing to answer.—Besides from looking into the question I am half convinced on the other side—For Ma'am if the Empress[4] can gain an ascendancy in Poland and by commanding the navigation of the Dnieper and the Dniester get complete possession of the Black Sea then Ma'am with the future connivance or assistance of the Emperor[5] She may certainly get actual Possession of Constantinople, and the European Provinces of Turkey which is all that's necessary and then Ma'am turning the Black Sea into a Wet Dock and floating down her Stores from the North fit out such a fleet when no one can peep at her that out they will come to the Mediterranean, swallow up all the States of Italy like larks, and at last a Russian Brigadier may

---

[1] *Richard III*, iv. iii. 54: 'Then fiery expedition be my wing, Jove's Mercury.'
[2] Lady Duncannon suffered a serious illness in Feb. 1791. See *Georgiana*, p. 180.
[3] Grey moved that it was in the interest of Britain to preserve peace, and he justified the claims of Russia upon Oczakow and the Dniester. His motion was seconded by the Hon. Thomas Maitland, M.P. for Jedburgh. S.'s speech in this debate of 12 Apr. is given in *Speeches*, ii. 329–40. Lord Belgrave moved the previous question, and this was carried.
[4] Catherine the Great.
[5] Leopold II.

be quarter'd at Roehampton[1] for aught I know within these
hundred years. So on your account Ma'am I am rather for
the Balance of Europe.

I will write [no] more now for I am worse than melancholy. E. too is very unwell she has been bled this evening—
and I have not been out. I will write again in the morn[2]

156. To——

Add. MS. 29764, ff. 49–50. Draft?

[*Apr.–May 1791?*]

Sir,

The various circumstances which prolong'd the passing
of the Corn-bill[3] occasion'd my deferring the answering the
favour of your Letter upon that subject at the time and as
many things too long put off are at last wholly omitted I have
now to apologize for that having been the case with me upon
this occasion and at the same time to express my hope that
you have not considered it any personal disrespect or neglect
of your application—which would be an imputation I should
be very sorry to have occurr'd.

Altho this Business is over I trouble you with this Letter
in consequence of my having been informed that there has
been a report circulated in Glasgow that I had not attended
to the wishes of the very respectable Bodies who had
honour'd me with their commands and entrusted me with
their Petitions respecting that Part of the Corn Bill which
affected Scotland. Nothing I assure you can be more untrue
than any such insinuation, I attended to the Bill with no
other object than to obtain the Relief desired in those
Petitions and had frequent conversations with the Managers
of the Bill for this Purpose. And I flatter'd myself not with-

---

[1] Lady Duncannon's country villa.
[2] This paragraph is on a slip of paper
attached to the letter.
[3] The Corn Trade Regulating Bill
was read a third time on 27 May 1791,
but S. had presented on 1 Apr. 1791
a petition 'from the trades house at
Glasgow, praying to be heard by

counsel against the clauses which respect
Scotland'. If the claims were not
altered, he proposed to present a petition against them signed by twenty
thousand people. The House of Commons then referred the petition to the
committee on the Bill. See *Speeches*, ii.
326.

out effect in assisting to their assent to the alterations obtain'd. It is unnecessary for me to add anything further on the subject, or to make more professions than to assure you that I shall at all times be happy to receive any communication from the same Quarter, and to be of every service in my Power in promoting their wishes. | S.

157. To the Duchess of Devonshire

Dufferin MS. *Pub.*: Sichel, ii. 432–3.

Wednesday evening July 20th[1] [*1791?*]

I was quite convinc'd that I should have sent you volumes whenever Craufurd[2] should really go[3]—and now I am in the greatest hurry possible so I shall reserve all I have to say for the Post—and it is a great deal. Pray don't think me negligent about M.[4] and I am afraid you have too but I assure you dear T. L. it has not been my fault. He is the most shuffling Fellow I ever knew—and after repeated Promises to send me every scrap of Paper in a Packet seal'd up, He at last affected a qualm about the Propriety of delivering these into my hands without an *express order* from *you*, which he said I had not—and this is so far true, tho' I told him he must understand that the same authority on which He gave me the bond was sufficient to justify his delivering up the rest. I could not shew him your letters authorizing me to get them because they spoke of him in such Terms. At last I told him how ill I thought he behaved

---

[1] The second figure is difficult to read. The letter is dated '1790?' by Sichel, and 'July 24th [1790]' in *S.C.*, 25 May 1954, lot 272. If the date is 'July 24th', then the letter belongs to 1793.

[2] John Craufurd (*c.* 1742–1814) was known in this circle as 'Fish'. See N. Pearson, '"Fish" Craufurd', *Nineteenth Century and After*, lxxv (1914), 389–400. Chatsworth MSS. 980 and 994.1 show that he was at Spa with the Duke and Duchess in Aug. and Sept. 1789.

[3] The Devonshires, Duncannons, and Lady Elizabeth Foster were at Bath. See D. M. Stuart, *Dearest Bess* (1955), pp. 56–59, for an account of their stay there.

[4] Probably Henry Martindale, to whom the Duchess owed gambling debts. His name is not, however, in the list of creditors compiled by the Duchess in Dec. 1790, but one Masters, to whom she owed £1,000, is mentioned. See *Georgiana*, p. 178; S. Rogers, *Table Talk* (3rd ed., 1856), p. 194.

and how unfair his trifling was—and that Lord Spencer and Mr. Coutes[1] would apply to him. This I thought had more effect with him than his Promises—and He says he will deposit the Papers with either under *two seals* affecting a scruple that it would be unfair to you to trust them into anyone's hands on any other terms—or he offers to burn them in the Presence of any of us upon a new Doubt whether there might not arise some inconvenience to *him* if they were not destroy'd.

I made him however promise to write a letter (which he has since sent me) disclaiming any remaining Demand whatever on you. But whether he has done this in the way he promised I would not swear as he sent it seal'd. I enclose it however—and I should think there would be no further difficulty if you send him a peremptory order to deliver the Papers under as many seals as he pleases.

. . .[2] I must not stop to say a million of things I ought to say about other matters—but only do you never write me Line?

There is one subject too I do want most vehemently want to talk to you about—tho' I am afraid—but don't you be afraid for it relates only to *yourself* and interests me only because it is so dangerous to you.[3]

But I will write you by the Post which will probably reach you before the Fish.[4] | Your very faithful and . . .[5]

She[6] is very well but you will have Letters of course. What do you do with all the fugitive Princes?[7] I never thought I should live to wish myself a Frenchman—but I would not hang the poor old foolish men. I will write to-morrow and to Bess.

---

[1] When the Duchess had needed £6,000 to pay her debts in Mar. 1789, she applied to the banker Thomas Coutts (1735–1822). He agreed to lend it on condition that her brother George, 2nd Earl Spencer (1758–1834), gave his bond for the sum.   [2] Erasure.
[3] Her intimacy with Grey? She had a child by him on 20 Feb. 1792.
[4] Craufurd.
[5] Illegible. Sichel reads 'obedient'.
[6] Mrs. S.? Sichel suggests Lady Dun-

cannon, and this is given some support by the fact that elsewhere in these letters S. refers to Mrs. S. as 'E.' If Sichel is right, my dating must be wrong.
[7] This phrase was used in Oct. 1791 with specific reference to the Princes of the House of Bourbon. See the *Pub. Adv.*, 27–28 Oct. 1791. S. appears to be using it more loosely and with reference to the French *émigrés* at Bath, for whom see D. M. Stuart, op. cit., pp. 56–57.

158. To the Prince of Wales

Windsor MSS. 41961–4.

[*31 July 1791*]

Sir,

I am extremely apprehensive that your Royal Highness may have been surprised at not having sooner received the Letters.[1] In obedience to your Royal Highness's commands I took them to Fox at St. Anne's[2] whom I could not see till wednesday. On thursday I gave the Packet to Mr. Burrows[3] a Friend of mine who was going to Brighton. It was returned to me on Friday evening, He having put off his journey, and Mr. Lamb[4] having fix'd to go this morning I have concluded that it will be safest that He should have the Honor of delivering it into your Royal Highness's own Hands.

As your Royal Highness commands I have of course permitted no Person to seet hese Papers[5] but Mr. Fox. Who is of opinion, as every body must be, that your Royal Highness's conduct in this important and delicate Business must command the applause of all descriptions of Persons, and unalt[e]rably secure to you, if any additional inducement had been necessary, the grateful attachment of the Royal Person most interested in the subject. Mr. Fox will write

[1] The Prince wrote to S. on 29 July 1791 (Osborn MS.) from Brighton, and asked for the return of his letter to the Duke of York: 'as in the first place I wish much to get it back into my own possession, and in the next place I fear very much that you will either mislay or lose it, let me know what Charles thinks of it'. The Prince adds that he would have liked Fox's advice but 'I was compelled immediately to decide'.

[2] His country house at Chertsey.

[3] He is mentioned in Mrs. S.'s letter (W.T.) of 28 July [1785] as dining with the Sheridans at Putney; and was probably Walter Borrowes, executor of Stratford Canning.

[4] Peniston Lamb (1770–1805)? The Sheridans were on friendly terms with the Melbourne family, and Mrs. S. twice stayed at Brocket Hall in Mar. 1791.

[5] Moore notes (ii. 139) that 'they referred to a very important and embarrassing question, which is known to have been put by the Duke of York to the Heir Apparent, previously to his own marriage this year;—a question, which involved considerations connected with the Succession to the Crown, and which the Prince, with the recollection of what occurred on the same subject in 1787, could only get rid of by an evasive answer'. The Duke had asked the Prince if he was likely to marry. The Duke's own marriage to the Princess Frederica of Prussia was announced (c. 3 Aug.) as taking place in the following Oct.

without Delay to the Duke of York, and the result I have no
doubt will be what I took the Liberty of humbly suggesting
to your Royal Highness. And on this supposition I beg
your Royal Highness to Pardon my presuming to hint that
it may be right to prefer that any communication of Your
Royal Highness's excellent Letter (unless where your Royal
Highness has perfect confidence) should come thro' the Duke
of York rather than from Those who have the Honor to be
more constantly about your Royal Highness's Person. I am
confident your Royal Highness's Discernment will see at
once the possible misrepresentation which this caution is
humbly meant to guard against, and in which Fox very
much agrees with me, without my trespassing on your Royal
Highness's Time by further explanation. When I have the
Honor of attending your Royal Highness's commands at
Brighton,[1] it will be my duty to mention other circum-
stanc[e]s of the long conversation I had with Fox, and which
I know he wishes to be convey'd to your Royal Highness in
the way most calculated for full explanation.

It may perhaps amuse your Royal Highness to have a
copy of the Note by which the Empress has desired to have
Fox's Bust.[2] Worenzof[3] has sent the original to Fox—it is
written in Pencil by the Empress, and address'd to her
secretary Besberodkow[4]— | I have the Honor, Sir | to be
ever your Royal Highness's | Most dutiful | and faithful
Servant | R B Sheridan.

London
Sunday morn.

[1] The Prince was there for the races
(1–6 Aug.), and from 19 Aug. onwards
(*Sussex Weekly Advertiser*, 8 and 22
Aug. 1791).

[2] S.'s copy is at Yale. It is printed by
Moore, ii. 134–5. *The Europ. Mag.* xx
(1791), 154, states under 10 Aug. 1791;
'The Empress of Russia . . . has written
with her own hand to her Ambassador,
to request Mr. Fox to sit to Nollekens
for a bust in white marble, which she
says, she means to place between the
statues of Demosthenes and Cicero.'
When the Triple Alliance insisted that

Oczakow, at the mouth of the Dnieper,
be given back to the Turks, Fox
strongly opposed the government move
to send troops to force Catherine to
comply. The country was clearly behind
him, so Pitt gave way. Catherine then
showed her gratitude.

[3] Count Semen Romanovich Woron-
zow (1744–1832) was Russian ambassador in London from 1785.

[4] Count Aleksander Bezborodko
(1749–99) was Catherine's 'plenipotentiary for all negotiations'; and later
Grand Chancellor of Russia.

Sir,

I reproach myself extremely on being obliged to open this Letter—finding that Mr. Lamb had set out sooner than I understood was [his] intention. If the Gentlemen I mention'd is not going to Day a messenger shall immediately take this. I entreat your Royal Highness's goodness to forgive this seeming Neglect of your commands.[1]

159. [To Parties concerned about the Dormant Patent?]

Gilmore MS. Copy. *Dock.*: Mr. Sheridans treatise on the | disposal of Mr. Harrises | dormant patent | Oct. 1791

Oct. 1791

Proposal respecting the disposition of Mr. Harris's dormant Patent in the present general arrangement of the three Theatres.

It has always been considered as a preliminary stipulation in this Arrangement that Mr. Harris should receive a valuable consideration for this patent, and that it should either be the authority with the Chamberlain's consent (and restricted to Operas) for the new Theatre in the Haymarket, or with the consent of the Duke of Bedford be surrendered to the Crown and a new patent for Operas granted.

There appear considerable objections both on the part of the Duke of Bedford's interest and that of the two present Theatres that this patent should be separated for any purpose from the Duke of Bedford's property, and, with whatever instructions, exercised elsewhere. The present idea therefore is that Mr. Harris should surrender this patent and that the whole of the consideration claim'd by him should be charged on the Haymarket property upon a new patent for Operas being granted to that place.

Without discussing the ability of the Haymarket property

---

[1] The Prince acknowledged S.'s 'kind letter' on 3 Aug. (Osborn MS.). Cf. Rae, ii. 241–2.

to bear this load in addition to the payment of the debts of the Pantheon as well as their own, the proprietor argues that the debts of the Pantheon being taken at so large a Sum as thirty thousand Pounds it is reasonable that the licence should be restored to the Haymarket[1] whence they are to be paid without further expence as it would have been continued at the Pantheon.

It certainly must be a desirable thing to the arbitrators in this business not to load the Haymarket undertaking with any unnecessary expence, or to make it pay for anything for which there does not appear an equivalent advantage. And this would in a great measure appear to be the case if that property is compelled to pay a large sum to Mr. Harris for an authority it is not to use, at the same time that it is supposed His Majesty is graciously inclined at the recommendation of the Lord Chamberlain to grant a free Patent or Licence for a term for the benefit of all parties.

The question arises whether instead of destroying it there cannot be some other use made of this patent equally beneficial to Mr. Harris, and less burthensome to the Haymarket, and affording at the same time an equal or rather an improved security to the Duke of Bedford's property.

The circumstance of the Duke of Bedford's being the proprietor of both the Winter Theatres and of all the property round them appears to point out a very obvious arrangement for the benefit and accommodation of all parties.

The Proprietors of Drury Lane Theatre have renewed their Leases for ninety nine Years and are engaged to Build a new Theatre on an extended Plan.

It has always been contended that the renewal of their patents, of which 27 years remain, was a matter of course, at the same time it is not to be concealed that events may arise which might either create difficulty in the renewal, or unreasonably load it with some additional charge which

---

[1] Taylor advertised, on 5 Apr. 1791, that the proprietors of the King's Theatre would not put on operas until the hardship of their case produced 'the proper influence upon His Majesty's benevolent mind' (*Morn. Chron.*, 5 Apr. 1791); but his two letters (24 Mar. and 1 Apr.) to the same newspaper, bitterly attacking the Lord Chamberlain for his covert support of Gallini and O'Reilly, were hardly calculated to bring Taylor into court favour. For the terms on which he received the licence in 1792, see Kelly, ii. 363–4.

would be equally prejudicial to the proprietors of the present patent and to the security of the Duke of Bedford's Rent.

It cannot be denied therefore that to fix this dormant Patent without further discussion of its validity to the Duke's Theatre in Drury Lane would be advantageous to the Duke's property there without injuring his security in his Theatre in Covent Garden, and advantageous also to the proprietors of the present Drury Lane patent.

In this arrangement it is not to be understood that the renewal of the present Drury Lane patents under the same authorities is to be neglected or given up. Still however the authority of the other annexed inseparably to Drury Lane Theatre may eventually be of essential service.

At the expiration of the Lease the dormant patent to revert with the Theatre etc. to the Duke and his heirs.

In this arrangement the Haymarket Theatre would undoubtedly receive a considerable advantage by the circumstance of the dormant patent (the exercise of which in a new Theatre always threatened the interests of the Opera House more even than those of Drury Lane) being permanently confined to a Theatre already established, and finally prevented from opposing or disturbing its interests.

The only remaining consideration seems to be the amount of the compensation to be made to Mr. Harris, and the proportion in which the expence of that compensation should be borne by the parties benefited.

During the Chamberlainship of Lord Hertford, Mr. Harris and Mr. Sheridan obtain'd His Majesty's full consent that this dormant patent should be exercised in a new Theatre which they then proposed to erect, *provided* it was done with the consent of all the Proprietors of the Winter Theatres and for the benefit of both. Mr. Harris and Mr. Sheridan in consequence purchased the shares of such of their partners as did not chuse to imbark in the plan at an advanced price. A subsequent suggestion from His Majesty respecting the Opera House occasioned their purchasing that property also. Although their plan was afterwards given up and their Interests separated, Mr. Harris appears always to have paid the fairest attention to the interests of Drury Lane in every plan for reviving the idea of exercising this patent, and during the late calamity in the Haymarket it is admitted that the property benefited by his forbearance. Upon these considerations it appears but equitable that Mr. Harris's interest should not be depreciated by his past justice and moderation or by the conditions upon which his Majesty's gracious approbation was originally obtain'd.

The present proposal offers middle terms between what has been understood to be the expectations of Mr. Harris and the idea of those who have proposed to treat for his Patent.

Let the price paid to Mr. Harris be £15,000.—£5,000 from the Duke of Bedford, £5,000 from the proprietors of Drury Lane Theatre, and £5,000 to be charged on the Opera House. The proprietors of Drury Lane Theatre also to pay a conditional rent to the Duke of Bedford for the Sum advanced by him and the patent to be made *over* to the Duke and to be *by him* leased and fixed to the Drury Lane property.

By this arrangement three evils will be avoided and three benefits obtained,—1st all possible future injury to either of the three Theatres by the erection of a fourth under this patent, it being manifest to any one who has well considered the subject that nothing can *ultimately* be so *ruinous* to all *Theatrical property* as any innovation of this sort, even though the proprietors of one Theatre should find a temporary advantage in it.—

2dly—All discussion or dispute on the validity of the patent would be avoided.—

3dly—All doubt or difference respecting Mr. Harris's claim to detach this patent without the Duke's consent would cease, this being a measure to be effected by the Duke himself.

As to the benefits arising—1st. Mr. Harris will obtain with general consent a greater sum than can be obtain'd or perhaps than ought to be demanded from the Haymarket property only.

2dly. The Haymarket property will be charged with but half of the Sum which they once offered for this arrangement.

3dly. Drury Lane Theatre will receive an advantage and a security fairly adequate to the payment proposed to be shared by the proprietors and the Patentees.

160. To Henry Holland

Gilmore MS. *Address*: H. Holland Esq. | Sloane-St: *Dock.*: Mr.
Sheridan | by Mr. Peake relating | to the Plan of the Theatre

[*1791–2*]
Monday [?] morning

Dear Sir,
Mr. Peake our under-Treasurer will give you this and
I send by him a Plan of our Theatre and the Houses[1]—of
which he will give you an explanation.
I wish very much that at least not a moment should be
lost in settling our *Plan*. I was in hopes that our principal
impediments were got over. As I am absolutely determined
on a new Theatres being built this summer no little difference in settling with Malthus or Wigge can be of such
consequence as to lose a week for it—I will meet you at any
time on Plans on Thursday | yours ever | R B Sheridan

Pray have the Plan copied[2]—as I want mine

161. [To Willoughby Lacy]

Shuttleworth MS.

Southampton
Jan. 28th [*1792?*]

Dear Sir,
A Letter of yours has follow'd me to Southampton,[3] in
which you mention having written me four others—certainly
but *one* has ever reach'd my hands and on receiving that I
immediately wrote to Westley to send what you desired—

[1] The proposals of S. and Linley
were to build a 'Theatre upon an insu-
lated plan to be surrounded by four rows
of Houses'. For 'Holland's Drury Lane'
see Ian Donaldson's article in *Theatre
Notebook*, xvi (1962), 90–96.
[2] Holland submitted the plans of
D.L.Th. to the Lord Chamberlain (for
the King's approbation) on 16 Jan.
1792: see *The Later Correspondence of*

George III (ed. A. Aspinall, Cambridge,
1962), i. 580.
[3] Mrs. S.'s tubercular symptoms had
grown more serious, and she was also
pregnant as a result of her liaison with
Lord Edward Fitzgerald. So she went
to Southampton for a change of air,
arriving on 15 Jan. 1792. S.'s visit to
her ended on 2 Feb. See her letter (W.T.)
of 3 Feb. 1792 to Mrs. Canning.

if it has not reach'd you before you receive this, you may
depend on it Wednesday's Post (when I shall be myself in
Town) shall bring it to you. I have been so entirely without
any fix'd habitation that many Letters have miss'd me—but
you ought always to be assured of my good will to assist you,[1]
and that it will be the more if I get more ability—| Yours very
truly | R B Sheridan.

162. [To William Taylor][2]

University of Kansas Library MS., Lawrence. [Ph.] *Dock.*: To
Mr. Taylor

[Jan.-Feb. 1792?][3]

Dear Sir,
    We must meet as soon as possible, as there are parts of
your letter quite incomprehensible to me. I wish you would
always apply to me and not listen to reports about my intentions. No person has so great an interest in expediting
the rebuilding D. L. Theatre as I have, and at the same time
no one has a greater stake in the future prosperity of the
Opera House. You ought to be assured that even were this
not the case, that I shall be very ready to forward the general
interests of the three Theatres and to fulfill the purposes of
the last and final settlement concerning them.—Nothing
shall be wanting in my power to expedite the re-establish-
ment of the Opera at the Haymarket[4]—the little delay that
has occurr'd, when explain'd to you, you will perceive to have
been unavoidable, and the consequence upon the terms of
our agreement cannot be said to be injurious to you or to
the Pantheon, the destruction[5] of which undoubtedly alters
no part of our settlement—I mean the final arrangement[6]

[1] Cf. Lacy's *A Memorial Humbly
Addressed to the Public* (1813), p. 8,
where he refers to S.'s 'friendly and
honourable conduct towards him on all
occasions'.
[2] Cf. P. & S. C., 19 Feb. 1874, lot
343, where the letter described tallies
with the above, and is said to be addressed to 'Mr. Taylor'.

[3] Dated from the allusion to Taylor's
letters to the Trustees.
[4] The Lord Chamberlain had granted
a licence for opera to the Pantheon, but
not to Taylor for the Opera House. See
Pub. Adv., 8 Sept. 1791.
[5] On 14 Jan. 1792. Cf. Kelly, ii. 20.
[6] Albany Wallis was uneasy about
the validity of the D.L.Th. patent for

sign'd by all the parties[1] which admits of no possible mis-understanding. I hope therefore you have written no such letter as you mention to the Trustees,[2] as, independant of the unfriendly appearance of such a proceeding, it must appear strange indeed to them to receive a notice directly in the Teeth of our covenant lodged in their hands.

I cannot think you can have done this from your own counsel after the explanations we have had—you may be assured however that every expedition, consistent with good faith to the D.L. Subscribers, however expensive to myself shall be employ'd for the general accommodation. | Yours very truly | R. B. S.

Wednesday

I shall be at the Theatre tonight

163. To——

Add. MS. 35118, f. 148.

[Early 1792]

Pray send me as exact an estimate as possible of the ex-pence of getting up Dido[3]—and the nightly expence.

a new theatre, and the Duke of Bedford would renew the lease only on the assurance that another patent would be obtained. S. therefore proposed to buy the dormant ('Killigrew') patent from C.G.Th. and to reconcile the interests of D.L.Th., C.G.Th., the Pantheon, and the King's Theatre in his carefully planned 'final arrangement'. This is dated 15 Oct. 1791 (Egerton MS. 2134, f. 75), and is printed as an 'Outline for a general Opera Arrangement' in the *Report from the Select Committee on Dramatic Literature* (1832), pp. 241–3. One of the clauses called upon all the parties to unite to obtain a licence for operas at the King's Theatre.

[1] The representatives were S., Thomas Holloway, and William Sheldon; but the Prince of Wales, the Duke of Bedford, and the Marquis of Salisbury also added their signatures to show that they approved of the arrangement.

[2] Taylor wrote to the D.L.Th. trustees on 21 Feb. 1792 (Dufferin MS.), to say that it was almost a month since he had written to them to urge them to rebuild the D.L.Th. He had leased them the Opera House until Dec. 1792, and 'it was impossible . . . your Patent could be exercised here after next Christmas without endangering the very existence of the Establishment of Italian Operas in this Country'. He had heard nothing from them since that date, so had asked the architect, Novosielski, how long it would take to rebuild D.L.Th. and had been told that it 'might be done inside six months'. If the proprietors would only get on with there building, he could hope and assume they would not need his theatre for the next season.

[3] *Dido, Queen of Carthage* was adapted by Hoare from Metastasio, and given with music by Storace on 23 May 1792.

Speak to Fosbrook[1] about the Papers[2]—it is very hard they will not send them punctually. | Yours | R B S.

Monday

164. [To His Wife]

Dufferin MS.

[*Feb. 1792*]

Pray tell Faddy[3] to write and tell me how you go on—

165. To Mehitabel Canning

The Earl of Harewood MS. [Ph.] *Pub.*: Sichel, ii. 215–16.

[*Jan.–Apr. 1792?*][4]
Saturday Night

Dear Mrs. Canning,

Altho' I do not think it likely that I shall miss you to-morrow morning, yet I am so anxious to prevent any accidental engagement interfering with my seeing you that I send this to reach you very early, hoping that you will give me a leisure half hour about twelve.

I wish exceedingly to speak to you about your Friend and your answer to Mrs. B.[5] I am confident you do not know what her situation is, or what effect may arise, and has indeed taken place on her mind, from the impression or apprehension that the Friend *she loved best in the world* appears,

---

[1] Thomas Fosbrook had become housekeeper at D.L.Th.

[2] In an undated letter from Southampton, Mrs. S. wrote to S. 'pray tell Mr. Reid I take it very ill of him not to make them send the Papers punctually' (Widener MS.). Cf. Rae, ii. 143.

[3] E. Faddy was Mrs. S.'s maid; she wrote four letters (Widener MSS.) describing Mrs. S.'s progress at Southampton, one postmarked 6 Feb. 1792.

[4] Sichel and Black date the letter 1789, but the allusions to Mrs. S.'s serious illness suggest the Spring of 1792.

[5] Mrs. Canning's moral strictness, frequently referred to in Mrs. S.'s letters to her, was outraged by Mrs. S.'s liaison with Fitzgerald. He seems to have tried to remove her objections through the good offices of Henrietta Bouverie ('The Bankrupt Beauty'), wife of Edward Bouverie (1738–1810) of Delapre Abbey: see *Leinster Corr.* ii. 71, Rae, ii. 143–4, and Sichel, ii. 214–17. Maggs Catalogue 314 (1913), item 3140, contains a suggestion, however, that the allusion is to one Mrs. Benwell, 'a lady of fashion of the period'.

without explanation even, to be cooled and changed towards her.

She has not seen your letter to Mrs. B. and I would not for the world that she should. My Dear Mrs. C. you do not know the state she has been in, and how perilous and critical her situation now is, or indeed you would upbraid yourself for harbouring one alter'd thought or even for abating in the least degree the warmest zeal of Friendship! of such Friendship as nothing in Nature could ever have prevented *her* heart shewing *you*. Pray forgive my writing to you thus, but convinced as I am that there is *no chance of saving her Life*, but by tranquillizing her mind, and knowing as I do and as I did hope you knew that God never form'd a better heart, and that she has no errors but what are the Faults[1] of those whose conduct has created them in her against her nature, I feel it impossible for me not to own that the idea of unkindness or coldness towards her *from you* smote me most sensibly, as I see it does her to the soul.

I have said more than I meant, when I have the satisfaction of seeing you tomorrow I am sure you will enable me to heal her mind on this subject, or real Love charity and candour exist nowhere | your's most sincerely | R B Sheridan.

166. [To Lady Duncannon]

Dufferin MS. *Pub.*: Sichel, ii. 433–5.

Friday March 2 1792

Two very late days in the House of Commons and sitting up late afterwards have destroyed all the Hours of the day all the Night and all the morning[2]—and now I return again to my journal[3]—which after breaking my last Promise I will

---

[1] Fitzgerald and himself? Maggs prints 'fault'.

[2] The debate on Whitbread's motion that Oczakow was not of sufficient importance to call for armed intervention from Britain took place on 29 Feb. and

1 Mar. 1792.

[3] On 5 Mar. Lady Duncannon wrote to S. saying she had just received 'the packets from you the only one I have had, since that first I got at Hiers which I have answer'd . . .' (Widener MS.).

not again swear never to interrupt but I am sure I never shall. Now I ought to renew my Complaints . . .[1] on your silence but I will defer it till I get to Southampton, because I have a millions of things to do before I leave town tomorrow. I again compare the time when you left of[f] writing with the time when you must have received my last and I am sure your silence could not have been caused by your not hearing from me—but I must some day argue this with you once for all. I cannot bear the footing you want to put it upon—yet . . .[1] do not be angry at my illustration of it—you will see that I was not serious—never, never can I be so when I seem to utter a word like unkindness to you.

My total incapacity of having a word like news to tell you continues—I am sure that instead of wishing it [not] so you must be more and more tired of many letters you receive from me. The Newspapers will tell you of our Debates and Division if you care about them—Grey spoke uncommonly well better much then ever. I spoke very well too Ma'am I know, but very late.[2] Whitbread[3] and Wyndham[4] remarkably well. Their side execrably—except your Jenkinson[5] whom we all agreed to puff to enrage Pitt tho' in fact it remains to be proved whether he has anything in him or not—I think he has tho' Pitt made a miserable figure yesterday after Fox. But what is the good of it all? Heaven bless you . . .[1]

Bagshot Sunday Morn. [*4 Mar. 1792*]

I came here very late last night with Dr. Moseley.[6] He could not leave town till eleven so I kept my dinner engagement with Tickell. The Party was Jack[7] and Lady John Fitz-

---

[1] Some erasures here.
[2] Grey's speech, supporting Whitbread, is given in the *Parl. Reg.* xxxi (1792), 309–20. S.'s oration, 'Armament against Russia', is in *Speeches*, ii. 398–403. The division was 116 to 244.
[3] Samuel Whitbread (1764–1815) said that it had been the invariable plan of her (Catherine's) reign to protect the commerce of friendly and neutral nations. See *Parl. Reg.* xxxi 282–96.

[4] William Windham. Ibid. xxxi. 324–8.
[5] Robert Jenkinson, later 2nd Earl of Liverpool and Prime Minister (1770–1828). S. complimented him on his 'more than promise of great abilities' in this maiden speech supporting Pitt. Ibid. xxxi. 299–306.
[6] Benjamin Moseley (1742–1819), physician.
[7] Townsend.

patrick[1] Adair[2] and Richardson[3] Mrs. Tickell[4] and her sister—we has a sufficiency of sparring of course. Lady John I thought looked remarkably well—and she has rusticated herself into a trick of colouring at everything like a milkmaid—and she does it very becomingly.—Moseley is ready.—I am taking him to see *E.* who is much better because I want to decide about moving her—The last time[5] Dame Frost threw her back for a time sadly—and I find she conceal'd it from me.—

Southampton. Sunday Night [*4 Mar. 1792*]

Moseley thinks very well of *E.* He returns early in the morn. I shall enclose this to Carrington by him that I may not miss a post—and then journalise on. . . .[6]

Tuesday Night [*Mar. 1792*]

I wrote to you in rather good Spirits yesterday . . .[7] for I like the Quiet of this spot and *E.* seem'd much better and I wrote in the morning when the gloom upon everyone's mind is lighter. But now I am just returned from a long solitary walk on the beach. Night Silence Solitude and the Sea combined will unhinge the cheerfulness of anyone, where there has been length of Life enough to bring regret in reflecting on many past scenes, and to offer slender hope in anticipating the future. . . .[8]

There never has been any part of your letters that have won my attention and interested me so much as when you

[1] She (Anne Liddell) was divorced from the 3rd Duke of Grafton; and in 1769 married John Fitzpatrick (1745–1818), later 2nd Earl of Upper Ossory.

[2] Fox's friend, Robert Adair (1763–1855), politician and diplomatist. Knighted 1809.

[3] Joseph Richardson (1755–1803), S.'s intimate friend in the next ten years. See iii. 290 for his share in D.L.Th.

[4] Tickell's second wife, the daughter of Thomas Ley of Gower Street. They were married on 24 Aug. 1789.

[5] Mrs. S. had been at Southampton since 7 Jan. and had met her lover, Lord Edward Fitzgerald, there. See *Leinster Corr.* ii. 65–66; *Wolverhampton Chronicle,* 15 Feb. 1792; and letters by Mrs. S. among the Widener MSS. Mary, her daughter by Fitzgerald, was born within the next month: Rae, ii. 144, gives the date of birth as 30 Mar.; *The Oracle,* 13 Apr. 1792, states that it took place on 10 Apr.

[6] Some erasures here.

[7] Some words obliterated.

[8] Almost three lines have been obliterated, not apparently by S.

have appeared earnestly solicitous to convey to my mind the Faith the Hope and the Religious Confidence which I do believe exist in yours.[1] Accomplish this . . .[2] if you can—and if there is any true merit in convincing selfish incredulity, or reclaiming those who tho' not quite hardened, can find no solace in seeking for truths they must dread . . .[2]

How many years have pass'd since on these unceasing restless waters which this Night I have been gazing at and listening to, I bore poor E., who is now so near me fading in sickness from all her natural attachments[3] and affections, and then loved her so that had she died as I once thought she would in the Passage I should assuredly have plunged with her body to the Grave. What times and what changes have passed! You . . .[2] what have been, what are your sufferings? what has the interval of my Life been, and what is left me— but misery from Memory and a horror of Ref[l]exion?—

167. To ——

Widener MS.

[*Apr. 1792*]

Sir Joseph Banks[4] and Family to go over the Stage.

168. To Samuel Parr

Pub.: Parr, *Works*, i. 798.

Monday, May 1. [*1792*][5]

My Dear Sir,

It is a bad thing for one so averse in general to writing to resolve to write a very long letter. This for a long time I have meant to do in reply to a former one of yours, and so have not written at all. At present I can only send a line

---

[1] This is confirmed by a passage in Fanny Burney's diary, of 31 Aug. 1791, when the Dowager Lady Spencer spoke of Lady Duncannon's 'prepared state for death and the excellence of her principles'.

[2] Some erasures here.

[3] Their channel crossing in 1772.

[4] Banks (1743–1820), President of the Royal Society, wrote to S. on 21 Mar. to say that his mother was so old she needed certain privileges to enable her to attend performances. He received no reply, so he wrote again on 10 Apr. (Widener MS.).

[5] It was a Tuesday.

with the enclosed. We had a furious wrangle on the notice yesterday in the House,[1] when Pitt steadily avowed his having in effect abandoned all his principles upon this subject. Each member of our association[2] proposes an honorary non-resident member on Saturday next. There are those who have persuaded me that it is not improbable that we might have the sanction of your name. I cannot myself form a decided opinion whether, supposing you approved our principle and proceeding, it would be prudent to appear to do so in this manner.

I have been much occupied by the state of Mrs. Sheridan's health. She is going to Bristol. A week ago we thought there was nothing to apprehend.[3] But my anxiety and apprehensions are greatly encreased. I leave town soon to follow her, for I can put nothing in competition with my feelings for her. Pray, my dear Sir, talk quietly to Tom on this subject, and desire him to write to her. He shall hear from me to-morrow. Yours ever most truly, | R. B. Sheridan

169. [To Lady Duncannon]

Dufferin MS. *Pub.*: Sichel, ii. 435–6.

Speen-Hill.[4] Thursday May 3rd [*1792*]

. . .[5] But I have often said . . .[6] grating to my mind to think or talk upon, and upon these it was no relief to my mind to communicate and I appear'd . . .[6] which never was my motive.

Why have I not written to you lately?—F.[7] I shall now

[1] Grey gave notice of a motion (which he would submit next session) for reform in the representation of the people and drew Pitt into expressing a 'suspicion that the motion for reform was nothing more than the preliminary to the overthrow of the whole system of our present Government' (*Parl. Reg.* xxxii (1792), 465).

[2] 'The Friends of the People for Parliamentary Reform' had met on 11 Apr. 1792 at the Free Masons' Tavern. S. was a member of the committee.

[3] But *The Times* of 18 Apr. 1792 had reported: 'We are sorry to learn that Mrs. Sheridan's health is still in that precarious state, as to make a journey to Bristol Wells absolutely necessary as soon as she is recovered of her lying in.'

[4] Just outside Newbury, on the London to Bristol road.

[5] Much of the writing on this page has been carefully obliterated.

[6] Further obliterations.

[7] Lady Duncannon's Christian names were Henrietta Frances.

prove what your regard for me has been and is. *Forgive my silence, and write kindly to me when you receive this.* In the most melancholy hours I have ever known, for I never felt so without Hope on a point that interested us before, I find my mind turning towards you as the only creature whom I find it a relief to think of, or with whom it is an ease to me to communicate, or from whose words I can look for anything consoling or reconciling. O . . .[1] however negligent, mysterious or unaccountable my conduct may have appeared to you let me now find that I am not deceived in the opinion I have of the unalterable kindness of your Heart and nature.

I am writing to you on the Road to Bristol[2]—while E. is in bed very very ill—eager to get there, and sanguine of the Event. But many gloomy omens have told me our Hopes will be disappointed. I have been in long and great anxiety about her—flying from my Fears and yet hoping, one event safely over, that all would be well. But this day se'nnight every favourable appearance exceeded our most sanguine hopes, since Friday when the infant[3] was christen'd and she has been steadily falling back. Her impatience to get to Bristol made all Delay impossible. I was to have follow'd her in a week, but yesterday she was so sunk and alarmed that she begged me not to leave her, tho' before, she had stipulated that I should settle my affairs in Town,[4] and I was only [to] come with her to maidenhead Bridge, so I returned to town for a few hours and have overtaken her today in this place. Her Friend whom she loves best in the world, Mrs. Canning I have prevailed on to accompany her and she is now with her.—There never was in the World a more friendly act than her doing so. She has left her daughter[5]

---

[1] Sichel thinks that the erasure here is possibly of 'T.L.' I question this.

[2] On the way to the Hot Wells at Clifton.

[3] *The Oracle*, 21 Apr. 1792, stated: 'The new born daughter of Mr. Sheridan is not yet christened. There are sponsors enough—the doubt is about its name.' She was named Mary Sheridan.

[4] On 5 May T. Westley wrote a letter (Harvard MS.) to S. to say that the treasury of D.L.Th. was 'exceed-

ingly straitened' because of demands made on it by Taylor, Holloway, and T. Linley.

[5] Elizabeth Canning wrote to her mother, Mehitabel, on 4 May: 'there is something particularly shocking in her [Mrs. S.] being so sensible of her Danger, I think however she might have been mistaken in what she spit. . . . I hope Mr. Sheridan will not be obliged to leave you again. I cannot bear the idea of your being left alone.' (Canning MS.)

and all her children whom she dotes on for this office. Poor E. feels such a difference in her conduct from her worldly Friendships, and in many ways her Society is the greatest blessing to her, and what no other Person could have been. Dear F., shall you I wonder think it selfish in me now to share so many gloomy thoughts and melancholy moments with you as I must if I write to you?—

170. To Samuel Parr

Pub.: Parr, *Works*, i. 799.

[*7 May 1792*]
Hotwells, Bristol, Monday morning.

My Dear Sir,
Dr. Bain[1] of this place has just seen Mrs. Sheridan for the second time. She is certainly in a most critical state, and I feel wholly disconcerted and dispirited. The affections of habit and of so many years various trial seem stronger from the accidental interruption of past dissipation or business, when such times as these come. I know not how to act about Tom.[2] In her low moments she is wishing anxiously to see him, and I can put no consideration in doubt with what tends to please or sooth[e] her. We will wait a day or two more however. She has borne the journey well, and all about her are very sanguine; but though I have said but little to Bain, I fear his manner, and he is said to be very skilful.[3] I am, Dear Sir, yours truly, | R. B. Sheridan.

I write to Tom.

[1] Andrew Bain (d. 1827) graduated M.D. at Edinburgh in 1780, and after beginning his medical career at Bath, moved to London and was admitted L.R.C.P. in 1802 and a Fellow in 1813.

[2] At Parr's school at Hatton.
[3] He said that Mrs. S.'s lungs were ulcerated but thought her condition might be improved if she drank the mineral water. See Rae, ii. 146.

171. To the Duchess of Devonshire[1]

Dufferin MS. *Pub.*: Sichel, ii. 436–7, with the note: 'endorsed, apparently by the Duchess, "Received Geneva June 21, 1792" '.

[7 May 1792]
Bristol. Monday Night.

We got here safely yesterday and she has borne the latter part of the journey amazingly well. And appears much better today. Dr. Bain a young Physician lately settled here and who came here himself in a consumption is reckon'd very skilful in these cases. I have avoided asking him distinctly what he thinks—but I flatter myself from Mrs. Canning's manner[2] he does not think so ill of her as I feared . . ..[3]

I do not feel as if I should pursue my plan of writing to you and sharing the melancholy moments I pass here, for the only time I am away from her at Night I get into such gloomy fits that I can do nothing. If you were with me now you would not think it necessary to bid me reflect or look into my own mind—I stopt yesterday evening as we came over King's Down, while poor E.'s Chaise was going slowly down the Hill—and went to the spot where my life was strangely saved once[4]—it is marked with a great Stone cut by the man who, I remember used to make a shew of our broken swords and a sleeve-button of mine and the setting of her Picture which was broke on my neck, and placed where He found the blood. At this man's cottage I remember I got some water—and I remember every thought that passed then in my mind, believing as I did that I was dying . . .[5] What an interval has passed since, and scarce one promise that I then made to my own soul have I attempted to fulfill. I looked at the carriage that bore her down the same road,

[1] The Duchess and Lady Duncannon were together, and had arrived at Genoa on 1 May.
[2] She seems to have written to her daughter immediately after Bain's first visit, and Elizabeth Canning replied on 9 May: 'Your letter gave me some hopes that poor Mrs. Sheridan will recover, if Dr. Bain had been struck as he was last year he would have told it at once.' (Canning MS.)
[3] Some words scratched out.
[4] In his duel with Mathews on 1 July 1772. [5] Some words obliterated.

and it wrung my heart to think over the interval, the present and the too probable conclusion. My nerves are shook to pieces. The irregularity of all my Life and pursuits, the restless contriving Temper with which I have persevered in wrong Pursuits and Passions makes . . .[1] reflexion worse to me than even to those who have acted worse. God bless you, T.L.

172. To Henry Holland

Gilmore MS. *Dock.*: Hot Wells | May 10. 1792 | Mr. Sheridan | concerning a Letter | to the Duke of Bedford.

10 May 1792

My Dear Sir,
I have written to the Duke to offer to come up any Day He pleases next week. Will they forward my Letter from Bedford House?—if not will you direct them to do so—as the sooner I have an answer and come the better.
Pray let me have a Line from you—are we proceeding?—not one word have I had from any one about White[2]—I can't help thinking a message from the Duke on the subject of the Leases would bring him to reason sooner than any thing. | your's truly | R B Sheridan
Hot-Wells
May 10th:

173. [To Lady Duncannon?]

Dufferin MS. *Pub.*: Sichel, ii. 437–8.

Thursday May 10th [*1792*]

My dear . . .,[3] I find it useless to think of writing to you anything but a repetition of the same course of symptoms hopes and apprehension. Each hour of each day has been

---

[1] Some words obliterated.
[2] George White, a clerk in the House of Commons, married Elizabeth Mary, elder daughter of William Powell, a former proprietor of C.G.Th., and so controlled one-eighth of the Killigrew and Davenant patents of 1662: see Winston's copy of an indenture of 21 June 1788 in C.G.Th. 'Scrapbooks, 1788–91' (Folger MSS.). On 9 May Troward wrote to S. to say that White refused to part with his share: 'Harris therefore proposes to sell you his share conceiving that the [Killigrew] patent might then be exercised' (Dufferin MS.).
[3] Sichel suggests the erasure is 'T.L.'

exactly the same since I have been here. We all think she is getting better—and she is certainly much stronger.[1] She drinks the Waters and goes on the Down twice a day tho' the weather is very unpleasant—I see no soul but get up very early and ride before she gets up. Lady Sarah Napier[2] is here with Mr. Napier who is very ill but getting well. If E. continues as well as at present I shall go to Town for a few hours—for I have left things of great importance, as far as business and one's affairs are of importance in most ruinous confusion[3] and just as all I have been about ought to be finally well settled.

Monday May 14th

She was so well on Saturday that I meant that Night to have gone to Town but in the Evening she grew very ill again—and was so all next Day and Monday. She wanted to receive the sacrament. Ever since she has been brought to bed, she has turned her mind wholly to think and talk and read on religious subjects and her Fortitude and calmness have astonished me. She has put by any other contemplation. I am confident if she can recover there never was on earth anything more perfect than she will be. And to be different, she says to me for ever, from what she has been makes her so seriously eager to live. But she cannot be deceived about the Danger of her situation. The affection and kindness of her words and manner to me make me more unhappy and do not Comfort.[4] Dear . . .[5] I know that either

---

[1] Elizabeth Canning wrote to her mother on 16 May: 'The Letter I received from you on Friday [i.e. 11th], gave us all much pleasure, and great hopes, of the recovery of your Poor Friend, a Letter from Mrs. Leigh which arrived at the same time, likewise gave us comfort by her saying she thought Mrs. S—— by no means *desperately* ill' (Canning MS.).

[2] Lord Edward Fitzgerald's aunt. She married first Sir C. Bunbury, and in 1781 Colonel George Napier. She noted later that S. dwelt on the idea that if his conduct had been good, his wife would not have died. See *Leinster Corr.* ii. 337.

[3] On 9 May, Richard Troward had written to S. to say that negotiations for the purchase of the C.G.Th. dormant patent could not go on without S. 'Let me know when we may expect to see you' (Dufferin MS.).

[4] Mrs. Canning described S.'s tenderness towards Mrs. S.: 'His whole time is devoted to her; he reads us a sermon every evening and does everything in his power to soothe and comfort her, keeps up his spirits wonderfully before her, but when she goes to bed is low and dejected' (Rae, ii. 147).

[5] Sichel suggests that 'F' has been erased here.

you or T.L. if you were to see her would be affected more than you would think possible. Last Night she desired to be placed at the Piano-Forte.—Looking like a Shadow of her own Picture[1] she played some Notes with the tears dropping on her thin arms. Her mind is become heavenly, but her mortal Form is fading from my sight—and I look in vain into my own mind for assent to her apparent conviction that all will not perish. I mean to send for my son and she wishes for him.[2]

174. To George White

Widener MS. Draft.

15 May 1792

I have only to add that as you informed me you had full Powers to treat and agree for Mrs. Warren[3]—and as I relied upon your amiable assurances I never have made the slightest application directly or indirectly to her or other Friends since I first spoke to you upon this subject. I then told you I would not. I now think it fair to assure you that I hold myself absolved from that restriction—and I have no doubt of receiving at least a direct and explicit answer from those to whom I shall apply.

I am sorry to trouble you with so long a Letter[4] but the matter is in many points of view of the deepest consequence to me and the injuries your conduct occasion[s] me are proportionable and I have but little time to give to the subject important as it is. Your share may be a Plaything to you, and to be trifled with from Pique or Caprice, but in this Business my whole credit Peace and hopes are embarqu'd[?], and the Property and security of many others for whom I act. If you put much value on your Theatrical Property

---

[1] The celebrated portrait by Reynolds of Mrs. S. as St. Cecilia, in which she is seated at the piano.
[2] Parr's sympathetic reply to the request is given by Moore, ii. 180–1.
[3] Ann, another daughter of William Powell, had married Thomas Warren.

White and Warren between them held fourteen-sixtieths of the Killigrew patent, and claimed £5,000 for it. This was thought too high a demand, because Harris was prepared to sell the forty-six-sixtieths for £11,500. See Watkins, ii. 122.
[4] The earlier part is missing.

I should have considered myself entitled to your thanks at least for the arrangement[1] which [by] trouble and pains certainly on my Part has been accomplish'd for the advantage of the three Theatres. This indeed you acknowledg'd to me, tho' you return the obligation by endeavouring by all means in your Power to injure the Property in which I am particularly engaged. For it is impossible for me now to think that your present object can be to stop Mr. Harris in his alterations of Convent-Garden Theatre[2] or in other words to prevent his improving your Property, and returning it to you at the end of[3] years wo[r]th a third more than when he took it.

I must necessarily be in Town for one Day in the course of this week—prior to on Sunday calling a meeting of the subscribers to propose an alteration of the security. I will assure you of the Day. I may then request that we may have one final meeting before any Persons you please—which I will yet hope may produce a satisfactory and friendly termination of the Business[4] | I have the Honor to be | Sir, | your obedient Servant | R B S.

Bristol Hot-wells
May 15th: 1792
To G. White Esq.

175. [To Lady Duncannon]

Dufferin MS. *Pub.*: Sichel, ii. 438–9.

Wednesday Night [*16 May 1792?*]

Very poorly to-day.—At two o'clock she was bled, and toNight she has put on a Blister. Yet Bain does not seem to

[1] 'The final arrangement': cf. p. 234, n. 6.
[2] 'In 1792, Mr. Harris expended £25,000 in the entire alteration of the interior and exterior parts of Covent Garden, which rendered it a new theatre' (T. Gilliland, *The Dramatic Mirror* (1808), i. 135).
[3] S. has deleted 'seven'.
[4] In June 1792 C. J. Fox acted as intermediary between S. and White, and

it was agreed that £5,000 should be paid for the fourteen-sixtieths of the Killigrew patent. S. confirmed this in a letter to White of 10 Aug. 1792. The money was not actually paid until 17 Dec. 1813. See Winston, 1810–11; P. Fitzgerald, *The Sheridans* (1886), ii. 196–9; and Fox to S., 24 June [1792], in the Osborn MSS. For its place in the general Opera settlement, see iii. 290 et seq.

think so much of this attack. While she slept this evening I rode to a Place where I remember she made me drive her when poor Mrs. Tickell was dying here—it is a spot on the side of Brandon¹ Hill where she and her sister used to play when they were at a boarding-school close by. And I remember how bitterly she cried here and lamented her sister's approaching Fate.—O . . .² I cannot describe to you how sunk I am and how horrid the solitude of the Night is to me. I now watch half the Night in the expectation of being called for by some new alarm.

Sunday Night [20 May 1792?]

Another dismal Day got thro'—but a day of more alarm. I was called up at 4 this morning—a shocking sensation such a message is—George³ telling me that for three hours she had had a violent Pain in her side.⁴ I went to Dr. Bain— he directed Leeches instead of bleeding—they have relieved her and she has been pretty well all Day but has not gone out. He has found fault this evening with her eating chicken for dinner—which I could not prevail on her to desist from and it has quicken'd her Pulse again but he thinks she shall have a good Night. She would read none of the books I got her to Day but we got Bain in the evening and I read to her again.

Tuesday 22d. [May 1792]

. . . ⁵ —one of the miseries of this Disorder is the uncertainty of the appearances—Altho' the week began so ill before the end of it she was much better than since she has been brought to bed if this will but last we shall all have the greatest Hopes. She frets herself at my not going to town on this business,⁶ so that tomorrow evening I mean to set off

¹ Overlooking Bristol.
² Two words scratched out.
³ George Edwards, S.'s manservant for many years.
⁴ The Leighs (friends of the Linleys) went to Bath on 28 May and told Ozias Linley that Mrs. S. was much better during the three days they were with her but had suffered the pain in her side

on the evening before they left. See the Humphry Correspondence, iv, no. 71, in the Royal Academy Library.
⁵ One word is erased.
⁶ S.'s absence from Parliament was noted there in speeches by M. A.Taylor on 14 May and by Fox on 25 May. See *Parl. Reg.* xxxiii (1792), 46 129-30. S. did not speak there between 1 May and

when she goes to bed. And stopping but a few hours in town return before she is up on Thursday. I shall take this disjointed scrawl with me. I should have sent before—but I thought to have gone, and I heard T.L. was coming immediately.[1]

Yesterday finding herself so well and collected she received the Sacrament. She first wrote a long Paper to be given me by Mrs. Canning in case she should not recover.[2] She said to her that she was grateful for the opportunity of being able to do this, that she yet hoped to receive it back from her, but at all events it was a great ease to her mind to have done it.

176. [To Lord Thurlow]

W.T.

Hot Wells, Bristol.
May 22. [*1792*]

My Lord,

It will be an indulgence almost unmerited if your Lordship pardons the liberty I take in making this application. I will not trespass on your Lordship's time with apologies, but state the motive of it.

Mrs. Sheridan has often wished me to endeavour to apply to your Lordship in favour of a brother of hers Mr. Ozias Linley[3] a Canon in Norwich Cathedral, to whom the smallest living would be a great promotion and acquisition. I have not failed to state how entirely without pretension I was

the prorogation of 15 June. 'This business' may refer to the Pitt–Portland negotiations begun in May; or to the dealings with William Taylor for the use of the Opera House, concluded with the agreement (Egerton MS. 2134, f. 75) signed on 27 July 1792.

[1] *The Oracle*, 2 May 1792, stated that the Duchess was expected in England next month. Return was contemplated, but she did not actually come home until Sept. 1793. See *Georgiana*, p. 192.

[2] Possibly her will, which begins: 'the Deceitfulness of this cruel Disorder is so well known to me I think it right

while I have strength to put down on this paper my Wishes in regard to some things which I believe I may call my own Property'. The copy among the Dufferin MSS. is dated 'April 14th 1792'; but she revised it later. Note Rae, ii. 147, under 15 May. For the agreement concerning the care of her daughter, see Moore, ii. 168–70; Sadler, p. 85.

[3] (1765–1831). He held several small livings in Norfolk before becoming, in 1816, Organist Fellow of Dulwich College. See Black, pp. 179–83, 280–91; Rae, ii. 256.

myself to request any such favour of your Lordship; and I never chose to do it circuitously. She has still however continued to entertain an idea that the application might possibly not have been unsuccessful, and it was my intention to take some opportunity of making it.

Hearing of an event,[1] which though it cannot lessen the power and influence of your Lordship's character, will deprive me of the opportunity of soliciting to be obliged by your Lordship in this instance, she has renewed the subject, and in her state of health it would be particularly gratifying to me, to accomplish anything she is interested to[2] have done. This is my only excuse for applying to your Lordship at such a time, or indeed for applying at all.

It is probable that I am too late in my request, or that your Lordship's engagements would render it impossible to comply with it even were your Lordship inclined to overlook the abruptness and intrusion of it.

I have only to entreat your Lordship to pardon the freedom I have used, and to believe me with the sincerest respect, your Lordship's very faithful and obedient Servant | R. B. Sheridan

177. [To Albany Wallis?]

Egerton MS. 2137, ff. 172–3. *Dock.*: Sheridan.

Hot-wells May 26th [*1792*][3]

Dear Sir,

I find that Mr. Taylor pretends that his only objection to executing the regular assignments of the other two Boxes which belong to me at the King's Theatre is that you oppose it. I am confident this cannot be the case—and I am sure

[1] News of Thurlow's coming resignation as Lord Chancellor was sent to S. by Fosbrook on 21 May: see Bodleian Library, English Letters, c. 132, f. 138.
[2] W.T. 'and'.
[3] Dated from the letter of Thomas Westley to S., of 21 May 1792: 'Mr.

Holland wanted very much to know when you would be in town says Taylor is going backward and forward to the Duke of Bedford endeavouring to do mischief. . . . Herewith I enclose you two Letters of Mr. Taylor' (Add. MS. 35118, f. 60).

if you consider the matter there ought not to be the shadow of an objection on *his* Part. I wish you very much to look at the *final arrangement* sign'd by the Duke of Bedford etc. and previously sign'd by Taylor. Here the 40 Boxes previously disposed of are recognized and it was known and stated thro' the whole settlement that *five* of them *belong'd to me*. Before my consent was given to the chancery proceedings[1] Mr. Taylor assured me that 7 Boxes were set apart for me, and he again authorized Mr. Richardson to write to me that this was done. He then apologized to me for having been only able to secure me *five*, and assured me the rest of my Debt should be otherwise taken care of. Mr. Troward[2] was then authorized to make out the assignments of these five for me. In the winter before last, during Gallini's[3] entertainments they were let for my Benefit,[4] and by Mr. Taylor's own order on Messrs. Hammersley I received the rent *for the whole five*—in the present Season *they are admitted to be my Property*: and Mr. Taylor nor any one else have pretended any claim to them. He constantly assured me He would execute the assignments as he had of the three as soon as they were ready, and laid the Delay on you. On what Pretence are two of them now to be forced back from me, and taken out of my actual Possession, and after I have received the Rents on them, and what is still stranger after Mr. Taylor expressly knew that I had mortgaged them to Mr. Hammersley[5] and in some respect for his accommodation. As for waiting for an account does he deny that he owes me a much greater Sum? but if it is said that by the Deed with Gallini these five Boxes are to pay only what I have

[1] Between Taylor and O'Reilly over the control of the King's Theatre. See *A Concise Statement of Transactions and Circumstances Respecting the King's Theatre in the Haymarket* (2nd ed., 1791), pp. 31–34.

[2] Richard Troward (d. 1815) was Wallis's partner, and solicitor to the Drury Lane Trust.

[3] Giovanni Andrea Gallini (1728–1805), dancing master and concert promoter. He ran the King's Theatre, Haymarket, from 1786 to 1789.

[4] Egerton MS. 2134, f. 75, states 'The actual Proprietors of the Boxes specified in the Deed or Agreement with Gallini of the twenty fourth of September 1790, [were] to be secured in the possession of them, both for Operas and Plays; those held last year [1791–2 season] by Mr. Sheridan as his own, or rented by him.' Cf. P.R.O., L.C. 7/4, 'Articles of Agreement between W. Taylor and S., 12 Aug. 1791.'

[5] Thomas Hammersley, banker, of the firm of Ransom, Morland & Hammersley.

advanced to Performers I say that in this way only my Debt will cover them, and he has admitted it. But I also contend that no Part of that Deed has been adhered to else who has the Boxes set apart for the £12,000 mortgage,[1] which I am also interested to see strictly taken care of?—all the appropriations should be literally adhered to if any.—But it is clear that no Trust has been created or exists under this Deed. The existing Rule arises out of the *final arrangement.* By this a fund is provided for the Performers Debts etc.[2] and it was my Proposal and arrangement that the Titles to the 40 Boxes should be submitted to a re-examination—so that my claim to the 5 Boxes then in my Possession must by my own Plan be made clear and just to the Renters. And if so I should be glad to know by what means (if I am to be paid at all) Mr. Taylor can pay me better? is it just that Sir John Lade[3] and others should have assignments of Boxes for subsequent Debts—before the Theatre itself is paid for? I shall be much obliged to you to talk this matter over with Mr. Hammersley who has advanced me as you know money on this security so unexpectedly and unjustly with-held. Every Day's experience with the Persons I have had to deal with determines me to be trifled with in this business no longer, and paid I will be the whole of my Debt some way or other. At least I will not look on and see every other Person paid before me—for no reason but because I have never press'd my claims, or because I have done the greatest service to the Property and been the principal cause of the other People getting paid at all.

pray excuse the haste with which I scrawl this—but my time is very much taken up here and my objects I cannot leave[4] for any business which renders these difficulties doubly distressing and irritating to me—| I am, Dear Sir | your's very truly | R B Sheridan.

[1] Gallini's mortgage. See p. 152, n. 3.
[2] This is not in the 'Outline of a general Opera Arrangement'; but by Clause 27, the outline was referred to John Maddocks and Arthur Pigott to prepare a proper deed, 'securing the rights and interests of the several parties'. They were also to examine all titles to boxes.
[3] 2nd baronet (1759–1838). He was a dissolute and extravagant member of the Prince's circle.
[4] 'Mrs. Sheridan, continues at Bristol, but we are sorry to add, with little prospect of recovery' (*Morn. Her.*, 26 May 1792).

178. To ——

Ericsbergsamlingen MS., Riksarkivet, Stockholm. [Ph.]

27 May [*1792*]

Sir,

I beg you to excuse the Trouble I give you by applying to you upon a subject which I some time since took the Liberty of mentioning to you at the House of Commons. It relates to the case of a poor Girl Mary Haydock, condemn'd at Stafford[1] for Horse-stealing. I have had the circumstances since particularly confirmed to me, and that she might have been saved if she would have own'd who the man was (her Lover), who instigated her to the crime and for whose advantage she committed it. After the obliging manner in which you seem'd disposed to attend to this application, I should not have delay'd to furnish you with the Particulars, but that I was informed that her Lancashire Friends had obtain'd a Promise of a Pardon for her so that I thought it unnecessary to give you further trouble. This appears to have been a mistake, and I understand she is actually on board. But if you will have the Goodness to procure her Release I will have her convey'd to her Friends.

I have found the first Letter I received on the subject which I will take the Liberty of enclosing—as it explains more of the case. The Writer is an Alderman of Stafford, and tho' a *self-electing Corporation* I assure you He is a Person whose account may be depended upon.

I must again request your indulgence for the Freedom I take in this request—but I am confident it will give you satisfaction to rescue the poor object if the circumstances are as stated, of which I have no doubt. | I have the Honor to be | Sir, | Your very obedient Humble Servant, | R B Sheridan

Hot-Wells
   May 27th:

[1] On 1 May the Home Secretary ordered that 'Mary Haddock' (sentenced to be transported) should be 'removed on board the Ship Royal Admiral, Capt. Bond, in the River Thames' (P.R.O., H.O. 13/8, p. 477). No pardon is recorded.

179. [To Thomas Westley]

Add. MS. 35118, f. 61.

> [*May 1792*]
> Hot wells.
> Monday

My Dear Sir,
  When you receive this come to me as expeditiously as you can. I can not quit this Place for a day, nor for any object however urgent. You will imagine that Mrs. Sheridan's State is not what you seem to think.[1] Pray set off tomorrow evening at least. | Yours truly | R B Sheridan.

Bring with you what money you can. You may return on thursday.

180. To Henry Holland

Gilmore MS. *Address*: Bristol May twenty-eighth 1792 | Henry Holland Esq. | Sloane-St: | Hans-Town | London *Fr.*: Free | R B Sheridan *Dock.*: May 28th: 1792 | Mr. Sheridan | concerning | White.

> *28 May 1792*
> Hot-wells
> Monday

My Dear Sir,
  I did not get your last Letter 'till my return to Bristol. I regret that it was not possible for me to wait to see you in Town. I perceive your Hint about Taylor was just. I should think it very curious indeed if this man whom with the utmost difficulty for a twelvemonth I prevented from most grossly and personally insulting the Duke of Bedford and whom every one of us find and declare unfit to be trusted or believed for a moment should at last be attended to and acted with in that Quarter. However I shall give up no

[1] In a letter of 21 May (Add. MS. 35118, f. 60) Westley had written: 'I have left a Line to inform Mr. Hammersley ... that you wou'd meet him at my house Wednesday at two oclock. I am very glad to hear of Mrs. Sheridan's Amendment. . . .'

Part of my Right—whatever I may do in amiable[?] compromise—and I certainly do not look to Taylor but to the other signing Parties for the honourable fulfilling of the real meaning of the *final arrangement*. The Duke of Bedford seems to me a little to forget that the Opera-Trust-Deed ought long ago to have been compleated, and that it is with the Trustees[1] I treat and not with Taylor.

Now for the more important concern of Drury-Lane. You will have heard that White refuses—and we have settled to close with Harris for his 3 fourths. This will answer almost every Purpose and White must in common sense soon come in. On this ground I trust the money at the Bankers will soon be released. In the interim it is of the greatest consequence to be doing what we can in forwarding the building.

Mrs. S. being better I will soon come to Town for another Day but I must be sure of meeting Harris.

I mention'd to the Duke a measure which I think might most justly be taken by him with respect to White. If He is not a Party to the new Leases why should not White have a formal notice from the Duke's Steward that as *He is endeavouring to destroy the Property and to stop its improvement and Rebuilding* the Duke will not continue him as his Tenant in any future Lease. Surely under such circumstances no Person could pretend to a *right* to be continued as a joint Tenant in such a Property—and I am sure He would be entitled to no indulgence. Pray consider this over. The Duke said He would talk it over with you and seem'd very ready to adopt it—I think it would bring White to Reason sooner than any thing. I think him a very good-for-nothing Fellow. I will send you a copy of my last Letter to him—which I shall be obliged to shew the Duke as it will part explain what has past. I wish some step could be taken in this before I come—and I should not be surprised to find White ready to agree— | I am, Dear Sir, | your's truly | R. B. Sheridan.

---

[1] By the terms of 'the Opera Arrangement', they were chosen 'one by Messrs Sheridan and Holloway, on the part of the Haymarket [i.e. King's Theatre]; one by Mr. Sheldon, on the part of the Pantheon; and one by the five directing noblemen'. They are named in the *Report of the Select Committee on Dramatic Literature* (1832), p. 104, as Sheldon, Needham, and Burton.

181. To Samuel Parr

Pub.: Parr, *Works*, i. 799.

[*May–June 1792*]

My Dear Sir,

My life is so irregular, and the present state of my mind so much so, that I pursue nothing almost that I ought; and among my omissions there is not one, for which I reproach myself so much as my seeming neglect towards you.

I give way unpardonably at times to gloom and fancifulness, and put off from day to day things which I ought immediately to decide upon. I am uneasy at not having a line from Tom. I send a servant for fear of further mistakes. I know not how to thank you for your goodness to Tom; but I will write when I am not so pressed for time, and explain myself more on this subject and entreat your counsel. Yours ever obliged, | R. B. Sheridan.

182. To Joseph Richardson

Harvard MS.

[*June 1792*]
Sunday [?][1]

Dear Richardson

I am sorry you thought I was huffish. I did not mean to be so because I am sure you have endeavour'd everything for the best.[2] But indeed you misconceive me and this business, or you would not listen to or enclose me such insolent nonsense[3] from Taylor.[4] It is impossible He can be serious

---

[1] Possibly 'Tuesday'.
[2] This is a reply to an undated letter by Richardson (Historical Society of Pennsylvania MS.) in which the negotiations with Taylor over leasing the King's Theatre for another season are described. Taylor was angry because the rent of £2,890 nominally paid him by S. on 17 Feb. 1792 (Folger MS.) had been used by S. to make up £6,000 to buy Vanbrugh's interest (purchase re-

ported in *Wolverhampton Chronicle*, 29 Feb. 1792) as ground landlord of the King's Theatre.
[3] Manuscript 'insolence nonsence'.
[4] In a letter with the postmark of 26 June 1792 (Harvard MS.), Richardson stated that he had earlier enclosed a letter from Taylor so that S. could see what was negotiated 'at Bedford House last Saturday'.

in any idea but that of evading the Trust. I am sorry you had so much talk with him—for I meant the Proposition[1] I gave you to be proposed to the Duke of Bedford—and not discussed before. I will write to you again tomorrow, at more length[2]—and 'till then do not say you have heard from me. My intention is to give them up the Theatre at least for Operas and bid them all go to the Devil. And perhaps to disperse our company for the next year.[3] The use of the Theatre for the next year is *my right* and the Duke of Bedford knows it. I offer to share the loss of leaving the Pantheon[4]—and to give them accommodation and they insolently desire all the Profits without a possible Risk. Are you aware what the Rent is they ask?—above £*14000* without a risk on their Part! which with above £2000 I am paying at Drury-Lane and for the new Purchase; and the interest of above £120,000 on an average for the next year['s] building subscription will make my rent £21,000. What can he mean but an insult in asking the exclusive right of appropriating *42 Boxes*? why twenty of them are *my Property* by purchase or lease! are you aware that this modest request alone is £4000 from me for my 20. The 3 Nights as He would chuse them is another £1000 and to trust them with letting the Boxes and the subscription and me to give them security from their Profits![5]—but I will write no more now nor while I

[1] The Duke of Bedford fostered Italian opera. Now that the Pantheon had been destroyed, S. probably proposed terms for a compromise which would allow the D.L.Th. company to use the King's Theatre but also permit independent opera nights.

[2] In the letter with the postmark of 26 June 1792, Richardson quotes from another by S.: 'You say explicitly . . . that (as an Alternative of getting rid of the Business) you will sell your Interest for the Price given to whomsoever Mr. Taylor or the Trust pleases.' This refers to the ground of the King's Theatre bought from Vanbrugh.

[3] Richardson replied warning S. of the serious consequences of disbanding the company. Nevertheless, *The World*, 2 July 1792, reported that 'all the performers of D.L.Th. have received the formality of discharges'.

[4] In an article on the 'final arrangement', *The Times*, 21 Nov. 1807, stated that under its provisions the King's Theatre contributed £30,000 (on recovering its licence) to the losses of the Pantheon undertaking.

[5] Agreement between the parties is embodied in Egerton MS. 2134, f. 75, and is dated 27 July 1792. The Duke of Bedford, Marquess of Salisbury, and S. were all to retain their boxes. D.L.Th. was to pay £5,000 for the use (to be decided by Taylor and Sheldon) of the King's Theatre; and to pay rents, taxes, and insurance, as well as £200 to O'Reilly. The D.L.Th. company would act for the winter season at the King's Theatre, except on the forty nights when Italian operas would be produced. The tenancy would end on 1 July 1793.

feel such disgust and indignations—upon such a subject and People I ought not to feel about at all. The Point that makes me write to you to Day is this. I could scarcely conceive that I understood rightly your last Letter in which you talk'd of my selling Vanbrugh's interest to him. Surely you could not misunderstand what I put on Paper on this Point after the distinct manner in which [I] express'd myself to you at Bristol[1] on this subject. You there told me I might get rid of the Purchase—and that He offer'd to take it—I did not enter into the Nonsense of his making such an offer because I observed to you that this Purchase turn'd out since his conduct to be the only security I had either for getting a shilling of my own debt, or his executing the Trust, or performing any one article of that agreement.—But I offer notwithstanding that if there is a Pretence for claiming any greater Payment for this Purchase I will either pay it or give up the Purchase. I am sure this explanation must be unnecessary to You but I do think that his saying He makes a sine qua non of my giving this up to him is matchless. He had better throw Drury-Lane in too. I who am still security for the Rent, who am dunn'd and look['d] to for the Payment of a great Part of the first mo[r]tgage, and have near £20,000 either by Debt, or pu[r]chase and engagements for Boxes. Pray if you have made any Slip on this Subject don't lay the cause to me. There was nothing I was so clear about to you tho' I certainly did not nor do wish you to tell him how I consider the matter—render'd so by his bad conduct. I beg Pardon for giving you so much trouble. But there are reasons. | yours ever | R B S.

If I could have sent a good account of Mrs. S. you should have had it—I will write again tomorrow.

[1] 'Mr. Sheridan is most deeply affected at the melancholy situation of his lovely Lady. Their friend Richardson has been down to Bristol, administering the most sensible consolation' (*The Oracle*, 22 June 1792). The *Wolverhampton Chronicle*, 27 June 1792, reporting from London of 20 June, stated that Mrs. S. was 'in a dreadful way. When the fickleness of our climate chears her with a sky unclouded, her mind as well as frame revive, and she converses with spirit that gives her friends the liveliest hopes; but with the changing elements, she becomes languid and silent, an affecting spectacle of beauty and accomplishments sinking to the grave.'

183. To Andrew Bain

Pub.: Moore, ii. 163.

My dear Sir,
[*1792*]

I must request your acceptance of the inclosed[1] for your professional attendance. For the kind and friendly attentions, which have accompanied your efforts, I must remain your debtor. The recollection of them will live in my mind with the memory of the dear lost object, whose sufferings you soothed, and whose heart was grateful for it. | Believe me | Dear Sir, | Very sincerely yours, | R. B. Sheridan.

Friday night.

184. To Henry Holland

Gilmore MS. Copy.

18 Aug. 1792

Sir

I hereby authorize and empower you to employ such persons as you think proper for the rebuilding Drury Lane Theatre and the intended adjoining premises and to make contracts for the same in the names of Mr. Linley and me and as the expense attending the rebuilding is to be paid out of a certain fund wherein Messrs Wallis Hammersley and Ford are the Trustees I request you will from time to time certify the work that shall be done to those Trustees for the purpose of procuring money on account | I am Sir | Your most obedient Servant | R B Sheridan

18th August 1792
Henry Holland Esqr.

[1] Mrs. S. lingered until 28 June, when she died at 5 a.m. This letter was probably sent on the following day. Bain had shown 'so much kindness, assiduity and solicitude that on the death of that accomplished lady ... Mr. Sheridan, though by no means in affluent circumstances, enclosed in a letter expressive of respect and gratitude, a hundred pounds' (Taylor, ii. 204–5).

185. [To Lady Duncannon]

Dufferin MS. *Pub.*: Sichel, ii. 439. *Dock.*: Ostia Sept. 12. 1792 [and also] 24th, l'ultima per sempre addio.[1]

27 Aug. [*1792*]

. . .[2] is it not strange that hearing so little from you for so long a time I yet own that your silence was not painful to me? even *your* Letters would not have been welcome tho' I must know how kindly they would have been meant. Even if I could have seen you I should have avoided you as yet. But I must think it fortunate that exactly as I began to feel a little hurt at your silence and found my mind looking for the relief of your kindness and attention to me I received your last short but most welcome Letter. I will write to you now constantly and now . . .[2] you cannot write too much to me. I shall know then that you are not estranged from me. And pray tell me a great deal and everything about yourself. How strange I feel it to be that I should know so little. I will tell you all my Plans and what I mean to do when I have settled things I have been fortunately forced to give my attention to. I will say little of the past when I have once sent you a melancholy Detail I wrote on purpose for you. I exert myself[3] in every way and avoid remembering or reflecting as much as possible, but there are Thoughts and forms and sounds that haunt my heart and will not be put away.

. . .[4] write to me now constantly. I entreat you do. I am sure you will.

Isleworth
August 27th

Pray remember me to dear T.L. Why are you separated?[5]

[1] Sichel notes that this was not the last farewell of either the Duchess or Lady Duncannon to S. Has it some hidden allusion to a last message from the dying Mrs. S.?

[2] Some words obliterated.

[3] The Leighs and Cannings spent a week with him at Isleworth early in August, and Mrs. Canning noted his attentiveness to everyone. Cf. Moore, ii. 171. He had rented this house from Mrs. Keppel at '£400 a year—an immense rate', since July 1791. See the *Journal and Corr. of Miss Berry* (1865), i. 319.

[4] Some words scratched out.

[5] Was S. misinformed? They were together at Lausanne on 10-11 Aug. See S.C., 24 May 1954, lot 297; and

186. To Henry Holland

Gilmore MS. *Address*: H. Holland Esq. | Sloane-St: | *Dock.*: Septr. 4. 1792 | Mr. Sheridan— | 'Fiery Expediton | be the word.'

4 Sept. 1792

My Dear Sir,

I cannot come to Town 'till tomorrow, and possibly shall not be able to get at you 'till thursday morn. I fear that if we do not give them a stout brick wall the Subscribers will think their security impaired by our past Delay—and present expedition. And tho I may be negligent in Forms and appointments I cannot bear being even doubted upon Points of good Faith. Let 'Fiery expedition' be the word and surely we shall do in the Time.—As for the ground I would risk the acting precisely as if we had our act of Parliament. On any other Points you wish to consult me I will now constantly be at your service for six weeks. But let me at the same time assure you that I have the most perfect confidence both in your ability and in your friendly attention to my interest. | your's sincerely | R B Sheridan

Isleworth
Tuesday morn.

187. To the Prince of Wales

Windsor MSS. 41698-9.

[*1792?*]

Sir,

In obedience to your Royal Highness's commands I had proposed to pay my Duty to your Royal Highness this morning at Carlton House but a very unexpected circumstance having prevented me I must entreat your Royal Highness's indulgence, and in the course of the ensuing week I will certainly have the Honor of attending your Royal Highness

Lady Bessborough and her Family Circle (1940), pp. 72–73. *The Oracle*, 27 Sept. 1792, reported that 'the Duchess of Devonshire is still at Lauzanne with Lady Duncannon'.

at Brighton.[1] I beg leave to assure your Royal Highness that I have the most grateful sense of the Kindness and consideration of the sentiments express'd in your Royal Highness's Letter. I should not have ventured to have omitted waiting on your Royal Highness, or to have explain'd my motives for what might have the appearance of inattention where least it would be pardonable in me, had I not had the most perfect conviction that the just and feeling turn of your Royal Highness's mind would view the subject and my situation precisely in the light which your Royal Highness had stated them. Permit me to assure you, Sir, that nothing will be more grateful to me in Life than any opportunity of evincing to your Royal Highness the sincere attachment and Devotion with which I have the Honor to be | Your Royal Highness's | most faithful | and obliged Servant | R B Sheridan

Isleworth
Saturday

188. To Henry Holland

Gilmore MS. *Address*: H. Holland Esq. *Dock.*: Mr. Sheridan | Oct. 28. 1792 | broke his appointment and observes that there is sufficient refacing[?] before the Piazza could be begun.

27 Oct. 1792
Saturday
At the Walls[2] of New Drury

My Dear Sir,
I was never more sorry at breaking an appointment than when I was last detain'd in the country the morning I had appointed to come to you, and now as I find you do not return 'till monday it must be the end of next week before I shall have the Pleasure of seeing you. But I hope I am not

[1] The Prince was at Brighton from 12 July to 1 Sept. (*Sussex Weekly Advertiser*, 16 July and 3 Sept. 1792). He returned there later in the month, and on 4 Oct. 1792 *The Oracle* reported: 'Mr. Sheridan came up from Brighton with the Prince. This is the pleasantest way of travelling that either PRINCE or PEER can take.' S. had interviews with the Prince at Carlton House (probably on the subject of the Prince's debts) on 16 and 28 Oct. See *The Oracle*, 17 and 29 Oct. 1792.

[2] Thirty inches high by 20 Nov.

deceived in observing that there is at least sufficient refacing[?] work for that time before the Piazza¹ need be begun.²
I shall not leave Town after next week | yours truly | R B
Sheridan.

189. [To Lady Duncannon?]

Pub.: Moore, ii. 183–4.

[*Dec. 1792*]

I am down here³ with Mrs. Canning and her family,
while all my friends and party are meeting in town, where
I have excused myself, to lay their wise heads together in
this crisis.⁴ Again I say there is nothing but what is unpleasant before my mind.⁵ I wish to occupy and fill my thoughts
with public matters, and, to do justice to the times, they
afford materials enough; but nothing is in prospect to make
activity pleasant, or to point one's effort against one common
enemy, making all that engage in the attack cordial, social,
and united. On the contrary, every day produces some new
schism and absurdity. Windham has signed a nonsensical
association with Lord Mulgrave;⁶ and when I left town yesterday, I was informed that the *Divan*, as the meeting at Debrett's⁷ is called, were furious at an *authentic* advertisement
from the Duke of Portland⁸ against Charles Fox's speech

¹ The *Europ. Mag.* xxiv (1793), 366, mentions that the Piazzas which formed a part of Holland's original design for D.L.Th. were not to be retained.

² Manuscript 'begone'.

³ At Wanstead, Essex, where he rented a house. See Sichel, ii. 229.

⁴ They were divided on several questions: on parliamentary reform, on war with France, and on the administration's attitude towards 'seditious' activities.

⁵ S. was said to have fallen in love with Pamela d'Orléans, daughter of Philippe Egalité, and afterwards the wife of Lord Edward Fitzgerald. She strongly resembled Mrs. S. She left the country, with Madame de Genlis, in Nov. 1792. See Moore, ii. 189–96.

⁶ Henry Phipps, Lord Mulgrave

(1755–1831), soldier and politician. With Windham and twenty-seven other members of parliament, he joined in a declaration vigorously supporting the administration and promising to reveal the authors of seditious writings. See *The World*, 8 Dec. 1792.

⁷ John Debrett (d. 1822), publisher and bookseller. His shop opposite Burlington House was a meeting place for political discussion.

⁸ *The World*, 8 Dec. 1792, declared that it had 'authority to contradict' a statement that Portland had acclaimed Fox's speech of 4 Dec. to the Whig Club. 'The fact is, the Duke was not there when it was delivered.' The paper then suggested that he would not countenance these 'innovations of speculative Politicians'.

in the Whig Club,[1] which no one before believed to be genuine, but which they now say Dr. Lawrence[2] brought from Burlington-House. If this is so, depend on it there will be a direct breach in what has been called the Whig Party. Charles Fox[3] must come to the Reformers openly and avowedly; and in a month four-fifths of the Whig Club will do the same.

190. To Henry Holland

Gilmore MS. *Address*: H. Holland Esq. | Sloane-St: *Dock.*: Mr. Sheridan on | the importance of | the Men being at | their Stations | May 6. 1793.

6 May 1793

My Dear Sir,
  It is impossible to state the importance of the Men being at work *tomorrow morning*. If they are not paid on saturday let them stop. Pray send me a Line to assure me it shall be so or I shall not be able to listen to the Debate—much less help the Reformers[4] | Yours ev[er] | R B Sheridan

Monday

191. To Henry Holland

Gilmore MS. *Address*: H. Holland Esq. | Sloane-St. *Dock.*: Mr. Sheridan | May 14. 93

14 May 1793
Tuesday morn

My Dear Sir,
  The Whole will be utterly ruin'd if you now abandon us—

[1] Where Fox had said that 'the tenets which he had frequently defended, both within and without Parliament, he continued to espouse with the same zeal' (*The Oracle*, 5 Dec. 1792).
[2] French Laurence, D.C.L. (1757–1809), politician and writer.
[3] Fox dined with Portland and his friends on 11 Dec., but moved away from them after this date and identified himself with those (like Grey and S.) who supported parliamentary reform. See G. M. Trevelyan, *Lord Grey of the Reform Bill* (1920), pp. 61–66.
[4] For S.'s speech supporting Grey's motion for parliamentary reform, see *Speeches*, iii. 158–68.

and there certainly is now not a difficulty left. After I saw you Palmer[1] came to me to fix the meeting with Harris for Wednesday one o'clock at C. G. Theatre instead of yesterday —and He was to apprize you of it. In consequence no meeting was held at Hammersleys and I call'd only on the chance of hearing of you—and understood you had not been there. Harris much wishes you to be present tomorrow and all vexations shall end. | Your's ever | R B Sheridan

192. To Thomas Bernard[2]

Harvard MS. *Address*: – Bernard Esq. | New-Square | Lincoln's Inn *Dock.*: Mr. Sheridan May 1793

May 1793
Isleworth
Sunday Night

Dear Sir,
I feel myself very materially obliged to you for your exertions in our late Theatrical settlements which I believe would never have got to an end without you. Harris has been with me this morning—and will sign tomorrow at two, when we meet at Wallis's. Yet He wishes something like what I enclose[3] to be added—on the ground of Wallis's scratching out of the Contract the approbation of the Trustees to the Title, which he thinks looks like laying in a claim to object to it hereafter. I think it of no consequence either way—but should be extremely obliged to you to look in on us for five minutes tomorrow | your | R B Sheridan

[1] 'J. Palmer' acted as intermediary between Harris, White, and S. in 1792: see his letter to S. of 22 Mar. 1792 (Harvard MS.).
[2] One of the lawyers who drew up the trust deeds for rebuilding D.L.Th. He is named in the Widener MS. 'Proposals' of 25 Nov. 1791, with Maddocks and Pigott, but not in the Gilmore MS.: cf. iii. 320.

[3] 'Something to be added to this Purpose | And it is hereby declared and to be clearly understood that the Council for the Trustees and Proprietors of D.L.Theatre having approved the Title to the Dormant Patent no future objection or doubt in that respect shall be raised on the Part of the said Proprietors or Trustees as a ground of impeding the fulfilling the Present contract.'

193. To Henry Holland

Gilmore MS. *Address*: H. Holland Esq. *Dock.*: Mr. Sheridan |
May 20

20 May [1793]
Sloane-St.

My Dear Sir,
I have just heard that the Workmen are stopt and were paid off on Saturday—I hope it is not so, for the mischief will be irreparable. We are just concluding every thing and no possible difficulty can again arise—but if the building is again stopt I should not be surprised or indeed I expect that the subscribers will all refuse their second Payment—which otherwise we might have next week. I entreat you will set them on again dircctly. I would not for five thousand Pounds lose a Day. This being Whitmonday, if they work again to-morrow may not seem so odd. Surely I could not have mis-understood you when you assured me they should go on for a Fortnight and that the Saturday's Payment was not an object—or we would have paid Parnams[1] People certainly. I cannot describe the consequence this is of. And I must hope you will make a friendly exertion for after getting over so many difficulties—it would be the cruellest thing on earth to have it all knock'd up by new Reports when no real Difficulty remain'd. | your ever | R B S.
Mond[a]y

194. To Thomas Parker[2]

Gordon N. Ray MS. [Ph.] *Address*: T. Parker Esq. | Brick-Court |
Temple *Dock.*: R. B. Sheridan Esq. | Recd. 25 May 93 | Ansd.
Same d[a]y | T P

24 May 1793
Friday Evening

Sir,
I am very sorry you should have had the trouble of calling

---

[1] Robert Parnham, Clerk of the Works at D.L.Th.
Middle Temple. See *Browne's General Law List for the Year 1793*, p. 93.
[2] An attorney of 2 Brick Court,

without my seeing you. Depend on it Mr. Glossip's[1] business shall be immediately settled—I told you the only contingency which retarded it, and that will certainly be removed on monday.—If you will do me the favour to call in L. G. St:[2] on sunday morn you will be satisfied there can be no further disappointment—and that your client will have no cause to regret the arrangement. If however you still think it right to require an appearance to be put in—let me know tomorrow morning and it will be done—yours etc. | R B Sheridan

195. To Henry Holland

Gilmore MS. *Address*: H. Holland Esq. | Sloane-St: *Dock*.: Mr. Sheridan with | an enclosed Letter from Mr. Harris | May 22[3]

[26 May 1793]

My Dear Sir,

yesterday we were to have met to sign the Patent contract—and the Advertisement was ready to have call'd tomorrow for the 2d: Payment.[4] I am confident the Delay is only 'till tomorrow when we meet at Hammersley's at two o'clock. Pray if possible look in on us, as the moment it is sign'd I trust the Bankers will advance the needful.[5] And the contracts for work etc. may be executed tomorrow. I assure you I have been following the Thing up very closely — | your's ever | R B Sheridan

Sunday

[1] Francis Glossop, a wax and tallow chandler. He was paid £676. 1s. 10d. by D.L.Th. on 27 Jan. 1794 (Folger MS.).
[2] Lower Grosvenor Street, where S. lived between 1793 and 1795.
[3] This date appears to be in error. Harris's letter of 'Sat.' mentions his efforts to get the lawyers to complete the contract, which would be in Wallis and Troward's hands by Monday at latest.
[4] The first part payment was made in Dec. 1791, when 300 subscribers took their shares of £500 each. Fosbrook was paid on 15 July 1793 for advertising the '2nd subscription'; and the third contribution was paid in Oct. 1793 when the theatre was covered in.
[5] The new D.L.Th. was vested in A. Wallis, R. Ford, and T. Hammersley, as trustees in a thirteen part indenture dated 13 June 1793.

196. To Thomas Parker

Text from a photograph in the Alderman Library, University of Virginia. *Address*: Thos. Parker Esq. | No. 2 Brick-Court | Temple

[*27 May 1793*]
Monday Evening

Sir,
I am this moment returned to Town and find your Letter. I hope you had not the trouble of calling in Grosvenor-St. to Day. As I must be in at the Impeachment Trial[1] early to-morrow I request the favour of seeing you on wednesday at the hour you mention. | Your obedient Servant | R B Sheridan.

I will have the appearance enter'd as you desire

197. To Henry Holland

Gilmore MS. *Address*: H. Holland Esq. | Sloane-St: *Dock.*: July 8. 1793 | Mr. Sheridan.

8 July 1793
Sunday

My Dear Sir,
I waited at Nerots[2] 'till this moment but I am afraid you call'd in Grosvenor-St: where I had lent all my beds to Mrs. Canning and her Family. I have been very impatient to see you—but I have not plagued you 'till all our difficulties are really over. Here is money Plenty—and all my Hopes are now on your super-natural exertions. Pray meet me to-morrow at Hammersley's at two, I shall come to Town on purpose and will now give my whole mind and time to this new[?] business | yrs | R B S.

---

[1] Of Warren Hastings. The evidence in his defence was brought to a close on 28 May, when Hastings also spoke.

[2] Nerots Hotel, King Street, St. James's.

198. To Henry Holland

Gilmore MS. *Dock.*: Oct. 27. 1793 | from Mr. Sheridan

27 Oct. 1793
D. L. Theatre—
Sunday—

My Dear Sir,
    As the Architect of an *English*[1] Theatre—believe me we shall be all found to be right—and your credit will be double—and you shall have a loftier Pillar to your favour[?] than the four of the Proscenium. I return to Town on tuesday—and am at your service on wednesday morning when we will talk of the contracts which I have no objection to be decisive[?] on Friday. I have met Mr. Carbanel[2] here—and after giving me the trouble to draw up a contract according to what I thought he at least proposed he broke off. I offer'd him 9 *guineas* a week for *a year certain*. Our People insist on it that they are masters of his whole Plan which was made for the Haymarket Theatre—and that working under Saunders[3] they could compleat it.—I further told Cabanel that he should have a compliment if he exerted himself on the Stage | yours truly | R B S.

If you see Cabanel perhaps you may bring him to reason.

199. To Charles James Fox

Goldsmiths' Company MS. Text from a transcription by the Archivist of the British Records Association. *Address*: To Mr. Fox.

27 Dec. [*1793?*]

Dear Charles,
    I will certainly exert myself in behalf of the Persons recommended to you by Mr. Adair whom I know you wish

[1] Holland replied, 'Italian before—English behind and French on Each Side!'

[2] Rudolph Cabanal was engaged to make drawings, plans, and a model for the new stage at D.L.Th., and later superintended the building of it.

[3] Master Carpenter under Henry Holland, at D.L.Th. Holland answered that Saunders could 'furnish men and Materials; But he has neither time nor intelligence to give any directions' (Gilmore MS.).

so much to oblige, and if they can be as useful as they represent themselves to be capable of becoming, I should hope that Kemble[1] would easily make them a situation, but I am sure you are also aware that I am really restricted from forcing Persons upon him who have not merit, at a time when he is discharging old Performers[2] on that account and refusing so many other applications. I will write a Line to Mr. Bissel and inclose him a Letter to Mr. Kemble who will soon be in Town.

No news but an account in the ministerial Papers of two more victories over the French on the Rhine—Yes—it is said that Lord Howe's expedition is yet to go on.[3] | Yours ever | R B Sheridan.

I hope Mr. A is well.
I wrote this yesterday as Mr. B. can testifie.

December 27th.

[1] John Philip Kemble (1757–1823), manager of D.L.Th., 1788–96.
[2] 'John Palmer and near forty others' (*Thespian Mag.*, ii (1793), 228).
[3] *The Times*, 26 Dec. 1793, reported that Howe's ships at Plymouth had been ordered to join his fleet at Spithead at once. On 28 Dec. *The Times* stated that Timms the messenger had heard on the continent that the Duke of Brunswick had defeated the French in Alsace. On 31 Dec. it censured the editor of an unnamed morning paper who had converted this vague report into an unofficial dispatch.

PRINTED IN GREAT BRITAIN
AT THE UNIVERSITY PRESS, OXFORD
BY VIVIAN RIDLER
PRINTER TO THE UNIVERSITY